Socialism and Failed States

Socialism and Failed States

Germinal Boloix

Germinal Boloix
2019

First Edition: 2019

ISBN 978-0-9958612-8-2

Front cover: "Feeding Socialists"

Germinal Boloix
email: gboloix@hotmail.com
Blog: gboloix.blogspot.com

Dedication

To those suggesting that Absurd (Twenty-First Century) Socialism follows a hidden agenda, using democratic institutions as parapets to perpetuate its ideology. Thanks to them this book was possible.

Contents

Acknowledgments

I want to thank all the libraries and coffee shops that had welcomed me during so many hours of thinking, reading, and writing.

Preface

This is the third book on the subject of Absurd Socialism, known by its partisans as Twenty-First Century Socialism. The first book was Socialist Bingo, Knowledge Distorted Journey [Boloix 2017] and the second Socialism is Dead, Nietzche is Eternal [Boloix 2018]. Both presented arguments against Absurd Socialism, the unsuccessful experience of Venezuela, a small country in South America that did not deserve so much suffering under such a regime. This third book keeps the tradition of criticizing Absurd Socialism, however, can be considered a research book covering historical information and highlighting those regimes born from socialist and communist ideals.

The first two books used fictitious names for countries and characters to make them universally applicable in any country affected by Absurd Socialism. One criterion was anonymity whereas another was fear to reprisals, Absurd Socialism has become a dangerous regime. Jeremy was a curious personage, very sensitive to suffering and injustice, who denounced the misfortune of Venezuela, a small country with 35 million inhabitants suffering so many miseries because of a bad political system called Absurd Socialism.

There are just a few countries in the world that have dared to implement another socialist or communist regime to make their people suffer a lot. The worse examples of those regimes are Venezuela and Cuba which followed different approaches to Absurd Socialism. Today, the luck of Mexico is uncertain with a leftist president that may follow similar erroneous political patterns. Hopefully, even leftists can learn from their friend's mistakes and do not repeat the same approach again.

The problem with those erroneous socialist regimes is that they want to impose autocratic policies against the will of the people, using democracy as a parapet. They do not want to yield and return back their power to allow better ruling governments. Some regimes may think they are making justice for the masses but because they have chosen mistaken ideals the result is unsuccessful. Their purpose is to remain in power primarily for stubbornness and collaterally to become rich by embezzling the treasures of the country for their personal use.

The purpose of this book is to demonstrate that wrong approaches of socialist or communist systems have implemented erroneous policies during their existence and have been unable to improve the life of their population. Some examples of wrong policies are collectivization and public property which were abandoned by all the socialist or communists states many decades ago. The aim should be to follow an approach that implements a free-market with more liberties for individuals to pursue their dreams. The Soviet Union and China are just two examples were socialism or communism was adapted to free-market policies and there are tangible improvements on the economy.

The countries identified in the book are just a small sample of those considered general state failures and socialist or communist failures. A detailed historical account of events is not presented in the book, only the events to fit the objectives of demonstrating that socialism and communism are mistaken approaches. To get a more historical perspective, please refer to many other sources and books that describe in detail the history of countries such as Russia and the Soviet Union revolution, China and Mao Zedong revolutions, Cuba and Fidel Castro events, Africa and its dictators, the North Korean dynasty, and Venezuela Absurd Socialism.

The book is supported by many references and links to web pages to make the work a research project. Some topics covered in the book are summarized as follows:

- Socialism and Communism
- Social Democracy
- Making the Revolution
- Authoritarian Regimes
- A Central Planning Society
- Failed States
- Collectivization and Individuality
- Equality
- Freedom
- Democracies
- Public versus Private Property
- The Party, Party Members
- Political System
- Economic System
- Ideological Sphere
- The Soviet Union, Nazi Germany, China, North Korea, Vietnam
- Europe and Asia
- Africa: Zimbabwe, Congo, Kenya, Nigeria, South Africa
- Venezuela and Cuba
- Stalin, Hitler, Mao Zedong, Mugabe, Kim Il Sung, Fidel Castro, Hugo Chavez
- Freedom of Thought, Expression, to Move
- Right to Life
- No Unfair Detainment

- The Right to Public Assembly
- Political Discrimination
- Race Discrimination
- Sex Discrimination
- Corruption
- Humanitarian Crisis
- End of Socialism and Communism

Introduction

I was surprised to find out that in a list of socialist countries, Canada was classified as 'socialist.' The list includes China, Denmark, Finland, Netherlands, Canada, Sweden, Norway, and Ireland. It is clear that the only country with socialist and Marxist-Leninist ideals is China. The rest of countries provide social assistance, such as Pensions, Public Health Care and social welfare, and are closer to a social democratic state than a socialist or communist state; additionally, their economy is run following primarily capitalistic approaches with a free-market economy.

There is another list with the countries that call themselves socialist today but that have followed primarily a communist ideal. They are China, Cuba, Laos, North Korea, and Vietnam. The most important country that called itself communist several years ago was Russia, in what was known as the Soviet Union, and we know its transformation to democracy after Perestroika. Countries following a socialist or communist view today, have primarily the party-state and the Strong Man, with a relatively free-market economy and state intervention. North Korea is the most backward country in the list because of its closed borders and limited free trade.

There were many other countries that called themselves socialists or communist at some point in time, but they abandoned the path to socialism or communism several years ago. For example, Russia, Afghanistan, Cambodia, Mongolia, Bulgaria, Czech Republic, East Germany, Hungary, Poland, Angola, Congo, and Mozambique. Today, there is only one country in the world that dared to become socialist or communist, more precisely Absurd Socialism, and its population is paying a high price for the mistake, Venezuela.

It is incredible that there still are some people in the world talking about how good is socialism or communism. After so many failures it is time to understand that they represent a wrong ideology based on wrong assumptions. One thing is to believe in a Utopia, anybody can do it, and another is to let it take roots in existent societies. All countries under socialism or communism have suffered extremely harsh living conditions. The case of Venezuela is the most recent collapse of a regime calling itself socialist. Using existent democracies' facade, make people believe in the rule of law but instead imposes the rule by law, forcing its ideas using the existent institutions.

Let us introduce two Latin American countries and let us try to guess what countries we are talking about. The first one has been the region's oldest and strongest democracy for over forty years. It boasts a stronger social safety net than any of its neighbors and is making progress on its promise to deliver free health care and higher education to all its citizens. It is a model of social mobility and a magnet for immigrants from across Latin America and Europe. The press is free, and the political system is open; opposing parties compete fiercely in elections and regularly alternate power peacefully. Thanks to a long political alliance and deep trade and investment ties with the United States, it serves as the Latin American headquarters for a slew of multinational corporations. It has the best infrastructure in South America. It is still unmistakably a developing country, with its share of corruption, injustice, and dysfunction, but it is well ahead of other poor countries by almost any measure.

The second country is one of Latin America's most impoverished nations and governed by a new style of dictatorship. Its schools lie half deserted. The health system has been devastated by decades of under-investment, corruption, and neglect; long-vanquished diseases, such as malaria and measles, have returned. Only a tiny elite can afford enough to eat. An epidemic of violence has made it one of the most murderous countries in the world. It is the source of Latin America's largest refugee migration in this generation, with millions of citizens fleeing in the last few years alone. Hardly anyone (aside from other autocratic governments) recognizes its sham elections, and the small portion of the media not under direct state control still follows the official line for fear of reprisals. By the end of 2018, its economy will have shrunk by about half in the last five years. Prices double every 25 days.

These two countries are in fact the same country, Venezuela, at two different times: the early 1970s and today, 2019. The transformation Venezuela has undergone is so radical, so complete, and so total that it is hard to believe it took place without war. What happened to Venezuela? How did things go so wrong? The short answer is Chavismo. Under the leadership of Hugo Chávez and his successor, Nicolás Maduro, the country has experienced a toxic mix of wantonly destructive policy, escalating authoritarianism, and kleptocracy, all under a level of Cuban influence that often resembles an occupation. Anyone of these features would have created huge problems on its own. All of them together hatched a catastrophe.

Today, Venezuela is a poor country and a failed and criminalized state run by an autocrat beholden to a foreign power. The remaining options for reversing this situation are slim; the risk now is that hopelessness will push Venezuelans to consider supporting dangerous measures, such as a U.S.-led military invasion, that could make a bad situation worse.

There are many reasons to establish why a country has been a failure. Among them, the leadership betrayed the society; the ideals were not accomplished; the political system did not promote the rule of law; the economic system did not perform well. Additionally, corruption, ignorance, discrimination, poverty, and laziness have helped to demolish many ideals.

States can be classified as Strong, Weak, Failed and Collapsed. Most countries are Weak because they are functioning but it is too difficult to eradicate poverty. Some are Strong because they have developed a prosperous society and their population has attained a high degree of wealth. Many countries have failed because they do not take care of their population as expected. Finally, Collapsed countries are those, most of the time in a war, that cannot provide any services to the population.

The GNP (Gross National Product) is usually used as an economic figure that shows economic performance. Countries that do not maintain a high GNP have their well being menaced. When countries enter into an economic whirlwind, where the population gets affected, suffering hunger and health difficulties, the country is definitively unsuccessful.

Nation-states exist to provide a decentralized method of delivering public goods to persons living within designated borders. It is according to their performance—according to the levels of their effective delivery of the most crucial public goods—that strong states may be distinguished from weak ones and weak states from failed or collapsed states.

There is a hierarchy of public goods. None is as critical as the supply of some security, especially human security. Another key public good enables citizens to participate freely, openly, and fully in politics and the political process. Other public goods typically supplied by states and expected by their citizens include medical and health care; schools and educational instruction; roads, railways, harbors, and other physical infrastructures; a beneficent fiscal and institutional context within which citizens can pursue personal entrepreneurial goals.

Strong states unquestionably control their territories and deliver a full range and a high quality of public goods to their citizens. Weak states include a broad continuum of states failing because of geographical, physical, or fundamental economic constraints. Failed states are tense, deeply conflicted, dangerous, and contested bitterly by warring factions. A collapsed state is a rare and extreme version of a failed state.

Venezuela is a small country in South America that followed the worse interpretation of socialism or communism. Its socialism is called Absurd Socialism (Twenty-First Century Socialism). It is an approach that has tried to impose a socialist or communist regime against the will of the people. Using a rigged electoral system, they started by taking power in a democratic country and little by little imposed socialist or communist ideals into the institutions to control the rest of the country.

It is incredible that the political leaders of Venezuela had chosen the worst socialist or communist approach to run the country, i.e., Cuba. The failures of regimes dominated by socialists or communists ideals have already been documented for over twenty or thirty years now. Why those leaders did not go through the exercise of reading the current experiences of other socialist or communist regimes? Just by browsing over historical books on socialism and communism, it is easy to identify their tendency to failure.

Venezuela had such a stroke of bad luck, getting related to Fidel Castro and his communist Cuba, instead of choosing another so-called socialist country promoting social welfare and some limitations in the power of the state. Hugo Chavez, the leader of the process in Venezuela, saw only his good personal relationship with Castro, without paying attention to what was going on in the rest of the socialist and communist world. Cuba is not a good example to follow regarding ideals, Cuba has been run under a communist regime where there was a Strong Man in charge, Fidel Castro, who concentrated all the power; the Communist Party had some participation but it was basically Castro who took most of the decisions in the country.

There are many socialist partisans who do not approve a Marxist-Leninist approach to socialism and communism. Those socialists believe in a parliamentary socialist solution where power is earned at the polls instead of by force. Those 'socialists' are currently called social-democrats. Social democracy is a political, social and economic ideology that supports economic and social interventions to promote social justice within the framework of liberal democratic policies and a capitalist economy.

In this book, most of the countries under surveillance are those which followed a socialist or communist approach such as Marxism-Leninism instead of social democracy. It is important to clarify that there is no country in the world that has followed a purely socialist or communist approach, these countries function with mixed ideals because it is impossible to implement a purely socialist or communist system. Most capitalist countries are basically run under some form of social democracy where the state has some limitations and there are some welfare provisions. It is possible to say that America has been more 'socialist' than the Soviet Union, just to give an example.

The problem with socialism, let us call it Absurd Socialism, is to follow a wrong interpretation of socialism where the state is in charge of everything, the party-state is in control of all decisions and the Strong Man manages all institutions; free-market is replaced by a state-controlled economy, private property has been kidnapped, and an authoritarian regime is imposed on the population. Absurd Socialism is much closer to communism than social democracy is to socialism.

Marxist-Leninist countries, such as the Soviet Union, China, North Korea, and Cuba, which are self-defined as socialists or communists are discussed in the book. Some other 'socialist' approaches will also be discussed, for example, Nazi Germany, a national socialist country; Zimbabwe, a country under the Strong Man approach; Venezuela under Absurd Socialism; and a few other African, European, or Asian countries which are not necessarily socialists but have been total failures. All these states represent unsuccessful states, some are complete economic failures while others are frustrated idealistic states that did not accomplish their promises.

Venezuela is a country that entered a negative economic whirlwind attributed primarily to its ideological, political and economic system. The government, non-democratically, has tried to pursue a socialist or communist approach that has made a mess on the economy and has hurt the population to extremes never seen. The hyperinflation was estimated at over one million percent per year (2018) and it may grow to over ten million percent next year (2019). The situation is unbearable but there is no solution because the government does not want to yield and does not accept a concerted solution. The solution must start by getting rid of the government and installing a provisional government to return to political democracy and free-market economy.

The first task in the book is to understand what socialism and communism mean and what are the main mistakes attributed to these regimes. There is too much confusion regarding whether the two approaches, socialism and communism, are different or similar. Jeremy was right in Socialist Bingo [Boloix 2017] by suggesting that the knowledge about socialism was distorted.

Many governments call themselves socialists when in fact they are pursuing communism; some call themselves 'socialists' but in fact, follow capitalist approaches, i.e., social democracies. Others call themselves communists but in fact are trying to promote a socialist society that eventually would become communist. And still others follow some communist approaches, such as total power to the party, but a big hunk of their economy is free-market oriented. The figure of the Strong Man surrounds most of the socialist and communist countries.

Another aspect that makes things still unclear is that there are no real socialist or communist states in the world. Most of the time, those countries that call themselves socialists or communists recognize that they are just in the initial stages of building socialism or communism. These countries believe human beings are perfectible, that with some effort people can become good and collaborative, and envy and egoism can disappear. Additionally, their socialism or communism is just their own interpretation of ideals, making available any possible type of government, most of the time a tyrannical system.

Chapter 1: Socialism or Communism?

Socialism and communism are political ideologies that advocate for an egalitarian redistribution of wealth and humanitarian justice in society through democratic ownership and distribution of society's means of production. Socialism, in the simplest of terms, involves making more efforts to balance the scales between the rich and the poor. Communism, on the other hand, proposes the same objectives as socialism but considers getting rid of the state in the final stages.

Anybody reading these statements becomes enchanted with these ideals, however, the reality is absolutely different. Knowledge of socialism and communism is absolutely distorted, there is a huge gap between ideals and practice. The worst part is that these ideals are mistaken, they are based in perfect humans. People supporting socialism and communism are biased towards ideas forgetting that in practice these ideas do not work. Human nature makes people absolutely different from what is expected in a socialist or communist society. Those that maintain a stubborn attitude defending these ideals demonstrate their irrationality.

The "social goal," or "common purpose," for which society is to be organized is usually vaguely described as the "common good," the "general welfare," or the "general interest." It does not need much reflection to see that these terms have no definite meaning to determine a particular course of action. The welfare and the happiness of millions cannot be measured on a single scale of less and more. The welfare of people, like the happiness of a man, depends on a great many things that can be provided in an infinite variety of combinations. It cannot be adequately expressed as a single end, but only as a hierarchy of ends, a comprehensive scale of values in which every need of every person is given its place. [Hayek 1994]

According to some sources, the term socialism was originally applied to a political-economic system with public ownership of large industries and corporations. Socialism is both political theory and a political-economic system that emphasizes the duty of society to ensure social and economic fairness and equality. In pure socialist theory, this means that society, or rather government, should own and/or control the means of production, private property, and wealth, all of which have to be used for the benefit of everyone and not simply for the benefit of a rich individual or a privileged minority. [Fleming 2008]

Socialists and communist have always dreamed of constructing a new society, a Utopian ideal that can never be attained. There are many reasons why that ideal cannot be attained, however, the main reason is their misunderstanding of human nature. Throughout the second half of the twentieth century, socialism came to be associated more with the welfare state and with step-by-step improvements in the living conditions of the majority of citizens than with an entirely new social order. [Brown 2009]

Communism and socialism have always shared common roots, initially it was the belief in the need to introduce universal public ownership of the means of production and the construction of the welfare nation. However, a fundamental division emerged between those who supported the revolution and those who favored evolutionary change. By the middle of the twentieth century, electorally successful socialist parties in Western Europe had accepted a 'mixed economy,' with public and private ownership co-existing. [Brown 2009]

Aiming at capitalism as the evil to conquest, socialists and communists have always look for ways of redistributing income, taking from some to give to others, instead of putting people to work. Notions of welfare in socialism, include a system of taxation to transfer wealth from the more affluent classes to the less affluent and to establish systems to provide pensions (social security) and health care, either for the poor or for the entire population. [Fleming 2008]

These ideologies prospered in the mid-19th century as a reaction to the rise of early capitalism and the economic inequality it induced. Throughout history, socialists have disagreed over how a change should come about; the alternatives been democracy or authoritarianism. Up to now, any country calling itself socialist has gone through the authoritarian road. Communists in the same tone have imposed the authority of the party in power and are usually called one-party-states. Social democracies are different from socialism and look for peaceful means of taking power.

The immense power given to the state or to the party in power by these regimes has always been a source of conflict. Some opposing viewpoints, such as anarchism, aim at a society without a state, where all human beings are capable of controlling themselves without coercive force. Many socialist theorists saw the essence of socialism not in centralized state ownership but in social or public ownership which could be in the form of co-operatives, guilds, or municipal control as well as nationalized industries. They saw these as inextricably linked with democratic institutions. [Brown 2009]

Economies calling themselves socialist economies can be divided into non-market and market forms. In non-market socialism the economy functions according to different economic laws from those of capitalism; it aims to circumvent the inefficiencies and crises associated with capital accumulation and the profit system. By contrast, market socialism retains the use of monetary prices, factor markets and in some cases the profit motive; profits generated by these firms would be controlled directly by the workforce of each firm. (Wikipedia) According to this definition, non-market socialism is more related with our understanding of socialism or communism, whereas market socialism is related primarily with social democracy.

Social democracy

Social democracy is the most common political system in the world, it provides welfare and free-market opportunities. Any capitalist system provides benefits for its citizens, therefore any capitalist system is related to social democracy. Social benefits involve a range of economic and social systems characterized by social ownership and workers' self-management of the means of production as well as the political theories and movements associated with them. There are many varieties of socialism and there is no single definition encapsulating all of them, though social ownership is the common element shared by its various forms. (Wikipedia)

There are many 'socialist' that do not approve a Marxist-Leninist approach to socialism and communism. Those 'socialists' believe in a parliamentary 'socialist' solution where power is earned at the polls instead of by force. Social democracy could be defined as the initial states of socialism, where the economy is mixed, some industries are under state protection and many other enterprises are run under private effort. These 'socialists' are currently called social-democrats, even though their final objective is to strengthen the state to dominate the economy and the people; it is possible to argue whether social democracy would become at the end another dictatorship of the proletariat.

When total or almost total control of the state is attained, the term socialism gets its full meaning. Compared to communism, which proposes the elimination of the state in its later stages, socialism sustains the idea of a totalitarian state during all eternity. Social democracy is based on parliamentary democracy, however, seeks a strong state similar to what we have identified as socialism. In recent decades social democratic parties have moved away from the idea that a radically different socioeconomic system bearing the name of socialism will ever be created. [Brown 2009]

Social democracy is a political, social and economic ideology that supports economic and social interventions to promote social justice within the framework of liberal democratic policy and capitalist economy. The protocols and norms used to accomplish this involve a commitment to representative and participatory democracy; measures for income redistribution and regulation of the economy in the general interest; and welfare state provisions. Social democracy thus aims to create the conditions for capitalism to lead to greater democratic, egalitarian and solidarity outcomes. (Wikipedia)

The terminology of social democracy, socialism, communism, and capitalism has never been perfectly defined. Socialism and communism require many generations governed by strong states to provide benefits to society. All these approaches, including capitalism, coincide in applying social measures to benefit people. According to Michael Lessnoff, a British political theorist, capitalism and socialism were conceptually compatible rather than irreconcilable opposites and also that states such as the USA and Britain 'are undoubtedly more socialist than the USSR or the People's Republic of China.' [Brown 2009]

Socialist and Communist Characteristics

Socialist and communist countries are characterized by strong states governed by the party in power and pleasing the desires of the Strong Man. Most, if not all, socialist and communist states are ruled in a tyrannical way, therefore, they use to spread fear among the population. Hundreds of thousands of people have been sacrificed in the name of the stability of those regimes. The main characteristics of a socialist or communist regime involve:

- Cult of the personality of the strong man
- Learning how to retain power from the masters, e.g., Stalin, Hitler, or Castro
- Gaining consent
- Crushing the internal and external enemy
- Use of propaganda to spread their doctrine
- Creating a culture of fear

- Use the rule by law instead of the rule of law

Socialist and communist systems promote a strictly regulated society. The control over the population implies how they think, where they work, as well as what they eat. The population is subject to fear making them obedient towards the government. Party members are constantly supervised to establish how submissive they are; those that do not fit the standards are purged.

One of the first things a socialist or communist regime is going to implement is a policy to gain the consent of the majority of the population. Usually, the regime is willing to demonstrate how good it is toward their people. Giving away ownership of the land to farmers or creating jobs in the governmental bureaucracy or in the military becomes an urgent policy. Distributing food and increasing salaries are also common strategies to gain support. However, the new elite must obey and be loyal to the new regime or it is going to be crushed.

The cult of personality is another strategy utilized by the strong man in charge. Human nature makes people believe in the benefactor that is capable of providing for the population; people love to have somebody to help them direct their lives towards the best possible path. In the same way people adore God, they want to adore a leader; people leave the responsibility of government to the strong man so that they can do their life without getting into the trouble of managing the society.

The strong man understands how weak people are and that knowledge is used to stay in power for the rest of his life. The strong man learn from the masters, his personal ambition makes him benefit from other leaders; how Stalin stayed in power indefinitely, Hitler was so popular, Castro was in power until death, and Kim Il Sung created a dynasty. The strong man gets information or finds out advisers to teach him how to proceed under difficult circumstances. Usually, the strong man has charisma, he comes from the poor and makes believe he understands their demands. The strong man has, most of the time, some skills, such as clear thoughts, interpersonal relations, easy speech, empathy, and so on. Some strong men can be ignorant but they are not dumb.

Propaganda is one of the strongest strategies used by socialist and communist regimes. The masses must support the regime; people's demonstrations are constantly present to support the regime. Spreading information that benefits the regime and eliminates opposition critics is constant, the government controls the media and can manipulate opinion.

Propaganda takes many forms, pushing the leader to become the father of the nation; looking for the adulation of the people; looking for people's loyalty; promoting self-criticizing sessions were defectors are identified; and looking for conspirators everywhere, internal or external.

Identifying the enemies is another strategy very common in socialist and communist regimes. This strategy demonstrates an image of power, constantly challenging the adversary. However, the enemy is not only from outside, but internal challenging of power also becomes a trauma for the leader. The party members and the population daring to go against the leader are going to suffer the most. Opponents that are lucky can leave the country, but in most cases, they are imprisoned or killed.

Creating a culture of fear is also a strong strategy for socialist and communist regimes. Violence, fear, and punishment are always present in those societies. The regime enforces the sense of loyalty towards the leader. The military and the secret police are the mechanisms of punishment. Socialist and communist regimes are characterized by big military support and a strong army using the most recent technology.

Controlling the people gets its maximum expression through gathering information about every single citizen according to their loyalty. People are classified into categories that determine what kind of work they are going to get, what education to pursue, and where to live. The regime controls every aspect of daily life, your eight hours work, your eight hours of study, and your eight hours sleep. Indoctrination is a constant activity several hours a week are dedicated to learning how to behave in that society. The regime organizes a kind of religious or mythical structure for the purpose of controlling individuals.

Another important consideration is how the law is enforced in these regimes. Rule of law and rule by law are totally different concepts. The rule of law refers to a state of constitutionalism where the law (nor parliament) is supreme and where all government's power is subject to the law. Rule by law means the opposite. It refers to a police state in which the government invokes the law (indeed creates law) to "justify" excessive use of government force. During a period of tyranny, leaders need to be visionaries, with prophetic voices, who are able to rise above the present crisis and take a principled stand against the rule by law.

Evolution of Socialism and Communism

It is clear that Christians are the first promoters of socialist ideas, which by themselves are not bad, but placed into the context of society are harmful instead of helpful. Why are still there some people pushing for those socialist and communist ideals that have been a long time demonstrated erroneous? Socialism and communism are very old ideas that have been evolving over many centuries it was not Marx who invented them. Common possessions were looked upon by many of the first Christians as an ideal to be aimed at. The disciples of Jesus 'were of one heart and of one soul: neither said any of them that ought of the things which he possessed was his own, but they had all things common.' [Brown 2009]

This reminds me about an anecdote of a lady that was very nice, always providing and pleasing her family members. She helped her daughters, grandsons, brothers, sisters, and many other people. She provided shelter for her brothers, daughters, and grandsons whenever they needed, without asking for compensation; her family lived gratuitously for years. Her husband did not agree, but she had always the last word on those issues.

Things started to change after a while, the first blow was her brother being caught as a drug trafficker, he is serving fifteen years sentence. The second blow was her daughters and grandsons mutiny; the daughters prohibited her to talk about their lives or criticize her grandsons, she could not explain to her sisters what was going on in her house. This demonstrates that people cannot be such a Samaritan one thing is to help during a limited time span and another very different making people irresponsible for their lives.

During the evolution of societies, some started to be organized along the lines of masters and slaves, however, people began to propose alternative solutions to attain justice. In the fourteenth century, only a minority challenged the monarchs and feudal lords and tried to create – or as they saw it, 'recreate' – a communist society which would combine freedom for all with broad equality. [Brown 2009] The serfs were the first to notice their disadvantage in the feudal society, therefore, they started to think of different arrangements of forces to handle the needs of human beings, however, they never succeeded to build a new arrangement of their society.

Since the fifteen century, the society knew how unproductive a communal society could become and it is unbelievable to find out in the twentieth-first-century some people still believing in those approaches. In the fifteen century, The Taborites, an extreme off shot of the Hussites, practiced a form of communism in anticipation of the imminent Second Coming of Christ. The principle that 'all people must hold everything in common, and nobody must possess anything of his own' was undermined by the practice whereby 'the Taborite revolutionaries were so preoccupied with common ownership that they altogether ignored the need to produce.' [Brown 2009]

The risks of a communist society are known since the beginning of history. For several centuries, the imagination of authors was plentiful, their dreams of better socialist or communist societies filled up the pages of manuscripts. Sir Thomas Moore wrote a book of an imagined communist society called Utopia, published in 1516. The narrator in his story says: '... I'm quite convinced that you'll never get a fair distribution of goods, or a satisfactory organization of human life until you abolish private property altogether.' And Moore objects that statement saying, 'I don't believe you'd ever have a reasonable standard of living under a communist system. There would always tend to be shortages because nobody would work hard enough.' [Brown 2009] If the problem was already identified in the sixteen century, is it wise to suggest socialism or communism in our days?

Italian Dominican monk Tommaso Campanella published The City of the Sun in 1602. He saw the family as the main obstacle to the creation of a communistic state and holds that parents, for the most part, educate their children wrongly and that the state must, therefore, be responsible for their education. He stressed the dignity of work, although, in his city of the sun, working hours had been reduced to four a day, with much of the rest of the time devoted to 'learning joyously.' [Brown 2009]

Campanella was absolutely wrong with the suggestion that the state was the mind changing generator of better citizens the society needs diversity rather than a monolithic view of society. The family we know is a source of diversity by showing children different ways of managing problems, each family decides the rules to apply in its own way; having a unique view from the state would produce a human robotized society. Regarding work and learning, Campanella looked much more advanced than socialists or communists by suggesting the importance of knowledge through better education.

Hopefully, better viewpoints were emerging in the most recent centuries and many of this opposed communism. The eighteenth-century Enlightenment – with its secularization, embrace of science, and belief in progress – paved the way for a different manner of thinking about the society of the future. The theory of stages of development provided the key to understanding the evolution of society. The four stages of development from hunting to pasturage to agriculture, and finally, commerce. [Brown 2009] This period was the beginning of capitalism, an economic approach that helps to integrate diverse points of view in society. These stages of development are opposed to a monolithic view of society, such as that proposed by socialism and communism.

There were many unsuccessful attempts to build a viable communal society. Many thinkers proposed alternatives, and in fact, there were a few attempts to put those ideas into practice. One of the Utopian socialists who was treated most seriously in his own lifetime was Robert Owen, from Scotland. He took over a mill that became a model factory. The factory workers were paid better than their competitors and worked shorter hours in far better conditions. Owen aspired to have complete equality of income in the community of New Harmony, with all residents enjoying similar food, clothing, and education. The self-governing community, however, found it very difficult to manage themselves and after a few weeks of trying, they had to call Owen to sort things out. [Brown 2009]

Making the Revolution

It has been mostly through wars, or what was thought as revolutions that socialists and communists took power; the use of force was always a dissuasive factor for those regimes. When communist parties took power, they were very ready to impose communism on the society. In at least half of the cases, this was a result of foreign support (usually, but not always, Soviet), backed by armed force. The parties certainly could not rely on coming to power through free elections. [Brown 2009]

"Our revolutions," said Mao Zedong, "come one after the other," a succession of mass movements "turned over" the Chinese society: the land confiscation and reform movement, in which at least a million landlords were executed (1950); the Marriage Law, which fundamentally changed the status of women, the Chinese family, and labor force (1950); sending three hundred thousand Chinese "volunteers" to fight in Korea against the United States (1950); the "Three-Anti" and "Five-Anti" campaigns to ferret out corrupt cadres and unreformed bourgeois elements (1951-52); the Agricultural Cooperative Movement to push millions of peasants into cooperatives (1952-53); and the Hundred Flowers Movement, when intellectuals were encouraged to speak out only to be brutally cashiered in the subsequent Anti-Rightist Campaign (1956-57). [Schell 2013]

Mao Zedong's concept of permanent revolution was his motto, claiming that in China the revolution could advance in an uninterrupted manner from the transition to socialism, which had been basically completed with the collectivization of agriculture, to the beginning of communism. Through the power of human consciousness and the strength of the human will – in which Mao had a profound faith – China could advance immediately to the next stage and become a country which was 'economically modern and socially communist.' [Roberts 2003]

In China, the Great Leap Forward is said to have exposed an ideological split within the leadership, a 'two-line struggle,' which dated back at least to 1949, and which was personified in the characters of Mao Zedong and Liu Shaoqi. It has been described as a romantic revolution against organized development, mass campaigns versus bureaucracy, slogans as opposed to plans, zeal vying with structure, purity struggling with pragmatism.

Another formulation of the same idea has been to contrast an 'engineering' approach to making a revolution, which is sequential, elitist and planned, and a 'storming' approach, which is simultaneous, egalitarian and spontaneous. The former was adopted by the managerial types, including Shaoqi, Deng Xiaoping and Zhou Enlai, and the latter by Mao Zedong. [Roberts 2003]

Authoritarian Regimes

Socialism requires some unpopular measures if justice, or more precisely socialist biased justice, must predominate. "The French writers who laid the foundations of modern socialism had no doubt that their ideas could be put into practice only by a strong dictatorial government. To them, socialism meant an attempt to 'terminate the revolution' by a deliberate reorganization of society on hierarchical lines and by the imposition of a coercive 'spiritual power'" [Hayek 1994]

Force is the only way to implement socialist justice; taking from some and give to others, instead of people working and building infrastructure to produce the goods required by society. Expropriation and confiscation are the main measures proposed by socialist and communist systems. In order to secure a fair distribution of wealth and income among the members of society, socialist governments typically confiscate or closely regulate major industries, the means of transportation and communication, and utilities (such as electricity and oil). [Fleming 2008]

Socialist governments must stay in power for decades because they are improvising all the time, always looking for the correct approach they dream about but is never found. Most of the time, socialism finds opposition not only from those that have been affected by expropriation and injustice but from common citizens that discover the multiple defects of socialist regimes, including the difficulties caused by lack of pragmatic approaches and lack of freedom of diversity. In the words of Adam Smith, socialism puts governments in a position where "to support themselves, they are obliged to be oppressive and tyrannical." [Hayek 1994]

A Planning Society

A well-deserved socialist society promotes central planning as the panacea to solve all the problems; socialists are not aware of the hidden problems that central planning presents. Centralism concentrates power into a few decisive planners that guarantee consistency of criteria. "Socialism means the abolition of private enterprise, of private ownership of the means of production, and the creation of a system of 'planned economy' in which the entrepreneur working for profit is replaced by a central planning body." [Hayek 1994]

There is a contradiction between a majority making decisions and a centralized society. In a society which depends on central planning, control cannot be made dependent on a majority being able to agree; it will often be necessary that the will of a small minority be imposed upon the people. Because this minority will be the largest group able to agree among themselves on the question at issue. [Hayek 1994]

In a planned society, the officials decide not whether a person is needed for a particular job but whether he is of use for anything, and how useful he is. His position in life must be assigned to him by somebody else. The unemployment or the loss of income which will always affect some in any society is certainly less degrading if it is the result of misfortune and not deliberately imposed by authority. [Hayek 1994]

Central planning has many disadvantages regarding diversity; to manage the system, simplicity must be imposed over variety. The modern movement for planning is a movement against competition as such, a new flag under which all the old enemies of competition have rallied. [Hayek 1994]

It is clear that central planners must decide what life the citizens would live; choice would not be part of the equation. What is the "just price" of a particular commodity or the "fair" remuneration for a particular service might conceivably be determined objectively if the quantities needed were independently fixed? If these were given irrespective of cost, the planner might try to find what price or wage is necessary to bring forth this supply. But the planner must also decide how much is to be produced of each kind of goods, and, in so doing, he determines what will be the just price or fair wage to pay. In deciding the relative importance of the different ends, the planner also decides the relative importance of the different groups and persons. [Hayek 1994]

I believe it was Lenin himself who introduced in Russia the famous phrase "who, whom?" This is the universal problem of a socialist society, who plans whom, who directs and dominates whom, who assigns to other people their station in life, and who is to have his due allocated by others? These become necessarily the central issues to be decided solely by the supreme power. [Hayek 1994]

Many politicians have enlarged upon Lenin's phrase and asserted that the problem of all governments is "who gets what, when, and how." Government affects the relative position of different people and all aspects of their lives are affected by government action. There are, however, two fundamental distinctions to be made. First, some measures may be taken without knowing how they will affect particular individuals. Second, it is the extent of the activities of the government which decides. Here lies the whole difference between a free and a totalitarian system. [Hayek 1994]

In the Soviet Union, planning was one of the most important activities during the communists years. Everything was planned and industries were just a tiny part of the plan. The Five-year plan was developed to transform the Soviet Union into an advanced industrial state capable of matching the country's capitalist neighbors. Each industrial unit was to be set predetermined quotas, minimum amounts that had to be achieved over a five-year period, and each worker had to produce a weekly amount. [Evans 2005]

The First Five-Year-Plan was placed on heavy industry factories were to produce capital goods such as machinery, machine tools, and tractors. Dams had to be built to provide hydro-electric power and increase production; new sources of essential raw materials, particularly iron, steel, coal, and oil were necessary. New areas such as chemicals, motor vehicles, synthetic rubber, and artificial fibers were also developed. [Evans 2005] It is clear that this type of planning does not promote innovation, things get done over and over without changes; it is impossible to improve on a static approach.

Failed States

Nation-states exist to provide a decentralized method of delivering public goods to persons living within designated borders. They organize and channel the interests of their people, often but not exclusively in furtherance of national goals and values. Usually buffer or manipulate external forces and influences, champion the local or particular concerns of their adherents, and mediate between the constraints and challenges of the international arena and the dynamism of their own internal economic, political, and social realities.

States succeed or fail across all or some of these dimensions. But it is according to their performance—according to the levels of their effective delivery of the most crucial public goods—that strong states may be distinguished from weak ones, and weak states from failed or collapsed states. Public goods are those intangible and hard to quantify claims that citizens once made on sovereigns and now make on states. They encompass expectations, conceivably obligations, inform the local political culture, and together give content to the social contract between ruler and ruled that is at the core of regime/government and citizenry interactions.

There is a hierarchy of public goods. None is as critical as the supply of the security, especially human security. The state's prime function is to provide that public good of security—to prevent cross-border invasion and infiltration, and any loss of territory; to eliminate domestic threats to or attacks upon the national order and social structure; to prevent crime and any related dangers to domestic human security; and to enable citizens to resolve their disputes with the state and with their fellow inhabitants without recourse to arms or other forms of physical coercion.

Another key public good enables citizens to participate freely, openly, and fully in politics and the political process. This good encompasses the essential freedoms: the right to compete for office; respect and support for national and regional political institutions, like legislatures and courts; tolerance of dissent and difference; and fundamental civil and human rights.

Other public goods expected by citizens include medical and health care (at varying levels and costs); schools and educational instruction (of various kinds and levels)—the knowledge good; roads, railways, harbors, and other physical infrastructures—the arteries of commerce; communications infrastructures; a money and banking system, usually presided over by a central bank and lubricated by a national currency; a beneficent fiscal and institutional context within which citizens can pursue personal entrepreneurial goals and potentially prosper; the promotion of civil society; and methods of regulating the sharing of the environmental commons. Together, this bundle of public goods, roughly rank ordered, establishes a set of criteria according to which modern nation-states may be judged strong, weak, or failed.

Strong states unquestionably control their territories and deliver a full range and a high quality of public goods to their citizens. They perform well according to indicators like GDP per capita, the UNDP Human Development Index, Transparency International's Corruption Perception Index, and Freedom House's Freedom of the World Report. Strong states offer high levels of security from political and criminal violence, ensure political freedom and civil liberties, and create environments conducive to the growth of economic opportunity. The rule of law prevails. Judges are independent. Road networks are well maintained. Telephones work. Snail mail and e-mail both arrive quickly. Schools, universities, and students flourish. Hospitals and clinics serve patients effectively. And so on. Overall, strong states are places of enviable peace and order.

Weak states include a broad continuum of states that are: inherently weak because of geographical, physical, or fundamental economic constraints; basically strong, but temporarily or situationally weak because of internal antagonisms, management flaws, greed, despotism, or external attacks; and a mixture of the two. Weak states typically harbor ethnic, religious, linguistic, or other communal tensions that have not yet, or not yet thoroughly, become overtly violent. Urban crime rates tend to be higher and increasing. In weak states, the ability to provide adequate measures of other political goods is diminished or diminishing. Physical infrastructural networks have deteriorated. Schools and hospitals show signs of neglect, particularly outside the main cities. GDP per capita and other critical economic indicators have fallen or are falling, sometimes dramatically; levels of venal corruption are embarrassingly high and escalating. Weak states usually honor rule of law precepts in the breach.

They harass civil society. Weak states are often ruled by despots, elected or not.

Failed states are tense, deeply conflicted, dangerous, and contested bitterly by warring factions. In most failed states, government troops battle armed revolts led by one or more rivals. Occasionally, the official authorities in a failed state face two or more insurgencies, varieties of civil unrest, different degrees of communal discontent, and a plethora of dissent directed at the state and at groups within the state.

There is no failed state without disharmony between communities. In contrast to strong states, failed states cannot control their borders. In most failed states, regimes prey on their own constituents. Driven by ethnic or other communal hostility, or by the governing elite's insecurities, they victimize their own citizens or some subset of the whole that is regarded as hostile. Another indicator of state failure is the growth of criminal violence.

Failed states provide only limited quantities of other essential political goods. Failed states are typified by deteriorating or destroyed infrastructures. Failed states offer unparalleled economic opportunity—but only for a privileged few. Corruption flourishes in many states, but in failed states, it often does so on an unusually destructive scale. An indicator of failure but not a cause of failure, are declining real national and per capita levels of annual GDP.

Sometimes, especially if there are intervening climatic disasters, the economic chaos and generalized neglect that is endemic to failed states lead to regular food shortages and widespread hunger—indeed, even to episodes of starvation and major efforts of international humanitarian relief.

A collapsed state is a rare and extreme version of a failed state. Political goods are obtained through private or ad hoc means. Security is equated with the rule of the strong. A collapsed state exhibits a vacuum of authority. It is a mere geographical expression, a black hole into which a failed organization has fallen.

Highlights for Chapter 1
- Socialism or communism is a political ideology that advocates for an egalitarian redistribution of wealth.
- Socialists have disagreed over how a change should come about; the alternatives been democracy or authoritarianism.

- Socialists and communist have always dreamed of constructing a new society, a Utopian ideal that can never be attained.
- The immense power given to the state or to the party in power by these regimes has always been a source of conflict.
- Those economies calling themselves socialist economies can be divided into non-market and market forms.
- Social democracy is based on parliamentary democracy and the free-market.
- Socialist and communist countries are characterized by strong states governed by the party in power that exercise the desires of the strong man paradigm.
- Most, if not all, socialist and communist states are ruled in a tyrannical way, therefore, spreading fear among the population.
- Hundred of thousands of people have been sacrificed in the name of the stability of the socialist or communist regime.
- Socialist or communist regimes implement policies to gain the consent of the majority of the population.
- The cult of personality is another strategy utilized by the strong man in charge.
- Propaganda is one of the strongest strategies used by socialist and communist regimes.
- Identifying the enemies is another strategy very common in socialist and communist regimes.
- Controlling the people through gathering information about every single citizen according to their loyalty.
- It has been mostly through revolutions that socialists or communists took power.
- Socialist governments typically confiscate or closely regulate major industries.
- "To support themselves socialists are obliged to be oppressive and tyrannical."
- It is according to the performance that strong states may be distinguished from weak ones.

Chapter 2: Socialist and Communist Features

Socialism and communism are so closely related that most of the time such governments call themselves using both terms. Worst of all, every country makes its own interpretation of socialism or communism, according to their own interests and understanding to justify its policies. It looks like without any theoretical support, the leadership defines its principles according to how things work in practice. It is well known that socialism and communism theories contain many flaws and have been heavily criticized over the centuries.

It is well known that there is no country in the world that has attained the ultimate objective of becoming a socialist or communist system. However, just because of their struggle seeking socialism or communism makes them deserve that label. Many of these regimes say that they are just moving towards the ultimate objective and that the failures in performance are due to not having reached the final destination. The suffering of a population should not be accepted on the grounds of an unattainable objective.

Socialism according to this book is the quest for a non-market based economic system where the state is the supreme power that controls everything. Communism is a workers or peasants oriented society with a ruling party that decide their destiny. Both socialism and communism require a strong state that decides the policies people must follow. Socialism and communism have always been intertwined, it is not easy to distinguish the differences between these two approaches. People participation in these societies is minimal and most of the time rulers make citizens believe that they are participating, when in fact the decisions have already been taken by the party-state.

In socialist or communist systems, there is a quest to get rid of capitalistic and egoistic ideals. Capitalism is associated with individuality where the actor is the entrepreneur. Common ownership of the means of production and the need of a strong state, at least during the initial stages of evolution, are required to attain those ideals; however, it is impossible to confirm that the state is going to disappear after many generations. For the state, it is going to be an immense task to take care of all the means of production, there is no successful experience in this regard yet.

A well-known argument against capitalism is 'In capitalism, there are two major classes, the working class, and the capitalist class. The working class, the majority within society, must work to survive. The capitalist class is a minority that derives profit from employing the working class through private ownership of the means of production.' Here we find an insane bias towards the working class, putting capitalists as the evil impersonated. In a more open mind argument, it must be recognized that a capitalist is just another person that has had the initiative to invent a new business that required additional workers to produce goods or services. If the business is profitable, the workers would take a bigger share, but if it is not, a reorganization of the business is due.

Another argument against capitalism proclaims 'The conflict between workers and capitalists classes is the root of all the problems in society and the situation will ultimately be resolved through a social revolution. The revolution will put the working class in power and in turn establish social ownership of the means of production.' It should be clear that when the workers take over, they will need to work to make the business productive, probably even hiring the eradicated capitalist. Marxism-Leninism is just one more recent socialist or communist proposal, which is biased towards the worker without considering the difficulties of making a business profitable for all.

Socialists and communists insist on the inconsequential nature of money. They believe that only capitalists impose the importance of money. If socialists or communists could do it, money would be eradicated; but of course, society would not work. However, if all rewards, instead of being offered in money, were offered in the form of public distinctions or privileges, positions of power over other men, or better housing or better food, opportunities for travel or education, this would merely mean that the recipient would no longer be allowed to choose and that whoever fixed the reward determined not only its size but also the particular form in which it should be enjoyed. [Hayek 1994]

It is incredible that people have so much faith in the positive evolution of human beings when, in many cases, new generations tend to be worse than older generations. The American writer Howard Fast, who joined the Communist Party in 1943, did so believing that the communist destination was 'the total brotherhood of man, a world-wide unity of love and creativity in which life is neither wasted nor despised. Regarding education level, it is well known that new generations are not necessarily better than older generations. Even within the same family where parents were overcome by their children, it is possible to find grandchildren that are worse than their parents or grandparents. These use to be children or grandchildren with no interests in advancing their knowledge and learning how to become useful to society.

Human nature is a much stronger factor than expected by socialist and communist idealists. Deciding from a desk how much help a person can give under pressure of hunger or injustice is unnatural. Many idealists believe that human beings are perfectible and normally good, that they are not selfish, always ready to help their fellow humans. Bakunin supposed that solidarity came naturally to people, making them capable when freed from the fetters of the state, of self-sacrifice and an ability to organize themselves in small autonomous communes, in which each person would have absolute freedom. [Brown 2009]

Communism is a dangerous approach, it is an all-encompassing system of beliefs that builds up upon desires, not realities. It purports to offer a key to understanding social development without understanding human nature. It has authorities whose word could not be questioned, and whose interpreters and guardians act also as gatekeepers, deciding who 'belongs' and who does not. [Brown 2009]

Socialist countries make us believe that social justice and ideals are paramount, however, economic considerations use to be their first priorities. Men are today more than ever before governed by economic doctrines, by the carefully fostered belief in the irrationality of our economic system, by the false assertions about "potential plenty," pseudo-theories about the inevitable trend toward monopoly, and the destruction of stocks of raw materials or the suppression of inventions, for which competition is blamed. [Hayek 1994]

The claims for social reconstruction are almost all economic in character: the "reinterpretation in economic terms" of the political ideals of the past, of liberty, equality, and security, is one of the main demands of people who at the same time proclaim the end of the economic man. The reinterpretation of political ideals is done with the aim of just taking power, believing that it is possible to do whatever they feel with human beings, thinking that humans are like robots that can be programmed.

According to the history of each country, it is possible to evolve towards unwanted approaches as socialism and communism. Some authors have had the cleverness to identify the importance of history when proposing new approaches for prosperous societies. Marx wrote: 'Men make their own history, but they do not make it just as they please; they do not make it under circumstances chosen by themselves, but under circumstances directly encountered, given and transmitted from the past. The tradition of all the dead generations weighs like a nightmare on the brain of the living.' [Brown 2009] When politicians keep repeating the same mistakes over and over again, societies are unable to prosper.

The principal principles under socialist or communist ideals are related to Collectivization and Individuality, Equality, Freedom, Public versus Private Property, and The Party.

Collectivization and Individuality

One important feature of socialist or communist systems is the vision towards collectivization instead of individualism. Everything for them is justified in terms of the collectivity, 'everything must be done for the good of all,' 'do not be egoistic, think about others,' 'work in groups instead of individually,' 'give as much as you can without expecting retribution,' are some arguments against individual's choices.

A collectivity is formed by individuals, not the other way around. And many activities require the concourse of many individuals working for the same objective. It is well known that individuals can get together and work for a business or noble cause independently of the type of society they live in (capitalist, socialist, or communist), therefore, forcing everybody towards some fixed objectives, invented by a group of bureaucrats, does not guarantee a better result. Freedom of choice should be paramount, the individual decides where he wants to work, it is not the state which decides.

Collectivization and individuality are complementary instead of opposites. The individualist view does not, of course, exclude the recognition of social ends, or rather of a coincidence of individual ends which makes it advisable for men to combine for their pursuit. Common action is limited to the fields where people agree on common ends. In fact, people are most likely to agree on common action where the common end is not an ultimate end to them but a means capable of serving a great variety of purposes. [Hayek 1994]

Collectivization

Collectivization has been one of the important concepts communists have integrated into their system. It happened in agriculture, industry, education, and in most of the common activities of citizens, such as food distribution, transport and so on. Arts were also collectivized, citizens were forced to produce works according to the needs of the revolution. The new culture had no use for individual 'inspiration,' which the communists viewed as a 'bourgeois' illusion. In a socialist society, based on the principle of collectivism, culture would necessarily assume a collective character. [Streissguth 2002]

Some positive and negative examples of experiences of collectivization demonstrate that it is possible to coexist with both collectivity and individuality viewpoints. The important point is to recognize that there is diversity within the collectivity, therefore, apply policies that benefit each group with appropriate measures that benefit each group. Treating everybody the same is unjustified, the context of each group must be taken into consideration, as well as the characteristics of the individual.

This reminds me of the experience of 'volunteers' in Cuba, were everybody was forced to go cut sugar cane. It was an egalitarian policy to force people to do a physical job independently of their skills and experience. The collectivity had to obey the request, nobody could avoid the task. They wanted to make everybody the same, this was justice for the regime. It did not matter if you had the physical strength or not, and if you hurt yourself was not their problem.

Over the centuries, individuals in capitalistic societies have always demonstrated the viability of working in groups to complete complex tasks, independently of how successful the distribution of wealth was performed. It has always been possible to manage a capitalistic society to attain collective objectives. On the other side, up to now, a socialistic or communistic society has never demonstrated tangible results to justify its existence.

The peasants benefited from the revolution because they came into possession of all agricultural lands. Never in modern Russian history was the peasantry as autonomous as in the 1920s. However, the revolution did not help to overcome the traditional problems of Russian agriculture: a backward peasantry, primitive methods of cultivation, and great agricultural overpopulation. In fact, the changes made by the revolution were a step backward. [Streissguth 2002]

The kulaks in Russia owned large farms and were capable of hiring labor and leasing land, they represented a collective enterprise that was successful. The Bolsheviks feared and mistrusted the peasant class, but it was impossible for them to say this aloud. Instead, they aimed their animosity at the richest layer of the peasant class, the kulaks, who made approximately 5 percent of the peasantry. On the one hand, the Bolsheviks needed the services of the kulaks to keep feeding the population. On the other hand, as communists, they feared that the increased economic power of the kulaks would inevitably lead to political power. They explicitly considered the richest peasants hostile; implicitly they feared the entire peasantry, still 80 percent of the population. [Streissguth 2002]

Christianity has had a large impact in socialist ideals, primarily collectivization. The notions of sacrifice, solidarity and collaborations have been surrounding religion for many centuries. The nineteenth-century saw many attempts to think about how society might be organized on a co-operative or, in some instances, communist basis. Etienne Cabet was the first person to use the term 'communism' in 1840. In his book Voyage en Icarie, an egalitarian community in which there is neither private property nor money and in which all goods are held in common. Cabet was opposed to violent revolution and his communism was inspired by Christianity. [Brown 2009]

Collectivization Backfiring

An argument against collectivization is the understanding of where wealth is being produced. Some areas of the economy can be much more productive than others, therefore, the distribution of wealth differs. Humans try to keep their benefits as much as they can, they prefer not to share. Thus, how to distribute wealth becomes a quest.

A fallacy of socialism is the promise that workers would take the means of production under their own hands, including the distribution of profits among workers. There are few socialists today who believe that in a socialist society the output of each industry would be entirely shared by the workers of that industry; for this would mean that workers in industries using a great deal of capital would have a much larger income. [Hayek 1994]

Despite their almost complete disappearance, there were successful experiences of collective management in China. The Liu Ling Lower Agricultural Producer's Co-operative was formed in 1954 with the enthusiastic support of the poor peasants and the grudging acceptance of the former wealthy members of the village. ... in the end everyone was agreed and understood that with a farmers' cooperative there was no question of one gaining at the expense of another, but that all should achieve prosperity together. [Roberts 2003]

At the beginning of the Chinese revolution, poor peasants were given ownership of land. However, over the years, peasants abandoned the original purpose and acted on their own, offering the land to the highest bidder. Soon after land reform, the more equal distribution of wealth began to be eroded. Within three years 20-25 percent of the population of some areas had sold land, most of the sales being from poor peasants households to those of rich peasants. The solution proposed by Mao Zedong was 'the socialist transformation of agriculture as a whole through co-operation.' Having encouraged peasants to join the revolution by offering them the ownership of land, it was an extraordinary reversal to start, within four years, the process of depriving them of that individual ownership. [Roberts 2003]

There were contradictions over the years in the path to follow regarding privatization or collectivization. It looked more of improvisation than ideological planning. The Great Leap Forward was one of the most striking examples of Mao actually putting his singular and radical theories into practice. All private farmland, which had been confiscated from landlords and redistributed to the peasants only a few years before in a bloody pogrom, was now to be forcibly abolished and the country's 740,000 agricultural cooperatives reorganized into 26,000 gigantic "people's communes." Not only would all land be communalized, but so would all houses, livestock, tools, meals, and even bathing. The plan also called on peasants to become a major source of iron production by forcing them to set up small backyard furnaces. [Schell 2013]

The first of Deng Xiaoping's local breakthroughs was the decommunalization of agriculture. A six-point proposal: take control away from the "people's communes" and collectivized production teams; "town and village enterprises" were essentially private enterprises in the form of local -public-private joint ventures; Special Economic Zones were manufacturing and industrial zones governed by special protocapitalist legal regulations and tax benefits designed to attract outside investment. [Schell 2013]

By the mid-1980s, collectivized agrarian socialism was withering away, while rural standards of living and household incomes were improving dramatically. Deng had made good on his slogan "Poverty is not socialism." He had liberated people from the rigidity of Maoist egalitarianism, arguing from the beginning that it was necessary to "allow some regions, enterprises, and people to become better off sooner than others." In 1983 he was even blunter, stating: "Some people in rural areas and cities should be allowed to get rich before others. It is only fair that people who work hard should prosper." [Schell 2013]

<u>Individuality</u>

It is impossible for any man to survey more than a limited field, to be aware of the urgency of more than a limited number of needs. Whether his interests center around his own physical needs, or whether he takes a warm interest in the welfare of every human being he knows, the ends about which he can be concerned will always be only an infinitesimal fraction of the needs of all men. [Hayek 1994]

The limitations of human beings is the fundamental fact on which the whole philosophy of individualism is based. It does not assume, as is often asserted, that man is egoistic or selfish or ought to be. The limits of our powers of imagination make it impossible to include in our scale of values more than a sector of the needs of the whole society, and that, since, strictly speaking, scales of values can exist only in individual minds, nothing but partial scales of values exist – scales which are inevitably different and often inconsistent with each other. [Hayek 1994]

Individualism has many applications within a society; human nature makes us more or less capable of interacting in isolated or populated environments. The various kinds of collectivism: socialism, communism, fascism, etc., differ among themselves in the goal toward which they want to direct the efforts of society. But they all differ from liberalism and individualism in wanting to organize the whole of society and all of its resources for this unitary end and in refusing to recognize autonomous spheres in which the ends of individuals are supreme. [Hayek 1994]

Equality

Equality was the most important principle dreamed by the intellectuals of socialism. Equality referred primarily to economic equality instead of an intellectual, educational, social or collaborative type of equality. A government which undertakes to direct economic activity will have to use its power to realize somebody's idea of distributive justice. But how can and how will it use that power? By what principles will it or ought it to be guided? What about the relative merits that will arise? Is there a scale of values? Does it justify a new hierarchical order of society to satisfy the demands for justice? [Hayek 1994]

There is only one general principle that provides a definite answer to the question of equality: complete and absolute equality of all individuals in those points that are subject to human control. It would give the vague idea of distributive justice a clear meaning and would give the planner definite guidance. What socialism promised was not an absolute equal, but a more just and more equal, distribution. [Hayek 1994]

For Gracchus Babeuf, during the French Revolution, equality was the supreme value, and they were ready to embrace 'a period of dictatorship in the general interest for as long as might be necessary to destroy or disarm the enemies of equality.' [Brown 2009]

In contrast to Babeuf, the French theorist Comte de Saint-Simon was no believer of equality, in his case, instead, he believed in a personal educational capacity. The most educated section of society would be in charge of the administration, based on the application of science, and subject to class co-operation instead of the inevitability of class struggle. He believed that free economic competition produced poverty and crisis and that society was moving inexorably to a stage when its affairs would be planned in accordance with social needs. [Brown 2009]

Even economical equality is difficult to attain, the transformation of human beings into unbiased justice seekers is an unattainable objective. John Stuart Mill wrote nearly a hundred years ago: "A fixed rule, like that of equality, might be acquiesced in, and so might chance, or an external necessity; but that a handful of human beings should weight everybody in the balance, and give more to one and less to another at their sole pleasure and judgment, would not be borne unless from persons believed to be more than men, and backed by supernatural terrors." [Hayek 1994]

When justice is defined by the political system in power, it can be twisted towards simple solutions that do not consider specifics, therefore implying injustice. Inequality is undoubtedly more readily borne and affects the dignity of the person much less if it is determined by impersonal forces than when it is due to design. In a competitive society, it is no slight to a person, no offense to his dignity, to be told by any particular firm that it has no need for his services or that it cannot offer him a better job. [Hayek 1994]

In socialist or communistic systems, the state is the only owner of all the means of production, therefore, there are no discretionary decisions, rules are applied equally to everybody. When there are many private owners, decisions can differ, allowing a balance of justice among participants. So long as the property is divided among many owners, none of them acting independently has exclusive power to determine the income and position of particular people – nobody is tied to any one property owner except by the fact that he may offer better terms than anybody else. [Hayek 1994]

Socialists promises of equality have failed, and after many examples with years in power, they have not been able to deliver. In the Soviet Union, the difference between the highest and the lowest salaries is of the same order of magnitude (about 50 to 1) as in the United States. Leon Trotsky estimated that "the 11 or 12 percent of the Soviet population now (1939) receives approximately 50 percent of the national income." This differentiation is sharper than in the United States, where the upper 10 percent of the population receives approximately 35 percent of the national income. [Hayek 1994]

In China, politicians have recognized that the economic system is unjust. Zhu Rongji has identified the unjust distribution of wealth in the population, where riches get benefited, and on the other hand, he appeared increasingly to identify with the other 99 percent of poor people. "I earn just around 800 yuan a month," he reportedly said. "How come I'm paying taxes and they [the nouveau riche] don't? Why is it that the super-rich pays the least taxes?" Zhu had always wanted to believe that China's "socialist market" economic model would guarantee greater equality. Now, though, his faith that state ownership would ensure "common prosperity" seemed far less certain. [Schell 2013]

Deng Xiaoping was clever on equality issues than his predecessors. Although Deng's immediate priorities were "pedestrian" ones, such as professionalizing the military, fixing the railroad system, reviving industry, and mending fences internationally, their combined implications were profound. Rejecting Mao's strict egalitarianism, Deng openly promoted material incentives in the form of increased wages in order to "encourage people's initiative" ... even if they did create inequalities. [Schell 2013]

"People's contributions do differ." Deng told his comrades in the leadership. "Shouldn't there, therefore, be differences in remuneration?" In the context of the preceding years of Maoist egalitarianism, these were almost heretical comments. [Schell 2013] It is clear from a human nature point of view that people are different, therefore, they must be treated accordingly.

The gap between rich and poor that Zhu Rongji had fretted about as he left office had only grown larger. China's Gini coefficient, the standard measure of economic inequality, already exceeded 0.4 by 2001, the last year that the government released an official number. And by 2010, the index was thought to be as high as 0.6, making China one of the most unequal major economies in the world. In 2010, even though up to five hundred million people continued to live in grinding poverty on less than $2 a day, China earned the dubious distinction of boasting more billionaires than Russia. [Schell 2013]

Some sources place Cuba as an egalitarian society thanks to using the control of all human activities. Thus by controlling most of the cultivated land in the country, controlling the output on the remaining private farms, eliminating most private property, using La Libreta (the ration book), decreasing the wages for all except the poorest paid Cubans between 1966 and 1970, guaranteeing employment and providing free health care, education and social security to all, the Cuban government created the most egalitarian distribution of income in all of Latin America. [Staten 2005]

Freedom

A planned socialist society has many disadvantages, including a lack of freedom. Walter Lippmann has arrived at the conviction that "the generation to which we belong is now learning from experience what happens when men retreat from freedom to a coercive organization of the affairs. Though they promise themselves a more abundant life, they must in practice renounce it; as the organized direction increases, the variety of ends must give way to uniformity. That is the nemesis of the planned society and the authoritarian principle in human affairs." [Hayek 1994]

The experience shows that socialism is based on a lack of freedom. Where freedom was concerned, the founders of socialism made no bones about their intentions. Freedom of thought they regarded as the root-evil of nineteenth-century society, and the first of modern planners, Saint-Simon, even predicted that those who did not obey his proposed planning boards would be "treated like cattle." [Hayek 1994]

Money is one of the greatest instruments of freedom ever invented by man. Socialism is against money because it represents capitalism. It is money which in existing society opens an astounding range of choice to the poor man – a range greater than that which not many generations ago was open to the wealthy. [Hayek 1994]

The connection between socialism and fascism has become increasingly obvious, the lack of freedom is common in fascists states. In democracies, the majority of people still believe that socialism and freedom can be combined. We can still hear such contradictions in terms as "individualist socialism" seriously discussed. [Hayek 1994]

Freedom and socialism do not mix, therefore, socialism must be authoritarian to stay in power. W. H. Chamberlin, who in twelve years in Russia as an American correspondent had seen all his ideals shattered, summed up the conclusions of his studies there and in Germany and Italy in the statement that "socialism is certain to prove, in the beginning at least, the road NOT to freedom, but to dictatorship and counter-dictatorships, to civil war of the fiercest kind. Socialism achieved and maintained by democratic means seems definitive to belong to the world of utopias." [Hayek 1994]

In the Soviet Union, by the late 1980s, glasnost had become almost identical to freedom of speech, and the flow of information had reached unprecedented levels. A free flow of information and a communist system were mutually incompatible. Highly authoritarian regimes need state censorship and give rise to self-censorship. [Brown 2009]

Glasnost was simple to implement in the Soviet Union because it implied less censorship. It soon appeared, however, that it was much easier to push through the glasnost reforms than the economic and social perestroika. Glasnost simply meant to limit the freedom of action of censorship – to give permission to publish Dr. Zhivago and other works. [Laqueur 2015]

World war II affected many Soviets, it was a harsh war that traumatized most of them, "The people weren't the same after the war. I myself came home crazed. Stalin didn't like our generation. He hated us. We'd tasted freedom. For us, the war meant freedom. We'd gone to Europe and seen how people lived there. When I would walk past a monument of Stalin on my way to work, I'd break into a cold sweat: what if he could read my thoughts?" [Alexievich 2016]

Deng Xiaoping was one of the greatest minds regarding economic freedom. He did not try to micromanage the changes he was unleashing. Instead, he gave local officials the freedom to experiment with new alternative economic models. "Under our present system of economic management, power is over-concentrated," he said. "So it is necessary to devolve some of it to the lower levels without hesitation, but in a planned way." [Schell 2013]

It is a pity that Cuba did not follow the Soviet Union and did not open up its society to the world. While the brothers Fidel and Raul Castro in Cuba would not recognize it as such, the biggest failure of the regime is the absence of political pluralism and intellectual freedom. While the abuse of human rights has been less than in some other communist states – and less than that at times in some right-wing Latin American regimes – it has been substantial and accompanied by political repression. [Brown 2009]

Democracies

Democracies have the great advantage over socialism and communism that when things go wrong, the incumbent government can be blamed and voted out. The political system itself is preserved as a result of the exercise of democratic accountability. An authoritarian regime which is driven to relying on economic performance for legitimacy faces special difficulties when that performance weakens. It was through simply being there as a better alternative to communist rule that democracies prevailed in the battle of ideas. The example of greater tolerance, of free elections, accountable government, and respect for human rights, plus substantially higher living standards, had a profound effect. [Brown 2009]

Democracies, once firmly established, are remarkably resilient. Consolidated democracies are hardly ever exchanged for a form of authoritarian rule, and however imperfectly they function, they have shown themselves more capable of delivering justice as well as freedom than any state built on the foundations laid by Marx and Lenin. [Brown 2009]

While democracy promotes freedom, socialism promotes authoritarianism. Nobody saw more clearly than De Tocqueville that democracy as an essentially individualistic institution stood in an irreconcilable conflict with socialism: "Democracy extends the sphere of individual freedom," he said in 1848; "socialism restricts it. Democracy attaches all possible value to each man; socialism makes each man a mere agent, a mere number. Democracy and socialism have nothing in common but one word: equality. But notice the difference: while democracy seeks equality in liberty, socialism seeks equality in restraint and servitude" [Hayek 1994]

Socialist and communist countries tend to maintain their population like ignorants. Studies of values in China have shown that the higher the education of respondents, the more likely they are to support political reform. They value China's social stability and recoil with horror at the memory of Mao's Cultural Revolution. Democratization, viewed as a development which could get out of control and give rise to instability, scares people to take the risk of pressing for political democracy. [Brown 2009]

Fear is too strong in totalitarian regimes. People do not dare to criticize the government, they fear for their life. However, obedient citizens are not welcomed in society; when the need calls, direct action is necessary. Active minorities are needed to start a fight against bad governments. Obeying majorities do not count, they just talk and comply, helping the government perpetuate.

Public versus Private Property

What our generation has forgotten is that the system of private property is the most important guaranty of freedom, not only for those who own property, but scarcely less for those who do not. It is only because the control of the means of production is divided among many people acting independently that nobody has complete power over us, that we as individuals can decide what to do with ourselves. If all the means of production were vested in a single hand, whether it be nominally that of "society" as a whole or that of a dictator, whoever exercises this control has complete power over us. [Hayek 1994]

The Party

Socialism and communism have followed the path of strong states, and are called one-party-states, obeying the unique command of the party in power. Between 1840 and the Russian Revolution of 1917, the terms 'socialism' and 'communism' were often used more or less interchangeably. Marx, however, made it clear that the communists espoused a revolutionary brand of socialism and the inevitability of the proletarian revolution. [Brown 2009]

The belief that the party brings more participation in the decisions of a government is false. Instead, the party facilitates the maintenance of the Strong Man impulsing decisions. Broad comparative studies of authoritarian regimes (embracing not only communist systems) have shown that personal rule tends to last longer when it is linked to a ruling party. The party organization can help keep in line potential rivals to the supreme leader and prevent them from endangering his power. The hierarchical nature of the party does, indeed, make it difficult for anyone to challenge the top leader, and it gives him an undoubted advantage in the determination of policy. [Brown 2009]

It is possible to affirm that communism is not the final stage of socialism, communism is a variant of socialism that perpetuates the party in power. Given that ruling communist parties described their existing systems as 'socialist,' it is reasonable to ask: what is our justification for calling them 'communist'? The members of the ruling parties described themselves as communists. The stage of 'communism' was to be the ultimate stage of socialism – that self-governing, stateless, co-operative society that has never existed anywhere. [Brown 2009]

In early 1989, during Perestroika, the questions were 'What kind of society did the Soviets have, and where are they now? Where are they going? One has a feeling that no one knows. Does this matter? After all, where are we going? In the Soviet Union, it did matter since the legitimacy of party rule rested upon its role of leading the people towards a goal.' [Brown 2009]

Political activity requires ethereal plans, it is impossible to predict the results of events, it knows 'neither starting-place nor appointed destination.' A political party could not claim the right to rule on the grounds that it had discerned how to guide society to an ultimate goal. Marxist-Leninist ideologists claimed that there was an appointed destination – that of communism, the classless, self-administering society – that they could justify the permanent exercise of the leading role of the communist party. It was that party which possessed the theoretical insight and the practical experience to guide less advanced citizens to this radiant future. [Brown 2009]

The Soviet Union was one example of party rule that had an influence on several other nearby states. The invasion of Czechoslovakia vividly illustrated the "Brezhnev Doctrine" to communist governments in the rest of Europe and around the world: No deviations from one-party rule and the party line as determined by the Soviet government would be tolerated. [Streissguth 2002] However, after Perestroika, the role of the party has almost disappeared.

Party Members

There were many different variants in communism, yet even more diverse than these regimes were the people who joined communist parties.

In non-communist states – especially fascist, right-wing authoritarian, or racist regimes – those who joined the party often did so for the best of motives. [Brown 2009]

Interest is one of the main drivers for human beings, the same happens to communists when they join the party. Some have the interest to help, others want to be powerful, still, others want to guarantee a job when the party takes over. Once a communist party did seize power, people of the most diverse views and personalities joined for a wide variety of reasons, but most commonly to further (or, at least, not retard) their careers. [Brown 2009]

When people suffer due to the wrong government, such as Absurd Socialism, they feel no sympathy for the members of the party in power. There may be hate toward those partisans. When people have been hurt, it is human nature at its best to consider every partisan a bad person. However, to be told that a person was a communist, meaning a member of a communist party, could convey surprisingly little about the person's basic beliefs and values. Even at the stage of a communist seizure of power, there were revolutionaries who joined the party with a burning desire to construct a just and harmonious society and others whose primary goal was to wreak vengeance on their class enemies and who were more interested in destroying than building. [Brown 2009]

Not only was there a wide diversity of opinion among individual members of communist parties, but there were also many different variants in communism. Some gave more importance to the party and the socialist economy while others used a more free-market approach. There were also substantial differences from one communist country to another, persisting to the present day, as the cases of contemporary China and North Korea clearly illustrate. The problem, of course, is that citizens suffer due to wrong policies and a country does not deserve to be bullied by misinformed politicians.

Characteristics of a Communist System

Marxism-Leninism used the class struggle as its main ideal. The originality of the Communist Manifesto, according to Marx, was: (1) the existence of classes is only bound up with particular, historical phases in the development of production; (2) the class struggle necessarily leading to the dictatorship of the proletariat; and (3) that this dictatorship itself only constitutes the transition to the abolition of all classes and to a classless society. [Brown 2009]

The idea of building communism, a society in which the state would have withered away, turned out to be a dangerous illusion. It is impossible to eliminate the state, the only thing that can be done is to reduce its power. What was built instead was communism, an oppressive party-state which was authoritarian at best and ruthlessly totalitarian at worst? Although it had some common features, it changed over time and differed hugely from one part of the world to another. [Brown 2009]

There are certain common features which make it entirely meaningful to call a political system communist. Features such as the ideology, the political system, and the economic system determine the degree of affinity with communist's precepts. Cuba is the only communist regime that has ever existed in Latin America. No African state has ever been communist, some have been under communist party command but none keeps communists ties today; some were called socialists or run under socialists parties. The Soviet Union ceased to be a communist system in the course of 1989. China is today a hybrid, possessing still some essential features of communism but having discarded others. [Brown 2009]

The defining characteristics of a communist system are related to the political system, the economic system, and the ideological sphere. [Brown 2009] Each characteristic is decomposed into features such as social measures to help the population, honesty of administrators, freedom of speech and market freedom, human rights considerations, and so on.

Political System

The first defining feature of a communist system is the monopoly of power of the communist party. There were other important institutions within a communist state besides the ruling party, among them government ministries, the military, and the security police. All institutions were overseen by the organs of the communist party, which had a higher authority than any other body. [Brown 2009]

The second defining feature of a communist system was the concept of democratic centralism. In theory, it means that there could be a discussion of issues – the 'democratic' component – until a decision had been reached, but thereafter the decision of higher party organs was binding and had to be implemented in a strictly disciplined manner throughout the party and society. [Brown 2009]

Economic System

The third defining feature of a consolidated communist system is non-capitalist ownership of the means of production, and linked to this is the fourth feature – the dominance of a command economy, as distinct from a market economy. Even in established communists systems, some private economic activity continued, whether on a legal or illegal basis – or quite commonly, as a mixture of both. [Brown 2009]

Ideological Sphere

The fifth feature of a communist system is the declared aim of building communism as the ultimate, legitimizing goal. It had an important place in the official ideology and motivational and inspirational significance for a substantial number of party activists. [Brown 2009]

The final goal was the justification for all the toil and hardship that might be encountered along the way. Once that goal was abandoned, communist regimes were in danger of being judged on the basis of their capacity to deliver more immediate results. Without the goal of communism, the 'leading role' of the party would become far harder to legitimize. [Brown 2009]

The sixth defining feature of communism was the existence of, and sense of belonging to, an international communist movement. The existence of that movement was of great ideological significance. It was the supposed internationalism of communism which attracted many of its adherents. For individual members of communist parties, the consciousness of belonging to a great international movement was of huge importance. [Brown 2009]

Communists believe in a communist universe where every other country is communist. They are not satisfied with a humble communist country isolated in a specific region, they want to install communism all around the globe. For communists themselves, 'communism' had two different meanings. It referred both to an international movement dedicated to the overthrow of capitalism systems and to the new society which would exist only in the future when Marx's higher stage of socialism had been reached. [Brown 2009]

Highlights for Chapter 2

- Socialism according to this book's viewpoint is a non-market based socialism.
- In socialist or communist systems, there is a quest to get rid of capitalistic and egoistic ideals.
- The capitalist class is a minority that derives profit from employing the working class through private ownership of the means of production.

- The revolution will put the working class in power and in turn establish social ownership of the means of production.
- Many idealists believe that human beings are naturally good, that they are not selfish, always ready to help their fellow humans.
- Everything for socialists is justified in terms of the collectivity, 'everything must be done for the good of all,' 'do not be egoistic, think about others,' 'work in groups instead of individually,' 'give as much as you can without expecting retribution.'
- Collectivization and individuality are complementary instead of opposites.
- For communists, collectivization happened in agriculture, industry, education, and in most of the common activities of citizens, such as food distribution, transport and so on.
- Christianity has had a large impact in socialist ideals, primarily collectivization. The notions of sacrifice, solidarity and collaborations have been surrounding religion for many centuries.
- At the beginning of the Chinese revolution, peasants abandoned the original purpose and acted on their own offering the land to the highest bidder.
- The first of Deng Xiaoping's local breakthroughs was the decommunalization of agriculture.
- By the mid-1980s, collectivized agrarian socialism was withering away, while rural standards of living and household incomes were improving dramatically. Deng Xiaoping had made good on his slogan "Poverty is not socialism."
- Equality referred primarily to economic equality instead of an intellectual, educational, social or collaborative type of equality.
- Socialists promises have failed, and after so many years in power, they have not been able to deliver.
- For Gracchus Babeuf, 'a period of dictatorship is in the general interest for as long as might be necessary to destroy or disarm the enemies of equality.'
- When justice is defined by the political system in power, it can imply injustice.
- In China, the Premier Zhu Rongji identified the unjust distribution of wealth "People's contributions do differ." Deng told his comrades in the leadership. "Shouldn't there, therefore, be differences in remuneration in the population?"

- In China, Deng Xiaoping openly promoted material incentives in the form of increased wages in order to "encourage people's initiative" … even if they did create inequalities.
- Freedom of thought was regarded by socialists as the root-evil of nineteenth-century society.
- Freedom and socialism do not mix, therefore, socialism must be authoritarian to stay in power.
- Democracies provide greater tolerance, free elections, accountable government, and respect for human rights, plus substantially higher living standards.
- A free flow of information and a communist system were mutually incompatible. Highly authoritarian regimes need state censorship and give rise to self-censorship.
- Fear is too strong in totalitarian regimes. People do not dare to criticize the government, they fear for their life.
- What our generation has forgotten is that the system of private property is the most important guaranty of freedom.
- In China, the regime abandoned its early egalitarian policies. Skilled workers now received much better wages than the unskilled.
- Most examples of socialism or communism have followed the path of strong states, called one-party-states, which obey the unique command of the party in power.
- Communist features such as the ideology, the political system, and the economic system determine the degree of affinity with communist's precepts.
- Defining features of a communist system: the monopoly of power of the communist party; the concept of democratic centralism; the non-capitalist ownership of the means of production; the dominance of a command economy; building communism as the ultimate goal; belonging to an international communist movement.

Chapter 3: The Soviet Union

According to the 2011 Census, Russians living in Canada amount to 550 thousand people claiming full or partial Russian ancestry. The closely related groups are Ukrainian, East Slavic and Belarusian. Many of them can be found in the metropolis of the English Province, in the north end neighborhoods of the city. Over the years, I have known a few sons of immigrants coming from Ukraine, but no Russian. I have no idea about Russian ancestor's culture.

I do not recall talking to a Russian in my life however I have an anecdote related with Russians. Many years ago, I was living in Montreal, the big metropolis of the French Province. It was a Friday night, relatively early evening, around 7 o'clock. I was strolling with my wife on a known street on the west of the city. When we were ready to take the bus back home, I told my wife to wait a few minutes, to give me a chance to withdraw some cash for the weekend at an ATM. She was outside the bank while I entered a line of about 8 people. I noticed on the line some men in leader suits and a couple of beautiful ladies on nice gowns. There were two ATM machines inside the building one beside the other; as people were withdrawing their money, the line was getting shorter however some other people were entering the ATM line. By the way, the bank was already close the offices were shut down for the weekend.

While waiting for my turn, I noticed one of the guys in the line talking to the one at the machine, saying things like why don't you move faster, we are waiting here. I did not suspect anything because, in Canada, people don't get scared of being rob in a bank, security and confidence with your neighbors are very high, so I was not afraid of anything. Finally, the guy at the machine finished his transaction and I was able to start my withdrawal process. I noticed another man getting close to me watching my transaction, I did not care very much, he is not going to rob me, I thought.

When I started the process at the machine, I noticed from the start that my debit card entered with some difficulty, but I kept going on anyway, I needed some cash, I was not afraid, why should I be? I pressed the keys to withdraw a hundred dollars, however, the money didn't come out and the debit card got stuck inside the machine. Suddenly I remembered a video I received from a friend a few months ago about some fraud committed in

ATM machines, in the video, the robbers placed some metal box in front of the bill dispenser and the customer could not get any bills.

Instantly, I thought about the possibility of being robbed at the machine by a bunch of thugs. The guy beside me simulated to help me, saying that the bank was closed and suggesting to better call the office to get my card back. The guy wanted me to abandon the machine, to call at the office, and complain about the card; the guys planned to get my card out and use it somewhere else to make some withdrawals. It seems the guy was trying to get my pin number while I was doing the transaction. Everything was clear, knowing the pin number and getting the card, they were able to steal money from my account at another ATM.

I acted extremely fast I understood I was being robbed. I started to shout loudly, calling my wife and telling her to call the police. My wife entered the bank and asked me what was going on while she moved outside pretending to call the police on a public phone. After I shouted, the whole gang of about 5 or 6 people started to abandon the bank fast and quietly and I was alone in front of the ATM. Close to the machine, it was dark, I barely was able to see and I started to scratch with my nail to establish if there was something to grab to recover my card. I noticed a small square piece of plastic and I pulled it out, it looked like a plastic label stuck on top of the cardholder; I continued to scratch and I was able to identify another very small piece of plastic or metal protruding from the hole, I pulled it out and my card came out at the same time, it was a metal centimeter of about 10 to 15 centimeters long. I remember getting cut in my finger when pulling the metal and a few drops of blood dropped on the floor.

At the time, I was suffering from a non-life threatening indescribable illness and I was not very happy with my discomfort. I was capable of getting into a fight with anybody trying to bother me, I did not care. Illness, as well as alcohol and drugs, is one of the reasons why people get into trouble easily; avoid getting in trouble with somebody that is sick, they defend themselves with any weapon or their bare hands. That was another reason for my quick reaction I was like a cat being attacked by a dog, ready to use my claws to make as much harm as possible.

I decided to check out if I was robbed by the thugs and entered my card again and tried to check out if some amount was withdrawn. I did it at the same machine and later on at the machine just beside; I thought nothing was stolen but decided not to make a withdrawal that night. I went out to meet my wife and she gave me a napkin to stop the bleeding on my finger. We took the bus home and on arrival called the bank to let them know what happened; the bank told me to call the police. Afterward, we talked to an officer that came to the apartment and prepared a report about the incident. A few weeks later the police told us that they saw the video surveillance records and found out about the Russian thugs; it was what the police said, that they were Russians. Later on, they said that the members were identified and warned about the issue. I was not contacted again, but I understood Russians could be quite dangerous when the mafia is involved. I do not know how bad Russians are when political issues are involved, but I am attentive to any wrongdoings.

While doing some research about socialism and communism for the book, a lady from the Russian community, living in the capital of the English Province, represented a good source of knowledge for this book. She was an expert on the evolution of Russia after the Soviet Union. Talking to her in one of the Russian community centers, the conversation evolved towards what was happening in Russia these days. She is a mature lady helping the needy, primarily East Europe emigrants, she knows people from Russia, Ukraine, and Slovakia. She also gives conferences about the situation in Russia today. She told me that to understand what happens in Russia you must understand the evolution of the Soviet Union.

She recommended the book by Svetlana Alexievich, "Secondhand Time, The Last of the Soviets" [Alexievich 2016] that contains several anecdotes related to Soviets and Russians. Svetlana spoke with a few hundreds of people to find out what they thought about the political situation in their country after the end of the Soviet Union. According to the book, there is a tendency to change the actual political scenario, a tendency to return to the old way of doing things in the Soviet Union. By the way, Svetlana won a Nobel Prize in 2015.

A joke in Svetlana's book, proposes a definition of a communist, "A communist is someone who's read Marx, an anti-communist is someone who's understood him." This joke reminds me another saying, "If you were not communist when young, you were insensible, but if you stayed communist when older, you were dumb." There are strong messages in those jokes, 'not because you read a book you understand the book.' and 'experience demonstrates that socialism and communism do not solve the issues.' Some effort is required to understand and build on experience, and most people do not enjoy learning. For example, Nietzsche is difficult to understand, therefore, the only way is to study his writings, taking the time to really learn. The same thing happens with Marx, if you are superficial, you will not be able to understand his writings. An additional effort is required annotation and study can help to grasp the meaning.

How has been my experience with Marx writings? Reading the first ten chapters of the Capital, it was too difficult to understand, it is repetitive in its arguments and biased towards workers, and if at the same time you are not a fan of Marx or communism, the impression with Karl Marx book is very poor. However, it has to be recognized that at the time of publishing, it was a contribution to the working class, helping them to improve on their working conditions.

The Soviet Union represents the quintessential example of a socialist or communist state. All the newly created socialist states used the Soviet Union as their idealistic model. Additionally, the Soviet Union financed and militarized other states with the purpose of expanding their socialist enterprise. The recent history of Russia can be summarized as follows [Freeze 1997]:

1. Revolutionary Russia, 1890-1914
2. Russia in War and Revolution, 1914-1921
3. The New Economic Policy (NEP) and the Revolutionary Experiment, 1921-1929
4. Building Stalinism, 1929-1941
5. The Great Fatherland War and Late Stalinism, 1941-1953
6. Stalinism to Stagnation, 1953-1985
7. Perestroika towards a New Order, 1985-1991
8. Yeltsin's Years 1991-1998
9. Modern Russia: Putin 1998-today

For the purpose of this book, the historical events are important to give some context. The survey of events starts on Revolutionary Russia, 1890-1914. A short timeline of Russia evolution events includes:

1904-05- Russian expansion in Manchuria leads to war with Japan - and the 1905 revolution, which forced Tsar Nicholas II to grant a constitution and establish a parliament, the Duma.

1914- Russian-Austrian rivalry in Balkans contributes to the outbreak of the First World War, in which Russia fought alongside Britain and France.

1917- Nicholas II abdicates. Bolshevik revolutionaries led by Lenin topple the provisional government and take power.

1918-22- Civil war between the Red Army and anti-communist White Russians.

1922- Bolsheviks reorganize remnants of Russian Empire as Union of Soviet Socialist Republics.

1945- Allied victory over Nazi Germany is followed by the swift establishment of Soviet hegemony in Central and Eastern Europe, and Balkans. The end of the war sees the start of decades of Cold War rivalry with the West.

1953- Death of dictator Joseph Stalin ushers in the less repressive rule at home, although Communist Party political dominance is firmly upheld.

1991- Russia becomes independent as the Soviet Union collapses and, together with Ukraine and Belarus, forms the Commonwealth of the Independent States, which is eventually joined by most former Soviet republics.

2000- Prime Minister Vladimir Putin takes over as president on the resignation of Boris Yeltsin, and begins steady re-orientation of Russia away from democracy and cooperation with the West towards a more nationalist and authoritarian politics.

Initial movements for revolution

The beginning of the twentieth century found Russia surrounded by trouble, bad social conditions, and poor economic performance. There was discomfort all over the country. The tzar was not able to design an organization to improve the conditions of the population. In early January 1905, some 120,000 workers were on strike in St Petersburg and Father Georgy Gapon took up their cause. In a petition to the tzar they asked for 'justice and protection,' saying that they were impoverished, oppressed, over-burdened and treated contemptuously. [Brown 2009]

Gapon led a vast unarmed procession – many of the marchers drawn from the ranks of the striking workers – in the direction of the Winter Palace to hand over their petition. The procession was fired upon by troops instructed to prevent them from reaching the palace. That day became known as 'Bloody Sunday.' It was rumored at the time that thousands had died. The real figures – approximately 200 dead and 800 wounded – were bad enough. [Brown 2009]

Unexpected events, happening outside its borders, made Russia get involved in a war to defend one of its neighbors. On 28 June 1914, Archduke Franz Ferdinand, heir to the throne of Austria, was assassinated in Sarajevo, Bosnia. Backed by Germany, it seemed likely that Austria would attack Russia's little ally Serbia. The tzar ordered a general mobilization to support Serbia. When Kaiser Wilhelm II of Germany appealed personally to Nicholas to cancel his plans for mobilization, the tsar refused. On 1 July 1914, Germany declared war on Russia. [Evans 2005]

World War I started in July 1914, it was unprecedented in the slaughter, carnage, and destruction. Well over a million Russian soldiers were killed in World War I, more than four million were wounded, and some two and a half million were taken prisoners. By the second half of 1916 and early 1917, the crucial factor was increasing disaffection in the Russian army. These 'peasants in uniform,' as Lenin called them, were sick of the war. When soldiers were brought in to suppress a strike in Petrograd (as St Petersburg had been named in 1914) in October 1916, they fired at the police instead of at the workers. The war ended in 1918. [Brown 2009]

Fall of the tzar

There was internal opposition against the monarchy. Some politicians received donations to fight the tzar; among those opponents was Lenin. The military was busy in World War I, they had to defend the country, and could not participate in other actions involving local politics. The fact that the army was not prepared to defend the regime was ultimately the decisive factor in bringing to an end monarchical rule in Russia. Nicholas II abdicated on 15 March 1917. 'The autocracy collapsed in the face of popular demonstrations and the withdrawal of elite support for the regime.' [Brown 2009]

News of Nicholas abdication was greeted with great enthusiasm across Russia. There was turmoil around the country. Provisional governments were not able to maintain order. At the front, discipline broke down as thousands of soldiers deserted and made their way home. In Moscow and other towns and cities, the workers formed soviets whilst in the countryside the peasants seized land. [Evans 2005]

The fall of the tzar also meant an end to the Russian Empire, a result long and fervently hoped for by Lenin and his followers in the lean years before the revolution. Among the opposition, there were Bolsheviks and Mensheviks fighting to consolidate their power. The Bolsheviks saw the Empire as a bastion of the corrupt and antiquated capitalist system, which they hoped to replace with an international order of communist nations existing cooperatively. [Streissguth 2002]

A month later, Nicholas II, Empress Alexandra, their four young daughters, and his younger son were killed. [Brown 2009]

The Bolsheviks

During the First World War, discontent was clearly manifested. On March 1917, all the factories in Petrograd were on strike, there was widespread looting and mutiny was spreading throughout the garrisons stationed in the Russian capital. The climax came when the Duma (legislative assembly) attempted to take power into its own hands and formed a committee which became the nucleus of a provisional government. [Brown 2009]

Bolshevik agitation set off further demonstrations and the slogan "All power to the Soviets' was put forward. But this first attempt to dislodge the Provisional Government failed to win enough popular support and, when it was reported that the Bolsheviks had received money from the German government, opinion in the streets turned against them. Lenin was forced to hiding in Finland. Bolsheviks contented themselves with propaganda work, especially in the army, and with the creation of their own illegal armed force. This was the Red Guard, consisting of factory workers equipped with rifles purloined from the army. [Streissguth 2002]

The Bolsheviks, although far from united in 1917, were organizationally stronger than the Socialist Revolutionary Party and much more ruthless than the Mensheviks. On 25 October 1917, the Bolsheviks seized power in Petrograd. Bolshevik troops took over public buildings and arrested ministers of the Provisional Government. Although that date entered history as the day of the successful Bolshevik revolution, in many respects it was more of a coup than a revolution. [Brown 2009]

Having settled the question of power, the Bolsheviki turned their attention to problems of practical administration. First of all the city, the country and the army must be fed. Bands of sailors and Red Guards scoured the warehouses, the railway terminals, unearthing and confiscating thousands of packs of food held by private speculators. [Streissguth 2002]

Russian troops did not do well on World War I. Before the end of 1914, the Russian armies had twice been heavily defeated at the Battles of Tannenburg and the Masurian Lakes and the disasters continued into 1915 when 4 million of the tsar's soldiers died on the battlefield. With inadequate food, clothing and weapons and the suffering of the soldiers, the Russian army appeared to be 'drowning in its own blood.' [Evans 2005]

Lenin compelled the Russian delegation to the peace talks in March 1918 to accept the harsh terms dictated by Germany. The 'indecent peace' was the price Lenin had to pay to acquire and retain power. [Streissguth 2002] By the treaty, Russia surrendered Poland, the Baltic provinces of Estonia, Latvia and Lithuania, Finland and parts of the Caucasus. And a promise to recognize the independence of Ukraine. Altogether Russia lost a quarter of all its territory in Europe, a third of its population, over half of its industry and four-fifths of its coal mines. [Evans 2005]

The civil war

Lenin explained the revolution, urged the people to take the power into their own hands, by force to break down the resistance of the propertied classes, by force to take over institutions of Government. Revolutionary discipline! Strict accounting and control! No strikes! No loafing! [Streissguth 2002]

The civil war was no doubt, a crucial period in the history of the new Soviet regime. It may be argued that the civil war began in November 1917 and ended in the middle of 1922. We are dealing therefore with a time-span of about four years, marked by upheavals, battles, slaughter – a protracted national agony during which the new system was created and took shape. [Streissguth 2002]

During the civil war, Lenin imposed an economic policy of "war communism," which included forced labor, grain confiscation, restrictions on trade unions, and state control of industry. Following the war, and to revive the devastated economy, Lenin eased his control of the economy by instituting the New Economic Policy (NEP), which allowed small-scale private business to operate free of government control. In addition, the Russian peasants, who made up 80 percent of the population, were allowed to keep their land and freely market their products. [Streissguth 2002]

We know that there was a nucleus of workers, poor peasants, and raznochintsy [intellectuals] on the side of the Reds and a core of members of the formerly privileged classes, richer peasants, and, especially, military officers on the side of the Whites. The problem was who would emerge as the better social and political strategist, who could mobilize the support of large circles of the urban population and, more importantly, the small-scale peasant farmers. In this crucial task of social strategy, the Bolsheviks proved superior. [Streissguth 2002]

Creation of the Soviet Union

The demobilization of the Red Army of five million played no small role in the formation of the bureaucracy. The victorious commanders assumed leading posts in the local Soviets, in the economy, in education, and they persistently introduced everywhere that regime which had ensured success in the civil war. Thus on all sides the masses were pushed away gradually from actual participation in the leadership of the country. [Streissguth 2002]

On December 27, 1922, the Tenth All-Russian Congress of Soviets accepted Stalin's motion to establish the Union of Soviet Socialist Republics or USSR. It was originally composed of four member-republics: Russia, Ukraine, Belorussia, and Transcaucasus. [Streissguth 2002]

Progress in the Soviet Union was slow, much slower than in the West. True, the devastation in the occupied territories was more extensive than the damage by the war in the West. This was adduced as the reason for the slow Russian recovery. It was a convincing argument for a decade or two, but it no longer seemed persuasive after that. By the 1970s, serious doubts arose about the efficacy of the system – something obviously was wrong with it, but what? [Laqueur 2015]

The Soviet Union had become a superpower with very strong military forces, and this caused much pride. But maintaining a strong military force was very expensive, and as the economy progressed only slowly and eventually stagnated, it became more and more difficult to keep pace with America and the West. From the 1960s onward, there had been manifestations of dissent, but their outreach was limited. The KGB had a society very much under control. [Laqueur 2015]

Perhaps most importantly was the failure to improve the quality of life. Air and water were polluted; the soil was poisoned; the Russian forest, traditionally the pride of the country, was partially disappearing in European Russia. Alcoholism, always a plague in Russian history, became worse. On payday in the villages and the cities, no work was done because everyone was too drunk to make their way to their places of work; the scenes were indescribable. The crime rate was rising, petty and not-so-petty theft was increasing all the time. [Laqueur 2015]

The Soviet system was, after all, a welfare state of sorts: people were paid pensions and had no fear of unemployment. This was true, but it was welfare at a very low level. Russia was and remained a poor country, and as the years passed, four decades after the end of World War II, blaming the war for most of the misfortunes became impossible. [Laqueur 2015]

The fall of communism

In the Soviet Union, reform produced crisis more than crisis forced reform. The fate of the Soviet system and of the Soviet state did not hang in the balance in 1985. By 1989 the fate of both did. The changes introduced by Gorbachev and the reformist wing of the party leadership had already made the political system different in kind. [Brown 2009]

One of the aims of the architects of Perestroika was to make the economy more effective: In most respects, this had been a failure. Another aim was to create a middle class, which would generate growth. A few people had become immensely rich during perestroika, and there was still much poverty; but if a middle class had come into being, it was certainly very different from the one in America or Europe. [Laqueur 2015]

If on March 11, 1985 someone other than Gorbachev had been made the general secretary of the Communist Party, and if ten or fifteen years later another had been the successor, they would have benefited from the oil and gas windfall that subsequently occurred, without any modernization effort. The Supreme Soviet would still exist, as would the Communist Party with its political monopoly. Some minor political and ideological reforms might have taken place, but no radical changes. The election of a leader who genuinely believed that the system could be reformed was an accident. [Laqueur 2015]

But Perestroika had achieved a great deal. Along the way, fear of the state authorities was removed, liberty was introduced, competitive elections took place, and democratic accountability emerged in the USSR. [Brown 2009]

1991 coup and Yeltsin

After the anti-Gorbachev coup in August 1991, the Soviet Union had two leaders. Gorbachev was still president of the Soviet Union, but Yeltsin had been elected president of Russia with 57 percent of the vote. It seemed only natural that Gorbachev should resign as president of the Soviet Union, for the Soviet Union had virtually ceased to exist. [Laqueur 2015]

Only three years earlier, Gorbachev had been generally considered the most popular Soviet leader. What had caused the quick downturn? The disastrous economic situation played a key role, but probably even more important was the impression that there was no strong hand in the Kremlin. [Laqueur 2015]

In 1991, the mood in the country was in favor of a market economy and privatization, even though no one knew what these radical changes really would mean and what effect they would have in practice. Yeltsin had appointed a small group of economists to prepare for the transition to a market economy, and this economic system became law in June 1992. [Laqueur 2015]

In April 1993, the government received a vote of confidence in a referendum, but it is doubtful that the majority of the population understood what was going on in the country. Ownership of 130,000 of the country's medium-and-large-sized enterprises passed into the hands of a small number of people, and the age of the oligarchs dawned. [Laqueur 2015]

The post-socialist crisis was rooted in the socialist model of industrialization and the profound disorganization of state finances, as well as the sharp decline in fuel prices. The task was to create the preconditions for a transition from recovery to investment growth, based on the growth of capital investments into the economy and the creation of new production capacities. [Laqueur 2015]

The Yeltsin era approached its end. This had been a lawless age during which the oligarchs could achieve, more or less, whatever they wanted – economically as well as politically. They could manipulate the president and had no reason to be afraid of the law. [Laqueur 2015]

Contemporary Russia

In mid-1998, Yeltsin decided that he would have to resign and another prime minister would be needed; for this, he chose the forty-six-year-old KGB operative named Vladimir Vladimirovich Putin, he was not well-known and not connected to any political party. [Laqueur 2015]

Of the last half dozen leaders chosen to govern the Soviet Union and Russia, all but the last came as no great surprise. All were members of the Politburo, the leading governing body. The choice of Vladimir Putin was far more accidental, but the policies he pursued were not. The Yeltsin years were chaotic, the emergence of a nationalist autocracy was far more likely than any other development even in the 1990s. The oil and gas income was decisive, it accounts for a rise in the economy in general, the various social and political schemes initiated by the Putin government and the foreign and military policy in 2014/15. [Laqueur 2015]

This was the time of renewed capitalism. People were suddenly invaded by a new political system that gave more importance to money instead of ideas. This was the new Russia, run by money interests. Soviets were affected by the change of government, "The first thing to go was friendship ... Suddenly, everyone was too busy, they had to go out and make money. Before, it had seemed like we didn't need money at all ... That it had no bearing on us. Suddenly, everyone saw the beauty of green bills – these were no Soviet rubles, they weren't just playing money." [Alexievich 2016]

After so many years of Soviet hegemony, the political changes were surprising, "Building communism ... We really did build it, too! We believed that everything was ahead of us! Ardent believers in the Soviet regime, we were. From the bottom of our hearts. But then we got old. Glasnost, Perestroika ... We sit here and listen to the radio. Communism doesn't exist anymore ... where did communism go? No more communists either." [Alexievich 2016]

What else can be said, those people that believed in communism should not be penalized, only those that helped the regime perpetrating injustices must be punished. The rest need just a brainwash: inundate them with arguments against communism or socialism 24 hours a day until they become convinced anticommunists.

Nostalgia from the past was constant remorse, "Mayday! Our favorite holiday in the world was May 1st. On that day, they would give us new coats and dresses. All of the coats and all of the dresses were identical. You'd start breaking in, leaving your mark on it. Just one little knot or crease to show that it's yours ... A part of you. We were told that our Motherland is our family and that it was thinking of us."

Human nature makes us different, we are genetically distinct. We want to be different, we want to be important, we want to be remarked, it is human vanity. People take charge of making their individuality show off, independently of the government that wants us all to be the same.

Russians feel nostalgia for the past, For us, communism was inextricably linked with the terror, the gulag. A cage. We thought it was dead. Gone forever. Twenty years have passed ... I go into my son's room, and what do I see but a copy of Marx's Das Kapital on his desk, and Trotsky's My Life on his bookshelf ... I can't believe my eyes! Is Marx making a comeback? Is this a nightmare? Am I awake or am I dreaming? [Alexievich 2016]

People were cheated by the wrong system, socialism is not the right approach, "I'm a Soviet, and so is my mother. We were building socialism and communism. Children were taught that selling was shameful and money couldn't buy happiness. Live honestly and give your life to your Motherland – the most precious thing we have. My whole life, I had been proud of being Soviet, but now I'm somewhat embarrassed about it like I was dumb for believing in it. We used to have communist ideals, now the ideals are capitalist: No mercy for anyone because no one has any mercy for you." [Alexievich 2016]

Soviets thought they were building a good society, what a big mistake. Have you ever seen any demonstration that socialism is viable? No way, nobody can demonstrate that it works, not even theoretically. Everything was just expectations, if you work for the collective good this is going to improve your life. Humans need a balance between individuality and collectivity, none can take command over the other. If we act all the time individually, society does not improve, but if we act all the time collectively, society does not improve either. Therefore, make some room for the freedom of individuals and groups, and make some room for individuals contributing to the collectivity.

Russia at the present time is a dictatorship with much popular support. The general trend of the Russian search for a new doctrine and mission would be toward the authoritarian Right, and it is going far and fast. The Left outside Russia has hardly been aware of the ideological and political changes in Russia and continues to think of Russia as a left-wing in some ways. [Laqueur 2015]

There are contradictions between idealism and pragmatism. Those ruling Russia today, the siloviki, have been described as the new nobility, selfless patriots motivated by pure idealism. It is indeed a noble vision, but how true is it? How important is ideology, and what is the specific weight of power and money? [Laqueur 2015]

The question why nations fail and decline has been frequently discussed in recent years, the question of why they recover – sometimes for a short period only, sometimes for longer periods – less often. It took Germany a mere fifteen years after the defeat in World War I to regain its military and political power. It took Russia two decades for its comeback after the desintegration of the Soviet Union. [Laqueur 2015]

How successful is Putin? To engage in a brief exercise of counterfactual history: The Putin regime owes its survival and success to one factor and one factor only – the export of oil and gas, which accounts for about half of the Russian budget. [Laqueur 2015]

What was the extent of political power that has been in the hands of those who grew very rich as the result of privatization in Russia? It all began with the decision to privatize the economy. No one knew exactly how to do this, but several astute individuals realized that state property was being sold or almost given away. Some were officials high up in government, including ministers and their deputies. [Laqueur 2015]

<u>Millionaires</u>

Russians started to look like wild capitalists, "For some reason, it was the number "one million" that sparked the imagination. To make a million! We had gotten used to the idea that Russians don't want to be rich, they are even afraid of it. So what do they want then? The answer is always the same: They don't want anyone else to get rich. That is, richer than they are. The magenta sports coats, the gold chains … that's all from films, TV shows … The people I met had steely logic and an iron grip on reality. They were systematic thinkers. All of them were learning English. Management. The academics and postgraduates were leaving the country … The physicists and lyricists too … But the new heroes, they didn't want to go anywhere, they liked living in Russia, this was their time to shine! Their big chance! They wanted to be rich. They wanted it all. Everything!" [Alexievich 2016]

It is clear that during socialism it is prohibited to be rich, therefore, in those years there were no rich. It is understandable that old generations do not want to get rich, however, younger generations see the opportunity of getting rich and they take that chance. It would be a good idea to combine capitalism with philosophy such that you live well and understand better how to live a healthier and productive life.

The cases of Boris Berezovsky and Mikhail Khodorkovsky were well known. Berezovsky, a talented mathematician, made his money first in secondhand car dealing, later became involved in the Russian media, and later still invested in a major oil company as well as Aeroflot, once the Soviet state airline. Subsequently, he went into the oil and gas business. These years of golden opportunities were quite violent, at least one attempt on his life by business rivals. [Laqueur 2015]

Khodorkovsky served as deputy minister of fuel and energy, which provided some useful contacts. He realized that he would need foreign capital to establish a truly major company. With the help of American investors, he acquired Yuko, the biggest oil company in the country, valued at about $15 billion. The business practices used during those years, whether they involved declaring bankruptcy, attracting new investors, not paying taxes, or acquiring companies, were not only unethical but considered criminal by many. [Laqueur 2015]

Government officials had also become rich – some of them immensely rich – but they had done so discreetly, such that no one knew exactly how great their fortunes were and where their money or investments had been deposited. Glaring contradiction between official propaganda and the actual state of affairs (the great and growing distance between the life of the rich and the rest) is a major weakness of the regime. It is bound to persist and to cause political tensions. [Laqueur 2015]

More billionaires reside now in Moscow than in any other city in the world. The 110 richest Russians own about 35 percent of the country's GNP, and if, on the other hand, 93 percent of Russian citizens own less than $10,000 then the creation of a strong middle class has not been achieved as the result of privatization. The number of Chinese billionaires is somewhat greater than Russia, but not by very much. Moreover, the Chinese GNP is four times as large (eight trillion dollars) as the Russian, which at present is about equal to that of France and smaller than the Brazilian GNP. [Laqueur 2015]

Putin's success rests mainly on two factors, above all the steeply rising demand for oil and gas and, correspondingly, a striking improvement in Russia's finances; this caused the emergence of the oligarchs. However, there has been a massive trickle down that has brought about a substantial rise in the standard of living of wide sections of society. These became the pillars of support for Putin and his regime. [Laqueur 2015]

Highlights for Chapter 3

- The beginning of the twentieth century found Russia surrounded by trouble, bad social conditions, and poor economic performance.
- Unexpected events, happening outside its borders, made Russia get involved in a war to defend one of its neighbors. On 28 June 1914, Archduke Franz Ferdinand, heir to the throne of Austria, was assassinated in Sarajevo, Bosnia.
- World War I started in July 1914, it was unprecedented in the slaughter, carnage, and destruction. Well over a million Russian

soldiers were killed, more than four million were wounded, and some two and a half million were taken prisoners.

- Nicholas II abdicated on 15 March 1917. 'The autocracy collapsed in the face of popular demonstrations and the withdrawal of elite support for the regime.'
- A month later, Nicholas II, Empress Alexandra, their four young daughters, and his younger son were killed.
- On 25 October 1917, the Bolsheviks seized power in Petrograd. Bolshevik troops took over public buildings and arrested ministers of the Provisional Government.
- In March 1918, the Russian delegation had to accept the harsh terms dictated by Germany to end the war. By the treaty, Russia surrendered Poland, the Baltic provinces of Estonia, Latvia and Lithuania, Finland and parts of the Caucasus. And a promise to recognize the independence of Ukraine.
- The civil war was, no doubt, a crucial period in the history of the new Soviet regime. It may be argued that the civil war began in November 1917 and ended in the middle of 1922.
- During the civil war, Lenin imposed an economic policy of "war communism," which included forced labor, grain confiscation, restrictions on trade unions, and state control of industry.
- At the end of the civil war, the demobilization of the Red Army of five million played no small role in the formation of the bureaucracy. The victorious commanders assumed leading posts in the local Soviets, in the economy, education, and in all institutions.
- On December 27, 1922, Stalin's motion to establish the Union of Soviet Socialist Republics or USSR, was approved.
- Progress in the Soviet Union was slow, much slower than in the West.
- The Soviet Union had become a superpower with very strong military forces, and this caused much pride.
- Perhaps most importantly was the failure to improve the quality of life.
- The Soviet system was, after all, a welfare state of sorts: people were paid pensions and had no fear of unemployment.
- By 1989 the fate of the Soviet state and the Soviet system changed. The changes introduced by Gorbachev and the reformist wing of

the party leadership had already made the political system different in kind.

- The election of a leader as Gorbachev who genuinely believed that the system could be reformed was an accident.
- But perestroika had achieved a great deal. Along the way, fear of the state authorities was removed, liberty was introduced, competitive elections took place, and democratic accountability emerged in the USSR.
- What had caused the quick Gorbachev downturn? The disastrous economic situation played a key role, but probably even more important was the impression that there was no strong hand in the Kremlin.
- Yeltsin had appointed a small group of economists to prepare for the transition to a market economy, and this economic system became law in June 1992.
- In April 1993, ownership of 130,000 of the country's medium-and-large-sized enterprises passed into the hands of a small number of people, and the age of the oligarchs dawned.
- In mid-1998, Yeltsin decided that he would have to resign and another prime minister would be needed; for this, he chose the forty-six-year-old KGB operative named Vladimir Vladimirovich Putin.
- In the 1990s, the oil and gas income was decisive, it accounts for a rise in the economy in general and the various social and political schemes initiated by the Putin government.
- Russians feel nostalgia for the past, For us, communism was inextricably linked with the terror, the gulag. A cage. We thought it was dead. Gone forever.
- What else can be said? Those people that believed in communism should not be penalized, only those that helped the regime perpetrating injustices must be punished.
- People were cheated by the wrong system, socialism is not the right approach, I'm a Soviet, and so is my mother. We were building socialism and communism.
- Russia at the present time is a dictatorship with much popular support. The general trend of the Russian search for a new doctrine and mission would be toward the authoritarian Right, and it is going far and fast.

- It took Russia two decades for its comeback after the desintegration of the Soviet Union.
- The Putin regime owes its survival and success to one factor and one factor only – the export of oil and gas.
- What was the extent of political power that has been in the hands of those who grew very rich as the result of privatization in Russia?
- More billionaires reside now in Moscow than in any other city in the world. The 110 richest Russians own about 35 percent of the country's GNP.
- Putin's success rests mainly on two factors, above all the steeply rising demand for oil and gas and, correspondingly, a striking improvement in Russia's finances; this caused the emergence of the oligarchs.

Chapter 4: Europe and Asia

For western and central Europeans, the Second World War began earlier than it did for Russians and Americans. German troops marched into Prague on 15 March 1939 but was not yet the beginning of European war. The Czechs, having been deserted by their democratic allies, offered no resistance. On 1 September 1939, Nazi Germany attacked Poland. The United States became a combatant country when the Japanese attacked the USA at Pearl Harbor later that same year – on 7 December. [Brown 2009]

Stalin was taken completely by surprise when German troops crossed the Soviet border on 22 June 1941. He had received a number of warnings of an impending attack but chose to ignore them. As a result of Soviet unpreparedness, the Red Army suffered horrendous initial losses. In their advance into the Soviet Union in 1941, the German army had reached the outskirts of Moscow by November. In the battle for Moscow, which lasted from September 1941 until April 1942, 926,000 Soviet soldiers were killed. [Brown 2009]

As Donald Sassoon has observed, the Second World War, after the German attack on the Soviet Union, turned to be the 'finest hour' also of Western communists. For the first time – and indeed, last – time: 'They could fight fascism and Nazism, be true internationalists, defend the USSR, be flawless patriots and all without inconsistency.' In occupied Europe, communists were particularly active participants in partisan resistance to fascism, whether in its German Nazi or Italian manifestations. [Brown 2009]

Indigenous Socialist Takeovers in Europe

In Eastern Europe, as distinct from the Soviet Union, most of those who worked to change the system from the inside had already joined the party before the communists came to power. The most active participants in the Czechoslovak reform movement, and in the Prague Spring of 1968 which was its culmination (and a forerunner of the Soviet perestroika), were party members who as young men and women in the immediate post-war years had joined the Communist Party full of revolutionary zeal for 'building socialism.' [Brown 2009]

If those whose names are associated with amelioration or reform of the communist system (in a few decisive cases amounting to transformative change) were, more often than not, leading members of the party; that was because the system was such that in normal times change could come from nowhere else. Poland was the great exception, although even there, Solidarity was effectively crushed as a mass movement at the end of 1981 and re-emerged as a force in political life only after the change had been instituted at the top of the Soviet political hierarchy. [Brown 2009]

The single most important reason for the establishment of communists regimes in Europe following the Second World War was the success of the Soviet army in ending Nazi rule in the region. Mao Zedong told communists that 'power comes out of the barrel of the gun.' In the immediate post-war years, the maxim applied, yet it was not the whole story. Socialism, whether in its democratic form or in its Soviet-style, had gained greatly in popularity. Capitalism, according to them, could offer only unemployment and misery. [Brown 2009]

The Soviet system only offered illusions. Collectivization had destroyed the lives of millions of peasants. Stalin, in his own country, was responsible for the imprisonment and execution of political opponents, real and imagined, on an even larger scale than Hitler in Germany, but all this was, for the time being, overlooked. Soviet secrecy and censorship meant that such facts were not known. [Brown 2009]

Where socialist parties of a democratic type were already strong, they received the egalitarian and anti-capitalist tide of opinion. In Britain and Scandinavia, the Labor and socialist parties had great electoral success while the communists received negligible support. In Italy, France, and Finland, communist as well as democratic socialist parties attracted broad support. Eastern and Central Europe had a different political inheritance. With the exception of Czechoslovakia, right-wing authoritarian regimes had been the norm in the 1930s and they were now thoroughly discredited. [Brown 2009]

In Albania and Yugoslavia, the success of the communists in resistance movements was on a scale which enabled them to prevail without Soviet support in the first case and with relatively modest help from the Soviet Union in the second. The coming to power of communists in these two countries, while largely independent of the feats of the Soviet army, rested, nevertheless, on the coercive power which the party leadership had already built up during the war. [Brown 2009]

The seizure of power by the Albanian Communist Party in the autumn of 1944 was facilitated by the lack of any clear Western policy. The Soviet

Union was clearly in favor of the communists coming to power in Albania, while the USA and Britain were relatively permissive and not particularly well informed. The Albanian communists' seizure of power is rivaled only by that of the Yugoslavs as the most indigenous of takeovers in Eastern Europe. Neither the Soviet army nor Tito's partisans set foot in Albania. [Brown 2009]

In Yugoslavia, Tito's partisans had by 1945 prevailed in the bitter civil war which had accompanied their struggle against the Germans. Yugoslavia was among the countries which suffered the most in the Second World War, losing 11 percent of its pre-war population between 1941 and 1945. The National Liberation Army of Yugoslavia was headed by Tito. In 1945 the monarchy was abolished and Yugoslavia was declared a Federal People's Republic. [Brown 2009]

In Yugoslavia, Milovan Djilas evolved into a democratic socialist, and he ended up hoping that 'monolithic ideological revolutions will cease, even though they have roots in idealism and idealists.' Civil war consisted of both ideological and military struggle between communists and anti-communists and bitter conflict among the country's different nationalities, especially between Serbs and Croats. In Croatia, a policy close to genocide was pursued against the Serbian part of the population as well as against Serbs in Bosnia and Hercegovina. [Brown 2009]

Josip Broz, 'Tito,' did succeed in establishing a communist state in Yugoslavia when the war ended. The communists, led by Tito, took power largely to as a result of their own efforts. The Red Army did play a very important role by liberating Belgrade, but by far the greatest part of the fighting on Yugoslav soil had been conducted by the partisans. It was not accidental that the first great split in the communist movement to affect ruling parties was that between the Soviet Union and Yugoslavia. [Brown 2009]

In Albania there was also limited Soviet participation, the communists came to power without any Soviet help at all. They did, however, get assistance from the Yugoslavs – both instruction on party organization and guidance on how to conduct guerrilla warfare. [Brown 2009]

The seizure of power in Czechoslovakia was a more gradual affair than in Albania or Yugoslavia. Czechoslovakia had been the most democratic, libertarian and tolerant country of any central and eastern Europe between the two world wars. In Czechoslovakia, there was no anti-Russian tradition. A positive attitude towards Russia and the Soviet Union was further engendered by the fact that most of Czechoslovakia were liberated by the Red Army. During the period of political pluralism (1945-1948), a number of socialist measures were implemented, including the nationalization of banks, insurance companies, and key industries. [Brown 2009]

By late 1947, the communist leadership in Czechoslovakia were determined to seize full power, and accordingly, they set about creating a crisis which would facilitate their takeover. In 1948, two concepts of socialism clashed and the communists took power arguing the 'parliamentary road to socialism.' Victory went to the communist variant that took the Soviet model instead of the pluralistic traditions. The system soon produced a wide range of Stalinist excesses, including the execution of communists and the persecution of the democratic opponents. [Brown 2009]

Soviet Impositions of Communism

The Soviet imposition of communist regimes on the countries of east-central Europe, with no regard for the wishes of their peoples, was the cause of the division of Europe – and that was the single most important manifestation of what became known as the Cold War. [Brown 2009]

Elsewhere in Eastern Europe, the Soviet Army played a decisive role in establishing the conditions for a communist takeover. It was the Red Army which captured the Baltic states from the Nazis. They had been taken into the Soviet orbit by Nazi-Soviet agreement before Hitler's invasion of the Soviet Union but were occupied by German forces during the conflict. The Red Army also liberated from Nazi domination Poland, Hungary, Bulgaria, and Romania. [Brown 2009]

Poland was important to the Soviet Union strategically, thus the local communists, with Soviet support, were cautious to capture power. The change in Poland's borders gave the communists the support of the Soviets. The alliance with the Soviet Union was in their favor in case of German possibly resurgent threat. What defined the limits of Poland's future was Soviet military strength and it became an obedient ally. [Brown 2009]

In Hungary, the communists got a breakthrough with the establishment of unity with the Social Democratic party. Soviet troops remained in Hungary and a great deal of pressure was exerted on the Social Democrats to co-operate. In an election in May 1949, the Popular Front was credited with 95.6 percent of votes cast. The communists were now able to move quickly to establish their monopoly of power. [Brown 2009]

Romania, under its right-wing authoritarian regime, had fought on the side of Nazi Germany in Second World War. The government of General Ion Antonescu, which had been formed in 1940, made clear to the monarch, King Michael, that he was to play a merely symbolic role and take no part in the making of state policy. When the Soviets forces were advancing into Romanian territory, the king arrested Antonescu who was looking for an armistice, but Romania was annexed to the Soviet Union anyway. The Romanian army was put back to war, now against Germany. [Brown 2009]

Bulgarian communists had taken part in partisan activities on a modest scale during the Second World War and they were able to gain influence in a Popular Front movement formed in 1943. The communists were in a minority in a coalition, however, they seized most crucial positions such as the police and the courts. The democratic opposition to communist rule ended with Nikola Petkov arrested and sentenced to death and hanged. In December 1947, Marxism-Leninism became in a few months the official ideology. The means of production were nationalized, and the communist party had by 1948 a monopoly of power. [Brown 2009]

What became the separate East German state known as the German Democratic Republic (GDR) began as the Soviet zone of Germany. It was the part of the country occupied by Soviet troops and thus fell under Soviet control. This meant that it was administered by German communists chosen by the Soviet Union. The German Communist Party's manifesto of June 1945 was modest, advocating neither a socialist economy nor a one-party state. It even included a commitment to 'complete and unrestricted development of free commerce and private enterprise on the basis of private property.' [Brown 2009]

Communists in Asia

Meanwhile, the Second World War had an effect also on the fortunes of communists in Asia, where it was linked to national liberation. Japanese expansionism became a catalyst for communist advance in China. Communists could respond to the desire for national liberation as well as to local peasant grievances. Thus in China, too, the war turned out to be the prelude to, and facilitator of, the communist seizure of power. [Brown 2009]

Four of the five states in the world today which counts as communist are in Asia. Apart from China, they are Vietnam, North Korea, and Laos. Two other countries which did have communist systems, and no longer have them, are in Asia: Cambodia (Kampuchea) and Mongolia, a much longer-lasting communist regime. Another country which, for a time, came close to establishing a communist system was Afghanistan, although it was not held to be a 'socialist country' by the Soviet Union. [Brown 2009]

In Asia and Africa, unlike Europe, the advance of communism has been linked not only with class struggle but, at least as crucially, with the movement for national liberation and anti-colonialism. Communist parties have been able to tap into patriotic and anti-imperialist sentiments as well as to the desire of the poor to reduce inequality and take revenge on those perceived to be their class oppressors. [Brown 2009]

Vietnam

A short timeline follows:

1859-83- France colonizes Indochina.

1940- Japan takes control of Indochina.

1945- Ho Chi Minh proclaims independence and establishes the Democratic Republic of Vietnam.

1946- French seek to regain control. Anti-French resistance war - or the First Indochina War - spread across the country.

1954- Vietnam is partitioned between North and South. The conflict between the two rival states rages for the next two decades, in what is known as the Vietnam War or the Second Indochina War. The US is heavily involved in support of the South.

1975- Southern cities fall one by one until communist forces seize Saigon.

1976- Vietnam is reunified as the Socialist Republic of Vietnam. Hundreds of thousands flee abroad, including many "boat people".

1979- Vietnam invades Cambodia and ousts the Khmer Rouge regime of Pol Pot.

For many Asian communists, hostility to colonialism and hostility to capitalism went together. For the kind of capitalist systems involved extreme exploitation of the local population by foreign business. In this context, therefore – even though nationalism and Marxism are poles apart – young intellectuals linked national liberation with the replacement of capitalism by a socialist or communist system. [Brown 2009]

The French rulers of Vietnam had dealt rigorously with sporadic strikes and demonstrations organized by the communists in the inter-war period, but with the Japanese surrender in August 1945, there was a power vacuum into which Ho Chi Minh and the communists moved rapidly. Having not succeeded in securing liberation from French colonial rule by peaceful means, Ho and the Vietnamese communists turned to force. [Brown 2009]

As well as using guerrilla tactics against the French, the communists were fomenting class war in the countryside. In fact, the communists controlled much of the North of Vietnam and were able to pass legislation which could be implemented in that territory. In late 1953 they passed a law enforcing rent reductions and 'extending the confiscation of landholdings to the entire landlord class.' [Brown 2009]

Moreover, when they took their struggle to the South, the communists were able to attract substantial peasant support, as they had done in the North. The communists had a better-thought-out strategy than the government in Saigon which American troops had been sent to support. Communists had some success in presenting as their ultimate goal a more just society. In the meantime, their redistribution of land in areas they controlled brought immediate benefits to many. [Brown 2009]

The United States was drawn into the conflict in Vietnam partly because of what it did not do in Laos; because of their non-intervention. Vietnam is a country of over eighty million people – a population over ten times greater than that of the economically backward, land-locked and mountainous Laos. [Brown 2009]

The Vietnamese communists maintained good relations with the Soviet leadership while China and the United States had some rapprochement. The Vietnamese communists emerged in 1975 as the winners in their struggle. There were some 700,000 Vietnamese casualties, and 45 percent of the country's towns were destroyed.

Laos

A brief timeline follows:

1893- Laos becomes a French protectorate until 1945 when it is briefly occupied by the Japanese towards the end of the Second World War.

1950- Laos is granted semi-autonomy as an associated state within the French Union.

1953- Independence restored after the end of French rule. Civil war breaks between royalists and the communist group, the Pathet Lao.

1975- Pathet Lao - renamed the Lao People's Front - replaces the monarchy with a communist government.

1986- Laos introduces market reforms.

1997- Laos becomes a member of Association of Southeast Asian Nations (ASEAN).

2011- New stock market opens in Vientiane.

2013- Becomes a member of the World Trade Organisation (WTO).

Already during the Eisenhower presidency, the United States was dropping supplies to anti-communist forces in Laos, but for more than one reason it avoided direct military involvement there. [Brown 2009]

The United States backed a compromise solution on Laos in 1962, abandoning their support for the most anti-communist forces and settling for a neutralist government. However, in the coalition government which was formed, the communists exercised increasing influence and finally gave way to outright communist rule in 1975. [Brown 2009]

The communist insurgents in Laos, the Pathet Lao, with the support of the North Vietnamese, were gradually able to take over the country territorially and to establish communist rule by the mid-1970s. Although the regime in Laos turned out to be milder than other communist systems in Asia – with few executions in comparison with Vietnam, not to speak of Cambodia – almost 10 percent of the people fled from the country. [Brown 2009]

Mongolia

A short timeline follows:

1206-63 Genghis Khan unites Mongol tribes and launches a campaign of conquest which eventually results in the world's biggest land empire.

1691- Mongolia comes under the rule of China's Qing dynasty.

1921- Wins independence but under strict Soviet control.

1990- Mongolia holds its first free multiparty elections.

2014- Prime Minister Norov Altankhuyag is dismissed by a parliamentary vote of no confidence and later replaced by Chimed Saikhanbileg.

Mongolia was the first Asian country to become communist. If Mongolia had not been under the protection and ultimate political control of the Soviet Union, it would hardly have survived as a sovereign state during its lengthy period of communist rule. [Brown 2009]

The communist party in Mongolia was known from 1924 until the end of communist rule as the Mongolian People's Revolutionary Party. In the inter-war period, collectivization of agriculture had been resisted by a reluctant and, in large part, nomadic population. In 1949 the leadership proclaimed that Mongolia was now a 'socialist' state – as distinct from merely building, or aspiring to, socialism. [Brown 2009]

Cambodia

A brief timeline follows:

802-1431 -Khmer Empire centered on Angkor. After the empire's decline, its heartland shifts south to Phnom Penh and becomes modern-day Cambodia.

1863-1953- French colonial rule.

1941- Sihanouk becomes king.

1941-45- Japanese occupation.

1970- Prime Minister Lon Nol mounts a successful coup against

1975-79- Lon Nol is overthrown by the communist Khmer Rouge under Pol Pot, who institute violent totalitarian rule until ousted by a Vietnamese invasion.

1981- The pro-Vietnamese Kampuchean People's Revolutionary Party wins elections, but its rule is not internationally recognized and later faces

1991- A peace agreement is signed in Paris, ushering in a power-sharing administration. Sihanouk becomes head of state.

1997- Hun Sen mounts a coup against the prime minister, Prince Ranariddh, effectively taking sole power

Cambodia had been part of French Indochina but gained its independence in 1953. When the French departed, Prince Norodom Sihanouk became prime minister. From 1960 to 1970 he governed as president. He was ousted by members of his own government in a coup in 1970. [Brown 2009]

Cambodia turned communist for some time, run by a regime of exceptional viciousness. Between 1976 and 1979, under Khmer Rouge, Cambodia slaughtered a higher proportion of its own citizens than any other communist or fascist state in the twentieth century. Under the leadership of Pol Pot, the idea of class war was taken to perverse extremes; the purges of the communist party itself exceeded the worst excesses of Stalin and Mao Zedong, and an attempt was made to leap into communism even faster than China's Great Leap Forward. [Brown 2009]

The overthrow of the Khmer Rouge government was very largely the work of the Vietnamese. After two years of border clashes, Vietnamese forces invaded Cambodia/Kampuchea at the end of December 1978. A communist government was established under Vietnamese supervision. For the next decade – until the Vietnamese troops withdrew in 1989 – Cambodia had a more orthodox communist system, with far less arbitrary violence. The Vietnamese incursion saved an incalculable number of lives. [Brown 2009]

Cambodia was the last country in the twentieth century to become communist, although well before the century's end it had ceased to be a communist state. The takeover occurred as late as 1975, and the system lasted – as a different type of communist regime from 1979 – until 1991. The Khmer Rouge, after being ousted from power, became once again an underworld organization, but in 1993 a peace process led to elections and a non-communist Cambodia. [Brown 2009]

Afghanistan

A short timeline follows:

1979- Soviet Army invades and props up a communist government. More than a million people died in the ensuing war.

1989- Last Soviet troops leave. US- and Pakistan-backed mujahideen push to overthrow Soviet-installed Afghan ruler Najibullah triggers

1996- Taliban seized control of Kabul and imposed a hard-line version of Islam.

2001- US intervenes militarily following the September 11 attacks on the United States. Taliban are ousted from Kabul and Hamid Karzai becomes head of an interim power-sharing government.

2002- Nato assumes responsibility for maintaining security in Afghanistan.

2004- Loya Jirga adopts a new constitution which provides for a strong presidency. Hamid Karzai is elected president.

Afghanistan is the only country which might conceivably be regarded as communist and which came to communism later than Cambodia. The Soviet involvement in Afghanistan was part of a policy aimed of ensuring that it would not acquire a regime hostile to the USSR. [Brown 2009]

The seizure of power by communists in Afghanistan came as a surprise to the Soviet leadership. The Soviet leaders made matters worse for themselves by invading their southern neighbor. Indeed, the war, with its aftermath of Taliban rule followed by further war, turned out to be one with no winners. [Brown 2009]

The Afghan regime, though led by people who regarded themselves as communists, had certainly not succeeded in creating a communist system prior to the Soviet invasion, and it was, if anything, even less successful in doing so after it. The regime's survival depended heavily on the Soviet military. [Brown 2009]

The decision to withdraw Soviet forces from Afghanistan was taken by Mikhail Gorbachev very early in his general secretaryship in 1985 but not made public at that time. Soviet perestroika has an impact on domestic reforms and the 'new thinking' on foreign policy. [Brown 2009]

Afghan communists had some achievements to their credit. They tackled the problems of widespread illiteracy and of gross gender inequality in educational opportunities. The government granted women equal legal rights and tried to ban forced marriage. They also attempted to introduce land redistribution. [Brown 2009]

Nazi's Germany

German Canadians – that is, Canadians who report their ethnic origin as solely or partly from Germany or of German ancestry – are one of Canada's largest ethnic categories of European origin. British North America, and then Canada, would receive six waves of immigration throughout their history, the most recent of which consisted of displaced people at the end of Second World War. In the 2016 Canadian Census, 3,322,405 (nearly 10 percent of the population) reported German origins, and 404,745 people in the country reported German as their mother tongue. A large proportion of these respondents lived in Ontario or Central Canada.

As it was mentioned in the book Socialism is Dead [Boloix 2018], I had already a bad experience with a German guy. I do not want to repeat the narrative and I prefer to shift towards nicer souvenirs. There is a German guitarist called Ottmar Lieber who plays nouveau flamenco and whom I enjoy very much during my daily walks in the park. I hear some songs at a pace that fits my walking speed and I usually listen repeatedly some to complete my exercise. One is called 'Barcelona Nights' that also reminds me of my ascendant family that lives in Catalonia, Spain.

A brief timeline follows:

1871- Otto von Bismarck unifies Germany.

1914-1918- World War I. Germany is defeated and becomes a republic.

1933- Adolf Hitler, head of the far-right Nazi Party, becomes chancellor.

1939-45- Second World War sees the defeat of Germany and its partition into the pro-western Federal Republic and the Soviet-controlled German

1955- West Germany joins Nato; East Germany joins the Warsaw Pact.

1957- West Germany is a founding member of the European Economic Community.

1961- Construction of the Berlin Wall to prevent the flight of East Germans to the increasingly prosperous West.

1970 - West German Chancellor Willy Brandt establishes relations with East Germany in an effort to ease tensions across the Iron Curtain.

1989- Mass exodus of East Germans as Soviet bloc countries relax travel restrictions. Berlin Wall is torn down.

Few people will deny that Germans, on the whole, are industrious and disciplined, through and energetic to the degree of ruthlessness, conscientious and single-minded in any tasks they undertake; that they possess a strong sense of order, duty, and strict obedience to authority; and that they often show great readiness to make sacrifices and great courage in physical danger. [Hayek 1994]

What the "typical German" is often thought to lack are the individualistic virtues of tolerance and respect for other individuals and their opinions, of independence of mind and that uprightness of character and readiness to defend one's convictions against a superior, of consideration for the weak and infirm, and of that healthy contempt and dislike of power which only an old tradition of personal liberty creates. They also lack kindliness and a sense of humor, personal modesty, and respect for the privacy and belief in the good intentions of one's neighbor. [Hayek 1994]

In Germany, distinction and rank are achieved almost exclusively by becoming a salaried servant of the state, where to do one's assigned duty is regarded as more laudable than to choose one's own field of usefulness. The alternative to security in a dependent position is a most precarious position, in which one is despised alike for success and for failure, only a few will resist the temptation of safety at the price of freedom. [Hayek 1994]

Nazis and Socialism

Nazi ideology regarded Russians (and Slavs more generally) – as well as Jews – as subhuman, and this dehumanization of entire populations led to brutality on the Eastern Front far in excess of that in the western war zones. Politically, the Nazis saw communists as their most bitter enemies, and so Communist Party members and Jews were killed in cold blood. [Brown 2009]

German had a different understanding of society's evolution compared with westerners. The structure of the English nation is based on the distinction between rich and poor, that of the Prussian on that between command and obedience. The meaning of class distinction is accordingly fundamentally different in the two countries. [Hayek 1994]

It is clear that socialists ideas were widespread in Germany for many years. However, the Socialist Party (SDP) did not agree with the Communist Party's loyalty to Russian-controlled Third International. The socialists were in power for some periods before the Nazis. Would it be possible to say that Hitler's empowerment was the fault of socialists? Because of their bad government policies? Because of not solving the problems? That is a real possibility. It is possible to state that the SDP was a model type of party, but it got stuck in impractical rhetoric and gained power before it had outlined a pragmatic party program. The SDP had dropped its extreme rhetoric and concentrated on practical programs, and was Germany's ruling party for many years. [Fleming 2008]

The Social Democrats managed to form governments (1918-1920 and 1928-1932) that wrestled with major problems of unemployment, inflation, and the reparations Germany was required to her victorious allies. An even more serious challenge emerged in the form of the National Socialist German Workers Party, which combined national resentments against German surrender at the end of World War I and an appeal to the patriotic members of the working classes. Under the circumstances, with few positive programs, the socialists were displaced by more conservative and more radical parties, paving the way to the rise of Adolf Hitler and the Nazi Party. [Fleming 2008]

There is, however, no simple straight line running from the Bismarck's Reich up to 1933. There were 'complex tendencies at work in Germany in 1914, which pointed towards both the development of a democracy and a more authoritarian solution. On the one hand, the paranoid tendency to see politics in terms of friends and bitter enemies, the role of pressure groups, the anti-democratic sentiments of the elites and the longing for a strong man who could unite the country. On the other hand, for all its imperfections, Wilhelmine Germany was very much a state where the rule of law was a reality, as was freedom of speech and the press. [Williamson 2002]

Nazis kept their opportunity to become notorious because of miscalculations of the socialists. Soldiers' and Workers' Councils sprang up all over Germany, and the new government, under the leader of the SPD, Friederich Ebert, could initially only survive by basing its power on these Councils. Consequently, there was briefly an opportunity to purge the ancient regime. Had this occurred it seems unlikely that Hitler would have been able to gain power in 1933. It allowed the enemies of the regime to stay in power and ultimately to act as 'stirrup holders for Hitler' in 1933. [Williamson 2002]

Enemies of the government on the Right also exaggerated the communist danger. The communist uprising in Berlin in January 1919 and the proclamation of the 'Soviet Republic' of Bavaria in April were inevitably judged against the background of the Russian revolution. Even though, in fact, they were quickly crushed, they struck terror into the minds of the Mittelstand (petty bourgeoisie) and property-owning classes and fueled their fears of Socialism and 'Jewish' Bolshevism. [Williamson 2002]

It was the economic crisis of 1930-33 that turned the Nazi Party into a mass party of protest. The great depression was felt in Germany, whose economy since 1924 had been dangerously dependent on short-term American loans. The fear of bankruptcy and unemployment affected all sections of society. [Williamson 2002]

The Nazis were well placed to exploit this misery, but they would have remained on the fringes of power if it had not been for the break-up of the Grand Coalition in March 1930, caused by the resignation of the SPD over the issue of increasing employees' national insurance contributions at a time when wages were falling. This triggered the long political crisis that ended in Hitler's appointment as Chancellor three years later. [Williamson 2002]

In the subsequent electoral campaign, the Nazis' main theme was that only Hitler could unite a Germany that under parliamentary democracy had become deeply divided and split into competing interest groups. [Williamson 2002]

In 1930 18.3 percent of the electorate (6.5 million) voted for the Nazis; in July 1932 this increased to 37.3 percent (13.7 million). Young voters contributed to the Nazi successes; Hitler's pledges to create work made the Nazis attractive to unemployed first-time voters. [Williamson 2002]

Hitler's anti-Socialism was increasingly appreciated by big business. When he met groups of leading industrialists, he was able to win their goodwill and considerable sums for his campaign funds by stressing the anti-democratic and anti-socialist nature of his campaign. When Germany went to the polls on 5 March 1933, Hitler did not secure the decisive majority he was hoping for. The Nazis won 43.9 percent of the votes and could only claim a majority with the Nationalist Party alliance. [Williamson 2002]

Nazi's Economy

Strenuous efforts were made to remove as many young people as possible from the labor market. In 1933-34 nearly half a million unemployed people joined the Voluntary Labor Service. In 1935, the introduction of conscription ensured that annually a million young men were taken out of the labor market for a two-year period. At the same time, the government reduced the length of the working week in order to spread work opportunities more widely. [Williamson 2002]

A new commission was created to ensure that job creation schemes did not result in inflation. In this, it helped the destruction of the unions and the introduction of controls, which fixed wage rates at their lowest level in 1932. Government subsidies increased industrial activity for house construction and the renovations of dilapidated buildings. The motor industry was also assisted with tax concessions. Fuel tax was abolished; not surprisingly, car sales improved in 1933 and doubled again in 1934. [Williamson 2002]

Unemployment declined steadily until the summer of 1934, but for the next 12 months it stabilized at 2.5 million and was only brought down to 1.7 million in the autumn of 1935 by the introduction of military conscription and increasing investment in rearmament. In 1938 full employment was achieved. Despite the initial priority Hitler gave to job creation projects in 1933, he never lost sight of his intention to rearm Germany as quickly as possible. He thus needed both to save foreign exchange to pay for imported raw materials and to raise the necessary money within Germany to finance rearmament. [Williamson 2002]

Schacht was given full dictatorial powers in the economic sphere, and in September 1934 introduced a New Plan, which set up the necessary controls for the government regulation of imports and currency exchange. He also saved vital foreign exchange by negotiating a series of bilateral trade agreements, mainly with the Balkan and South America. German purchases in these countries were paid for in German currency which could only then be used to buy German goods or to invest in the construction of plants which would later produce goods required for the German economy. [Williamson 2002]

Using the Four Year Plan, within four years both the German economy and the army were to be ready for war. The key to the plan was to increase production of synthetic rubber, fuel oil and iron ore. To prevent the economy from overheating, tighter controls of prices, wages, and labor were introduced. The Four Year Plan gave Hitler not only defensive strength but large-scale preparation for aggressive imperialism over which the armed forces were to have less and less say. [Williamson 2002]

The introduction of the Four Year Plan emphasized that capitalism could continue to thrive in Germany provided it was ready to subordinate itself to the Nazi government. The chemical industry welcomed the plan and subsequently prospered, whereas the steel industry was more critical. By 1938, 17 percent of Germany's gross national product was spent or rearmament, which was a sum far greater than any other European power was spending on armaments. The Four Year Plan really was 'a decisive step towards preparing Germany for total mobilization.' Obviously, Hitler hoped for a brief war, as he told his generals in May 1939, but simultaneously stressed that 'the government must … also prepare for a war of from ten to fifteen years duration.' [Williamson 2002]

By 1939 the German economy was the second strongest in the world and much less vulnerable to world pressure than either the French or British economies. It was the diplomatic rather than economic situation that determined the timing of the war in 1939, 'the mounting economic problems fed into the military and strategic pressures for expansion.' [Williamson 2002]

Some historians see Nazism as a consciously modernizing force. It both anticipated Keynesian economics by creating full employment, with all the potential for social mobility that this entailed, and, by destroying the trade unions while simultaneously controlling the employers, it decisively changed the structure of German society. Hitler justified the dissolution of the trade unions and the political parties of the Left by claiming that he had liberated the workers from their bureaucratic and corrupt Marxist leaders and given them a more respected place in society. [Williamson 2002]

Hitler's rise to power occurred in the context of the political, economic and social crisis of the early 1930s. The Nazi amalgam of volkish, authoritarian and nationalist ideas provided a solution for both the middle classes and the elites. It could promise an element of 'restoration' but also of change and dynamism without destroying the actual structure of society in the way Bolshevism had in Russia. [Williamson 2002]

Highlights for Chapter 4

- The Second World War, after the German attack on the Soviet Union, turned out to be the 'finest hour' also of Western communists. 'They could fight fascism and Nazism, be true internationalists, defend the USSR, be flawless patriots and all without inconsistency.'
- The single most important reason for the establishment of communists regimes in Europe following the Second World War was the success of the Soviet army in ending Nazi rule in the region.
- In Albania and Yugoslavia, the success of the communists in resistance movements was on a scale which enabled them to prevail without major Soviet support.
- In Yugoslavia, civil war consisted of both ideological and military struggle between communists and anti-communists and bitter conflict among the country's different nationalities.
- Elsewhere in Eastern Europe, the Soviet Army played a decisive role in establishing the conditions for communist takeover.
- What became the separate East German state known as the German Democratic Republic (GDR) began as the Soviet zone of Germany.
- Four of the five states in the world today which count as communist are in Asia. Apart from China, they are Vietnam, North Korea and Laos.
- Having not succeeded in securing liberation from French colonial rule by peaceful means, Ho and the Vietnamese communists turned to force.

- The Vietnamese communists maintained good relations with the Soviet leadership.
- The Pathet Lao, with the support of the North Vietnamese, were able to take over the country and to establish communist rule by the mid-1970s.
- Mongolia was the first Asian country to become communist.
- In the inter-war period, collectivization of agriculture had been resisted by a reluctant and, in large part, nomadic population.
- Cambodia turned communist, run by a regime of exceptional viciousness.
- The overthrow of the Khmer Rouge government was very largely the work of the Vietnamese.
- Afghanistan is the only country which might conceivably be regarded as communist and which came to communism later than Cambodia.
- Politically, the Nazis saw communists as their most bitter enemies, and so Communist Party members and Jews were killed in cold blood.
- It was the economic crisis of 1930-33 that turned the Nazi Party into a mass party of protest.
- Despite the initial priority Hitler gave to job creation projects in 1933, he never lost sight of his intention to rearm Germany as quickly as possible.
- Using the Four Year Plan, within four years both the German economy and the army were to be ready for war.
- By 1938, 17 percent of Germany's gross national product was spent or rearmament.
- By 1939 the German economy was the second strongest in the world.

Chapter 5: China

Chinese Canadians are one of the largest ethnic groups in the country. Despite their importance to the Canadian economy, including the historic construction of the Canadian Pacific Railroad, many European Canadians were hostile to Chinese immigration. Since 1900, Chinese Canadians have settled primarily in urban areas, particularly in Vancouver and Toronto, and have contributed to every aspect of Canadian society. The 2011 census reported that Chinese language speakers numbered slightly over 800,000, emerging as Canada's third most common mother tongue group after English and French.

A brief China's timeline would be:

1911-12- Military revolts lead to the proclamation of Republic of China under Sun Yat-sen and the abdication of the last Manchu emperor, but much of the country is taken over by unruly warlords.

1931-45- Japan invades and establishes a brutal regime of occupation across large parts of China.

1949 1 October- Communist leader Mao Zedong proclaims the founding of the People's Republic of China after the defeat of the nationalist Kuomintang in a civil war.

1958-60- Mao's "Great Leap Forward" disrupts agriculture, producing an economic breakdown, and is quickly abandoned after the loss of millions of lives.

1966-76- Mao's "Cultural Revolution" produces massive social, economic and political upheaval.

1976- Mao dies.

1977- pragmatist Deng Xiaoping emerges as the dominant figure and undertakes far-reaching economic reforms.

1989- Troops open fire on pro-democracy protesters in Beijing's Tiananmen Square, killing hundreds of people.

2010- China becomes the world's second-largest economy after the United States when Japan's economy shrank in the final months of the year.

China faced several invasions during many centuries making people distrust foreign cultures. In recent centuries, China has tried to reinforce its own culture, however, keeping some regard towards Western cultures. Towards the end of the nineteenth century, the intellectual Yan Fu wrote, regarding importing Western ideas to restore their country to greatness, "If one course leads to ignorance and thus to poverty and weakness ... we must cast it aside. If another course is effective in overcoming ignorance and thus leads to a cure of our poverty and weakness, we must imitate it, even if it proceeds from barbarians." [Schell 2013]

The dominant tradition of reform in China evolved from a utilitarian source. Its primary focus was to return China to a position of strength because of its innumerable defeats against the invaders. What "liberté, egalité, fraternité" meant to the French Revolution and the making of modernity in the West, "wealth, strength, and honor" have meant to the forging of modern China. [Schell 2013]

Confucianism is a system of social and ethical philosophy rather than a religion. The traditional Chinese society established its social values, institutions, and ideas around a way of life based in Confucian well-being for all. Legalists offered a radical alternative to the Confucian notion of harmonious agrarian idealism. They argued that the key to national strength was to invest in a technologically advanced military, encourage commerce through a mixture of private enterprises and state monopoly over key industries, and maintain social order through a brutal set of laws enforced uniformly by an authoritarian state. (Their list of priorities and principles bears a sometimes uncanny resemblance to today's "China model" of authoritarian, state-led capitalism.) [Schell 2013]

Legalism was egalitarian in that all stood equal before the law, and, true to their name, Legalists prized the "rule of law," rather than the Confucians' political philosophy of the "rule of virtue." Unlike Confucianism, Legalism stressed the need for strong leadership, rigid authoritarian controls, strict centralism, and an uncompromising system of laws and punishments, all "to enrich the people and strengthen the state." Almost anything done in pursuit of these basic goals was considered justifiable. [Schell 2013]

Revolutions

The Chinese learned a good deal from the West, but they could not make it work and were never able to realize their ideals. Their repeated struggles, including such a countrywide movement as the Revolution of 1911, all ended in failure. But then a new force burst onto the world stage: "The Russians made the October Revolution and created the world's first socialist state," wrote Mao. "Under the leadership of Lenin and Stalin, the revolutionary energy of the great proletariat and laboring people of Russia, hitherto latent and unseen by foreigners, suddenly erupted like a volcano, and the Chinese and all mankind began to see the Russians in a new light. They found Marxism-Leninism, the universally applicable truth, and the face of China began to change." [Schell 2013]

"Our revolutions," said Mao, "come one after the other," a succession of mass movements "turned over" the Chinese society: the land confiscation and reform movement, in which at least a million landlords were executed (1950); the Marriage Law, which fundamentally changed the status of women, the Chinese family, and labor force (1950); sending three hundred thousand Chinese "volunteers" to fight in Korea against the United States (1950); the "Three-Anti" and "Five-Anti" campaigns to ferret out corrupt cadres and unreformed bourgeois elements (1951-52); the Agricultural Cooperative Movement to push millions of peasants into cooperatives (1952-53); and the Hundred Flowers Movement, when intellectuals were encouraged to speak out only to be brutally cashiered in the subsequent Anti-Rightist Campaign (1956-57). [Schell 2013]

These revolutionary outbursts culminated in Mao's Great Leap Forward (1958-61), which communized Chinese agriculture, completely reorganized rural Chinese society and saw upward of thirty million farmers die from famine. After this catastrophe, for a while, it was difficult for Mao to launch new campaigns. Nonetheless, by 1963 he was able to initiate the Socialist Education Campaign, which sought to make all Chinese more proletarian. [Schell 2013]

Cultural Revolution

In the early stages of this Cultural Revolution (1966), Red Guards organized themselves without official backing. Mao wrote an open letter to rebellious students at Tsinghua University, thereby providing them with a carte blanche to criticize and attack any authority figure – their teachers, officials, even parents – whom they suspected of harboring bourgeois tendencies. "you say it is right to rebel against reactionaries," wrote Mao. "I enthusiastically support you." [Schell 2013]

Mao allowed the attack to the Chinese Communist Party itself. Although the bourgeoisie had already been overthrown, stubborn elements had nonetheless "gained a foothold in the Party and have set out on the capitalist path" by trying "to use the old ideas, culture, customs and habits of the exploiting classes to corrupt the masses, capture their minds and endeavor to stage a comeback." [Schell 2013]

The cost of this last revolutionary hurrah was astonishing: eviscerating the Communist Party; impeding the country's economic development; bringing the Chinese educational system to a standstill; splitting up countless families by sending millions into rural exile; and causing the death of untold numbers by murder, suicide, executions, and even acts of ritual cannibalism. From the perspective of conventional nation builders, these years of revolutionary turmoil represented a lost decade. [Schell 2013]

The Cultural Revolution began as a general investigation into rural conditions, then became a rectification campaign directed at rural Party cadres, and finally developed into a mass campaign against cadre corruption, known as the 'four cleanups,' involved the dispatch of outside cadres to the countryside. [Roberts 2003]

A notable consequence of the Cultural Revolution had been the intervention of the People's Liberation Army into politics. In April 1969, at the Ninth Party Congress, Lin Biao's position as Mao's successor had been confirmed and new appointments to the Politburo were dominated by the military. However, Mao Zedong had not intended that China should become a military dictatorship, new criteria were established for Party membership, a fresh emphasis was placed on the relationship between the Party member and the masses. In late 1969 the army was instructed to pay greater attention to military training, an indication that it was about to be relieved of its political role. [Roberts 2003]

Economy

The economic strategy adopted in 1953 was intended to achieve the following objectives: a high rate of economic growth through a concentration on industrial progress and a particular emphasis on heavy industry; a high rate of saving and investment to serve the previous objective; and the construction of large-scale, capital-intensive industrial plants using advanced technology. [Roberts 2003]

An aspect of the First Five-Year Plan concerned industrial management. A committee composed of technicians, cadres, and representatives of the workforce, exercised collective leadership, while the factory management organized the production operations. A Soviet model of 'one-man management' was introduced, it was a 'coldly rational arrangement of individual workers commanded by an authoritarian manager.' [Roberts 2003]

In 1955, in the context of the collectivization of agriculture, a harder line was adopted towards intellectuals who persisted in claiming the right to express their own views. In 1956 Zhou Enlai promised intellectuals an improvement in their standard of living and a reduction in their political study. In May Mao Zedong went further, announcing a relaxation of the policy towards intellectuals, declaring 'Let a hundred flowers bloom, a hundred schools of thought contend.' [Roberts 2003]

The first task was to restore agricultural output. From 1959 the production brigade was again made the basic unit of ownership and commune facilities such as the communal dining halls were abandoned. At the same time, a small proportion of the collectivized land was returned to peasants to be farmed as private plots. These plots, it was estimated, produced on average twice as much as community-owned land. In 1962 the communes were subdivided into smaller units, each corresponding approximately to the marketing area. [Roberts 2003]

Political

Unwilling to see Party control weakened, and aware of pressing economic problems, Mao supported the decision to divert criticism away from the Party and on to the intellectuals. For Mao, this shift was to prove decisive, for thereafter he abandoned the intellectuals as the key to economic development and looked to the next generation of educated youth to carry the revolution forward. [Roberts 2003]

In October 1957 the slogan 'more, faster, better, cheaper' was adopted to urge an increase in both industrial and agricultural output. In factories 'one-man management' was rejected in favor of workers' congresses and many cadres in middle-sector management were 'sent down' to participate in labor on the shop floor. Ideological exhortation increasingly replaced material incentives as the means to encourage workers to redouble their efforts. In 1958 production targets were raised dramatically and state investment greatly increased. Within three years, from 1957 to 1960, the numbers employed in state industrial enterprises doubled to over 50 million, placing an immense strain on the system of procurement of food from the countryside. [Roberts 2003]

Market Openness

When Deng Xiaoping took power, there were big changes in the way the country was run. Deng was unafraid to acknowledge the toll taken by the Cultural Revolution and China's relative inferiority. "We are at least

40 years behind the countries in the West," he reported. "We've got to work hard." [Schell 2013]

Paradoxically, Mao's savage revolution did prepare the ground for Deng Xiaoping to build not the proletarian paradise imagined by his predecessor, but a strong and prosperous, if unequal, nation in which the Chinese people, at last, could take pride. [Schell 2013]

Despite Deng Xiaoping's very different political agenda, his goals would be the same: wealth, power, and prestige for his nation. "The purpose of socialism is to make the country rich and strong." Deng was not interested in changing China's identity or arguing about culture and the political system. Instead, he was hell-bent on transforming the economic "means" by doing whatever was necessary to strengthen the state and enrich the people. [Schell 2013]

Deng proclaimed: "Speaking about the best system of production, I would support whatever type can relatively easily and rapidly restore and increase agricultural output, and whatever type the masses are willing to implement should be adopted. If it is not yet legal, then it should be legalized. Yellow or white, a cat that catches mice is a good cat." [Schell 2013]

On December 13, 1978, Deng gave arguably the most important speech of his life. At this historic turning point, Deng called on the Chinese people to "emancipate their minds." Seizing on the language of wealth and power, he proclaimed. "Let us advance courageously to change the backward condition of our country and turn into a modern and powerful socialist state." "Our fundamental task," he would later explain, "must be to develop the productive forces, shake off poverty, build a strong, prosperous country, and improve the living conditions of the people." [Schell 2013]

After all these decades, Deng was ready to turn to Mr. Science (if not Mr. Democracy). And, in the choice between "Reds" and "experts," Deng was ready to take the experts. "How can we dismiss nearly 10 million of China's intellectuals with one stroke?" he asked rhetorically in 1977. Indeed, his newest, and not very orthodox, slogans - "Practice is the sole criterion of truth" and "Seek truth from facts" - enhanced a sense that he was turning irrevocably from ideological faith to empirical reality. [Schell 2013]

"I am just a layman in the field of economics," Deng confessed. "I have proposed China's economic policy of opening to the outside world, but as for the details or specifics of how to implement it, I know very little indeed." Deng wanted to incentivize productivity and efficiency by allowing individuals and households to earn and retain any surplus profits they made. He was also willing to make room for private entrepreneurialism, and he was ready to decentralize economic decision making. [Schell 2013]

Deng was convinced that what he called a "socialist market economy" could be China's salvation. As he told American visitors in 1979, "Of course we don't want capitalism, but we don't want socialist poverty either; what we want is socialism that is advanced, that develops productive forces, and that makes our nation wealthy and powerful." [Schell 2013]

After a decade of castigating anyone with the slightest bourgeois affectation as a "capitalist-roader," now the popular slogan "To get rich is glorious" was widely touted by the party itself. Zhao Ziyang, the country's economic tzar of the 1980s testified to the depth of Deng's commitment to opening up. "Xiaoping believed in bringing in large-scale foreign investments." "He believed it was difficult for a developing economy like China's to take off without foreign investment. Of course, he only dealt with major issues and didn't intervene much as to how this might be brought about. But he supported all of it: preferential loans, non-preferential loans, joint ventures." [Schell 2013]

In a country that was post-Confucian, post-Maoist, and post-communist, it was no longer clear exactly what its essential core was. China had become a welter of contradictions created by the way its revolt against tradition was fusing with its revolt against the revolution. The only real constants were the yearning for a strong, prosperous, respected nation, and the faith that it could be achieved through strong leadership and a strong party, as well as a more open China. "No country can now develop by closing its door," Deng told party leaders in October 1984. "Isolation landed China in poverty, backwardness, and ignorance." [Schell 2013]

Deng openly praised dictatorships for being able to act quickly, mocking the United States for having "three governments" (executive, legislative, and judicial) in one, which collectively often rendered it incapable of dealing with serious problems in a timely and decisive manner. "The greatest advantage of the socialist system is that when the central leadership makes a decision, it is promptly implemented without interference from any other quarters." In other words, his dream was to perfect Lenin's concept of democratic centralism, but in the context of an increasingly capitalistic China. [Schell 2013]

Early in 1991, in an article placed in Shanghai's Liberation Daily, made Deng's agenda clear: "Reform and opening is the only path to making the nation wealthy and the people strong." "If the economy cannot be boosted, over the long run, we will lose people's support, and a collapse of the Communist Party." [Schell 2013]

Deng demanded that the core of China's new political system – Communist Party rule – be left untouched. If he surrendered socialism's dreams of egalitarianism and social welfare, he defended the political core of Chinese Leninism: single-party dictatorship. He saved China from the deadly elixir of Maoism with a heady cocktail of neo-authoritarianism and state-led capitalism. [Schell 2013]

Modernization

In August 1977 the Party had committed itself to the Four Modernization: the modernization of agriculture, industry, science, and technology, and national defense. The political context in which economic development would take place was defined by Deng Xiaoping in March 1979 as the 'four cardinal principles:' the socialist road, the democratic dictatorship of the people, the leadership of the Communist Party, and adherence to Marxism-Leninism and Mao Zedong Thought. [Roberts 2003]

From 1978 an industrial version of the responsibility system was introduced. Enterprises, which previously had been required to pass all their profits on to the state, were now allowed to retain a proportion of their surplus and distribute it as incentives. In some enterprises new management techniques were introduced, allowing managers much greater freedom of operation. Price controls were removed from many products, leading to moderate inflation. The development of private industrial and commercial enterprises was permitted. A stock market opened in Shanghai in 1986. [Roberts 2003]

From 1994 Deng Xiaoping ceased to appear in public, but until his death – and thereafter – the essence of his programme, the maintenance of a political dictatorship while transforming China into a 'socialist market economy,' prevailed. Deng Xiaoping's political reputation will always be clouded by his responsibility for the Tiananmen Square massacre, but his achievement in transforming the Chinese economy will secure him a high position among the creators of modern China. [Roberts 2003]

The first agricultural reforms encouraged peasants to produce more on their private plots for sale on the free-market. The next step was to introduce the 'household responsibility system.' Under this system, the ownership of the land remained collective, but individual families contracted to cultivate specific plots with nominated crops and to hand over a proportion of the harvest to the production team. The family could retain the surplus or sell it as it wished. This system spread rapidly and led to a sharp increase in output, diversification of production and rapid growth in rural marketing. [Roberts 2003]

Zhu Rongji

In June 1998, Jiang Zemin as President and Zhu Rongji as premier were trying to lead the country. Jiang tried to show a more open, even "democratic" China, while Zhu was accomplishing with extraordinary results in the economic realm. He was making his country "the factory of the world," therefore ensuring that Deng's vision of reform and opening up would outlive Deng himself. [Schell 2013]

Zhu created the Shanghai Foreign Investment Commission and endowed it with unprecedented authority to streamline the approval process for foreign investment, with no more interminable waits or need to grease the palms of countless bureaucrats. He lashed out at corruption among cadres even as he was pushing for faster growth and greater openness to foreign capital. By the end of 1989, Zhu had helped attract over $400 million in foreign direct investment (FDI) and secured a $3 billion loan from the World Bank to expand housing and transportation in Shanghai. Zhu had rendered his city an oasis of exactly the kind of reform that Deng had hoped to see before the rude interruption of Democracy Spring in 1989. [Schell 2013]

The implicit new post-1989 social contract between the party and the people: if the party would help people create wealth, the people would let the party keep power. "If we can increase the speed of economic construction, and continually raise the people's living standards," Zhu preached to a crowd of local cadres, "then the Party will be trusted and respected, and the people will support us." [Schell 2013]

A trademark of Zhu's leadership was a heavy reliance on economic experts who were, especially by Chinese standards, technically sophisticated, worldly, and daring. As Zhu and his aides crafted hard-driving reforms, they stuck to Deng's most essential principle: economic methods were in need of constant, structural transformation, while the political core – the system of one-party political control – should be left alone. [Schell 2013]

But an even greater challenge still faced Zhu: reforming China's massive, bloated state-owned sector itself, whose eighty thousand State-Owned Enterprises (SOEs) soaked up the lion's share of China's indigenous investment capital and bank loans. "As late as 1993, most scarce economic resources were still in the hands of the government and SOEs, despite the fact that the state sector accounted for less than half of the GDP," Wu Jinglian explained. In other words, China was suffering from a hugely wasteful misallocation of capital. [Schell 2013]

Zhu also challenged the "iron wage" principle, freeing managers to base salaries on performance and market competitiveness. Perhaps most controversially, he tried to destroy the notion of the "iron chair" that allowed incompetent officials to hold on to management positions once they got them. Now, profitability and productivity, not just party loyalty, longevity of service, or cronyism, were to help determine managerial and executive promotions. [Schell 2013]

After thirteen years of tedious and sensitive negotiation, China finally joined the World Trade Organization in December 2001, setting the stage for a decade of even faster growth, fueled by an exponential rise in its global trade and investment. Zhu's vision had finally and emphatically won out. [Schell 2013]

Zhu's quest was to remold China back into a strong state with a wealthy populace. He made unprecedented room for private enterprise, which left many foreign investors with the illusion that they were invited into an economy in the process of being liberalized piece by piece. However, that was never Zhu's end goal. His reforms were traditional, selectively borrowing Western methods and techniques in pursuit of wealth and power but on Chinese terms. The party-state's ultimate ownership rights of the national economy and the total monopoly of political power were no more to be changed. [Schell 2013]

Zhu wanted to emphasize the importance of the rule of law. "We are not afraid of democracy, we're not unwilling to implement the rule of law, and we certainly don't want to infringe on human rights," he insisted. "But based on conditions in China, we need to gradually do better and gradually turn China into a country that is completely under the rule of law." [Schell 2013]

Zhu flatly rejected, however, the relevance of liberal democracy to China, saying that the problem was not just that the Chinese people were unready for democracy, but rather that democracy had never been, and would never be, suitable for China. "We absolutely will not copy the Western model as we reform our political system," said Zhu defensively in 2001. "That is, we won't have different political parties taking turns running the government, nor will we have a bicameral legislature." [Schell 2013]

Contemporary China

In 2009 China overcame Germany to become the world's largest exporter. The next year China's economy surpassed Japan in total size to become second only to that of the United States. It seemed that Lenin's warnings about the dangers of international finance monopoly capitalism were being inverted. The Chinese Communist Party had become not only the darling of Wall Street but bankers to the world. [Schell 2013]

The "Beijing Consensus" is a new model in which free-market economic development becomes divorced from political liberalization, and capitalism delinked from democracy. In 2010, Premier Wen Jiabao did suggest that one of the reasons Chinese authoritarianism had been so successful was that it allowed leaders "to make decisions efficiently, organize effectively, and concentrate resources to accomplish large undertakings." [Schell 2013]

Despite all its obvious shortcomings and defying most predictions, the Communist Popular Party has managed to create three decades of rapid growth under a relatively stable political system. Many Chinese made a bargain with the party: as long as they are allowed to enjoy growing wealthier and to pursue a better life, and as long as their country is edging ever closer toward wealth, power, and a modicum of greatness in the world, they will not seek to challenge authoritarian rule. [Schell 2013]

When it comes to "core values," China's leadership is both lost and somewhat deaf and mute, neither wanting to accept the West's democracy and human rights as the birthrights of all people nor having any other "universal values" of their own to now offer as an alternative. [Schell 2013]

Self-inflicted humiliations have severely undercut China's bid for soft power, acclaim, and global respect. It includes the awarding of the Nobel Prize to jailed dissident Liu Xiaobo in 2010; the blind legal activist Chen Guangcheng's flight into the U.S. Embassy in Beijing after a daring escape from house arrest in 2012 just as Secretary of State Hillary Clinton was arriving in Beijing; and the announcement in early 2013 that the hundredth young Tibetan protesting Beijing's coercive policies in their homeland had immolated himself. [Schell 2013]

Xi Jinping

"We must achieve the great revival of the Chinese nation, and we must ensure there is unison between a prosperous country and a strong military." Said Xi Jinping as party general secretary in a trip to Guangdong Province. [Schell 2013]

But having touched on economic and military strength, there was an important piece left missing in this evolving new Chinese dream-escape, the question of political reform. The only realistic pathway forward to a comprehensive and long-lasting "revival" now lay in greater openness, the rule of law, and even constitutionalism. But this part of Xi Jinping's slowly pixelating dream for the future was left tantalizingly blurry. [Schell 2013]

Highlights for Chapter 5

- The tradition of reform in China and its primary focus was to return China to a position of strength.
- Confucianism is a system of social and ethical philosophy rather than a religion.
- Legalists offered a radical alternative to the Confucian notion of harmonious agrarian idealism.
- After the October revolution, all mankind began to see the Russians in a new light. Marxism-Leninism became the universally applicable truth, and the face of China began to change."
- Mao's Great Leap Forward (1958-61), which communized Chinese agriculture, completely reorganized rural Chinese society, and saw upward of thirty million farmers die from famine.
- Mao allowed to attack the Chinese Communist Party itself.
- A notable consequence of the Cultural Revolution had been the intervention of the People's Liberation Army into politics.
- The economic strategy adopted in 1953: a high rate of economic growth and heavy industry; saving and investment; and the construction of large-scale industrial plants.
- In 1955, in the context of the collectivization of agriculture, a harder line was adopted towards intellectuals.

- From 1959, a small proportion of the collectivized land was returned to peasants to be farmed as private plots.
- "We are at least 40 years behind the countries in the West," reported Deng Xiaoping. "We've got to work hard."
- Despite Deng Xiaoping's very different political agenda, his goals would be the same: wealth, power, and prestige for his nation.
- Deng wanted to incentivize productivity and efficiency by allowing individuals and households to earn and retain any surplus profits they made.
- Deng was convinced that what he called a "socialist market economy" could be China's salvation.
- Now the popular slogan "To get rich is glorious" was widely touted by the party itself.
- "The greatest advantage of the socialist system is that when the central leadership makes a decision, it is promptly implemented without interference from any other quarters."
- In 1977 the Party had committed itself to the modernization of agriculture, industry, science and technology, and national defense.
- The ownership of the land remained collective, but individual families contracted to cultivate specific plots.
- Zhu lashed out at corruption among cadres even as he was pushing for faster growth and greater openness to foreign capital.
- The party-state's ultimate ownership rights of the national economy and the total monopoly of political power were no more to be changed.
- "We are not afraid of democracy, we're not unwilling to implement the rule of law, and we certainly don't want to infringe on human rights,"
- In 2009 China overcame Germany to become the world's largest exporter. The next year China's economy surpassed Japan in total size to become second only to that of the United States.
- "We must achieve the great revival of the Chinese nation, and we must ensure there is unison between a prosperous country and a strong military." Said Xi Jinping.
- The only realistic pathway now lay in greater openness, the rule of law, and even constitutionalism.

Chapter 6: North Korea

The history of North Korea, and the entire Korean peninsula is really a history of the Korean people seeking to survive domination by greater powers. For centuries, Korea resisted foreign invasions, first by the Chinese and later the Japanese. [Miller 2004]

The history of the Korean peninsula reveals a series of Chinese invasions followed by Korean dynasties that continued to follow Chinese traditions, philosophy, and religion. In 1392, Korea entered its only golden period, 518 years of peace, independence, and unity during the Yi, or Choson, dynasty. [Miller 2004]

Japanese influence in Korea began in the late 1800s; Japan emerged as the winner for control of Korea, after overcoming both Chinese and Russian interests in the peninsula. In 1910 Japan formally annexed Korea, which became a Japanese colony for four decades, until Japan's defeat in World War II forced it out of the country in 1945. [Miller 2004]

The March First Movement of 1919 was an independence proclamation. Landowners, capitalists, religious representatives, intellectuals, well-known men from every walk of life signed the proclamation. It stated that Korea, through the kind help of the powerful nations of the world, hoped to gain independence. The Japanese military police used gunfire against the demonstrators and called even the army and navy for help. All over Korea resounded the cry: "Long live independence." [Miller 2004]

The March First Movement taught Koreans that you cannot free your country by merely shouting and marching around. We must learn from the Russian revolution and mobilize and arm the people of Korea, in order to free our nation and build a new Korea of equality, freedom, and justice for all. [Miller 2004]

The end of the Second World War opened the prospect for different countries in Europe, the cradle of communism, and in Asia, the forefront of the national liberation struggle, to build a new society on a democratic basis. [Miller 2004, Kim Il Sung]

When World War II ended on August 15, 1945, with the bombing of Hiroshima and Nagasaki and the surrender of the Japanese, the Russians had already entered the northern part of Korea to fight the Japanese after the defeat of Germany. Shortly thereafter, the United States moved into the southern part of Korea. [Miller 2004]

A recent North Korea's timeline would be:

1945- Japan's colonial rule over Korea ends with its Second World War surrender.

1948- Korea is divided between the Soviet-backed North and the US-backed South.

1994- Founding President Kim Il-sung dies, succeeded by his son Kim Jong-il.

2002- The US names North Korea as part of an "axis of evil" in a stand-off between the West and North Korea which lasts for decades.

2018- Kim Jong-un becomes the first North Korean leader to enter the South.

The nationalist movement that had developed in Korea during the Japanese occupation blossomed after the Japanese were ousted, pressing for unity and independence. Nationalists in Korea and the surrounding areas were primarily communist or left-leaning, supported by workers, students, and intellectuals. Korea was divided in half and subjected to military occupation in the area above and below the 38th parallel. [Miller 2004]

In the north, after the war, the Russians hastened to set up a communist government led by Koreans. A Russian-style communist regime was organized with Kim Il Sung. [Miller 2004]

In October came the shocking news that the Allied Powers had decided that Korea was to be ruled by a trusteeship system for a maximum of five years. A provisional government was to be formed under the trusteeship of the United States, Britain, the Soviet Union, and China. [Miller 2004]

Resistance was instantaneous and practically unanimous. After all the years of longing and fighting for independence, the Korean people simply could not accept the idea of even benevolent foreign rule. [Miller 2004]

When the Russians refused to allow the commission to oversee elections into North Korea, the UN held elections only in South Korea, resulting in the creation of an independent Republic of Korea (ROK) on August 15, 1948. [Miller 2004]

In North Korea, things were very different. When the Soviet Red Army departed North Korea in 1948, it left behind some advisers as instructors and much of its weaponry and equipment. After 1949 the formation of a field army went ahead rapidly. In March 1950 there was a further infusion of Russian equipment, following Soviet leader Joseph Stalin's tacit permission to invade. [Miller 2004, Michael Hickey]

In September 1948, the so-called People's Republic of Korea was formed. Almost immediately it began harassing guerrilla raids on the south, together with a propaganda campaign and fomenting of riots. Behind the scenes, serious military preparations were pushed forward as fast as possible. [Miller 2004]

The Republic of Korea immediately protested to the United Nations. In response, the Security Council passed a resolution ordering the communists to withdraw to the thirty-eighth parallel and encouraged all member nations to give military support to the Republic. [Miller 2004]

North Korea's Kim Il Sung and his Soviet backers misread the mood of the United States, believing that it would accept a communist invasion of South Korea since American troops had been withdrawn. With only the poorly prepared South Korean army left to defend the South, Soviet leader Joseph Stalin felt comfortable authorizing a military invasion. Not surprisingly, the South was crushed, and by June 28, 1950, the North had captured Seoul, the capital of South Korea. [Miller 2004, Michael Hickey]

On Monday the 26th of June 1950, Kim Il Sung broadcast to the Korean people from Pyongyang. He told them that the southerners had invaded the north, but that the NKPA was now counter-attacking successfully across the 38th parallel. He called for increased guerrilla activity in the south, for its workers to go on strike, and for the peasants to call for immediate land reforms. [Miller 2004, Michael Hickey]

The UN Security Council met in New York on the afternoon of 25 June to consider a draft resolution hurriedly tabled by the United States calling for collective action against 'unprovoked aggression' and an immediate cease-fire by the North Koreans. [Miller 2004, Michael Hickey]

Truman went a step further by authorizing the wider use of American ground forces in Korea on 30 June with the rousing words: 'We have met the challenge of the pagan wolves.' [Miller 2004]

MacArthur was authorized to commit all four of 8th Army's divisions if necessary, subject only to the need to safeguard the security of the Japanese islands. The President also gave authority for a naval blockade of North Korea, [Miller 2004]

North Korea faced enormous challenges after the Korean War. North Korea suffered almost complete destruction during the war because of the 'scorched-earth' tactics used by the United States and other United Nations countries. After the Korean War ended without unification of Korea, both sides faced massive economic reconstruction and problems of political instability. [Miller 2004]

Given the continuing hostilities and the vastly different ideologies, North and South Korea developed as totally separate countries, each supported by their respective superpowers and linked to their fates. [Miller 2004]

In the words of Kim Il Sung, We resolved to build the Party, state and armed forces, and also the national economy, education and culture, and develop science and technology by relying on our people's strength. In order to rouse the people to build a new country, we needed the staff of the revolution and state power which would educate, organize and mobilize them, as well as an army which could protect the building of a new society with arms. [Miller 2004, Kim Il Sung]

North Korea's world changed with the end of the Cold War and the collapse of the Soviet Union in 1991. Its alignment with communism, helpful during the early years, now became a liability. The absence of aid from the Soviet Union contributed to a sharp economic decline, and China's policy of economic modernization and opening to the United States also undercut North Korea's centuries-old reliance on that country for protection and support. [Miller 2004]

At this crucial time, 1991, Kim Il Sung, the deified 'Great Leader" of North Korea, died leaving the country to struggle under new leadership, that of his appointed successor and son, Kim Jong Il. [Miller 2004]

South Korea finally established a democratic government in 1992 under president Kim Young Sam. South Korea has developed along Western lines into a democratic nation with a thriving, modern economy, due largely to its ties with the United States. [Miller 2004]

The Economy

Kim Il Sung announced his "Three-Year-Plan" for reconstruction and successfully rebuilt North Korea in a remarkably short time. He also consolidated his grip on power by eliminating all his opponents and creating an authoritarian "cult of personality" around himself. Later, when the Soviets reduced their support, North Korea emphasized a political philosophy of Juche, or self-reliance, and learned to play the Soviets against the Chinese to reinforce North Korea's independence. [Miller 2004]

In April 1956, a new Five-Year-Plan was launched for the building of a socialist framework in North Korea. The plan, starting in 1957, was designed to establish agricultural co-operatives and to begin the socialist transformations of private trade and industry. [Miller 2004]

In 1984, Kim Jong Il said, "After having experienced about thirty years of socialism, I feel we need to expand to the Western world to feed the people. The reality is that we are behind the West." In July 1994, Pyongyang radio referred to Kim Jong Il as "the Dear Leader, the sole successor to the Great Leader." It took Kim Jong Il a few years before taking the high posts. In 1997, he was named the secretary of the Korean Workers Party and he consolidated his power with the title of National Defense Commission Chairman in 1998. [Miller 2004]

An inefficient economic model, the collapse of the Soviet Union, and droughts and floods in the mid-1990s left the country unable to recover without massive food aid from the United Nations and other countries. Yet the famine is only one part of a larger economic collapse. Domestic power shortages and an inability to import raw materials and replacement parts have exacerbated the declines in industrial and agricultural production. [Miller 2004]

The value of Soviet exports to North Korea plummeted from US$1,97 billion in 1990 to US$0,58 billion in 1991. By 1993 Russia's exports to North Korea were only 10 percent of what had been received from the Soviet Union prior to 1991. The value of China's exports to North Korea (primarily coal, petroleum products, and grain) rose from $0.39 billion in 1990 to $0,58 billion in 1991 and $0.66 billion in 1993, but thereafter declined to $0,47 billion in 1994. [Miller 2004]

Even under ordinary climatic conditions, North Korea has been barely able to feed itself. Its geography and climate permit only one season for growing food, lasting from about June to October. A 12 percent shortfall of grain can be expected in any given year. Campaigns such as "let's eat only two meals a day" were common in 1991. The flooding in 1995 and 1996 affected mortality reducing food availability and through the destruction of health infrastructure. It resulted in a 60 percent drop in pharmaceutical output between 1995 and 1998. [Miller 2004]

Those covered under the public distribution system were ostensibly guaranteed a certain amount of food. Prior to the famine, official daily quotas of grain for urban dwellers were typically about 600-700 grams per person, Larger quotas of 700-800 grams per day were established for high officials, the military, public security personnel, and heavy laborers. During the famine, rations had fallen to 150 grams per day. [Miller 2004]

International aid came through the World Food Programme, rising from 5,000 tons in 1995 to 387,000 tons in 1998. The United States also emerged as a major bilateral donor. Regrettably, the North Korean government had limited monitoring of the distribution of this aid, so there was little assurance that it reached the most in need of it. [Miller 2004]

The Military

The imperative of system survival requires the defense of the country from military provocation, the preservation of system legitimacy vis-a-vis South Korea, and the protection of the population from disruptive, capitalist, decadent culture. A series of policy strategies and tactical maneuverings include information control. North Korea views the reforms and "democratization" in the Soviet Union and East Europe as mistakes that only worsened the situation. "Countries, where capitalism is restored, presented a serious lesson to the people … if one defends socialism, it is victorious and if one discards socialism it is death." [Miller 2004]

Following the death of Kim in 1994, the junior Kim's efforts were devoted to the promotion of the military in the belief that defense preparedness precedes any other national goal, including even the people's livelihood. North Korea's development of nuclear weapons and long-range missiles, viewed in this light, provides critical bargaining leverage for the small country, and will not be abandoned lightly. [Miller 2004]

The Korean peninsula is the most heavily armed area in the world in terms of both manpower and weaponry. There is pervasive mistrust between the two systems that make the security system all the more precarious. Many have concluded that the country is pursuing a foreign policy of nuclear blackmail, in which it seeks to survive by extorting benefits from other countries by "rogue" threats. This view comports with the long Korean history of surviving by resisting and manipulating hostile world powers. [Miller 2004]

Pyongyang has never forgotten the stark reality that the Korean War has never ended. It is in a state of temporary truce. The continuing presence of U.S. forces in South Korea, including some 36,000 ground troops, is keenly felt in North Korea as a formidable and direct threat to the security of the region. North Korea began to develop missiles in the early 1980s to compensate for the lack of a long-range strike capability in its air force. North Korea relies on the missiles for more than security. For more than a decade, North Korea has sold missiles and missile technology to countries such as Iran, Syria, Egypt, and Pakistan. These exports have provided with much-needed hard currency. [Miller 2004]

Where is North Korea heading

Since October 2002, North Korea has admitted that it is once again developing nuclear weapons. The nation quickly moves between aggressive and diplomatic postures and threatens with weapons of mass destruction to achieve its strategic goals of aid or security. [Miller 2004]

By all accounts, modern North Korea is in crisis, suffering from widespread famine, an almost completely collapsed economy, and overspending on the military. The country continues to live as an isolated Cold War communist state under a highly repressive totalitarian dictatorship concerned mainly with its own survival. To survive, North Korea sells arms and pursues an erratic foreign policy seeking peaceful reunification with South Korea and following aggressive military and nuclear threats. [Miller 2004]

It is believed that the North Korean government is bound to change or to fall in the long run. However, a "soft landing" is preferable than a "crash-landing." South Korea does not have the economic capability to absorb North Korea's collapse. The South Korean people cannot afford to lose their hard-earned economic prosperity for immediate national unification. [Miller 2004]

North Korea's soft landing, or gradual adoption of a market economy and liberal democracy, is desirable and feasible. North Korea is trying to implement calculated economic reforms and an open-door policy, following China's model, to cure its chronic economic illness and end its diplomatic isolation. [Miller 2004]

The "Sunshine Policy" of South Korean President Kim Dae Jung, proclaimed in February 1998 has consistently promoted a message of reconciliation with the North: first, never accept unification through communization; second, never attempt to achieve unification by absorbing the North; and third, South and North Korea should seek peaceful coexistence and cooperation. [Miller 2004]

The national goals of the North Korean system have been remarkably salient and consistent. The decision makers seem to have a clear sense of goals, strategies, and tactics. People from all walks of life share their perceptions. Once the center (meaning the Party) makes a decision, it will be efficiently transferred to the rank and file through the most effective channels of Party cells, community residential units, workplaces, and all the aforementioned agents of socialization. In other words, North Korea has a set of goals shared by any system: survival, prosperity, and identity. [Miller 2004]

It is a huge dilemma for North Korea that it cannot participate in the global market to make the best use of its high-quality labor force, rich mineral resources, and strategically placed geographical location, which may well bring the necessary comparative advantage in market competition. [Miller 2004]

Highlights for Chapter 6

- Japanese influence in Korea began in the late 1800s.
- The March First Movement of 1919 was an independence proclamation. Landowners, capitalists, religious representatives, intellectuals, well-known men from every walk of life signed the proclamation.
- When World War II ended on August 15, 1945, with the bombing of Hiroshima and Nagasaki and the surrender of the Japanese, the Russians had already entered the northern part of Korea.
- In the north, after the war, the Russians hastened to set up a communist government led by Koreans.
- After the Korean War ended without unification of Korea, both sides faced massive economic reconstruction and problems of political instability.
- Kim Il Sung, relying on large amounts of Soviet aid, announced his "Three-Year-Plan" for reconstruction and successfully rebuilt North Korea in a remarkably short time.
- In April 1956, a new Five-Year-Plan was launched for the building of a socialist framework in North Korea.
- In 1984, Kim Jong Il said, "After having experienced about thirty years of socialism, I feel we need to expand to the Western world to feed the people. The reality is that we are behind the West."
- The junior Kim's efforts were devoted to the promotion of the military in the belief that defense preparedness precedes any other national goal, including even the people's livelihood.

- North Korea's development of nuclear weapons and long-range missiles, viewed in this light, provides critical bargaining leverage for the small country, and will not be abandoned lightly.
- The Korean peninsula is the most heavily armed area in the world in terms of both manpower and weaponry.
- By all accounts, modern North Korea is in crisis, suffering from widespread famine, an almost completely collapsed economy, and overspending on the military.
- It is a huge dilemma for North Korea that it cannot participate in the global market to make best use of its high-quality labor force, rich mineral resources, and strategically placed geographical location.

Chapter 7: Cuba

According to the 2011 census, there were 21,440 Canadians who claimed full or partial Cuban ancestry. Canada is home to the third largest Cuban immigrant community in the world after the United States and Spain.

Cuba is an unusual communist state. It is the only case of communism prevailing either in the Americas or in the Caribbean. It is the only Hispanic communist state, and also the only 'Third World' country outside of Asia to have constructed and sustained a communist system. [Brown 2009]

The evolution of Cuba toward communism was gradual, and it reflected the evolution in the thinking of the foremost leader of the revolution, Fidel Castro. Faced by the new challenges of managing, as distinct from seizing, state power, Fidel Castro turned to the only available long term example of non-capitalist, post-revolutionary governance, that offered by the Soviet Union and other communist states. [Brown 2009]

Cuban leaders over the years invoked the memory of the hero of their country's struggle for independence from colonial rule, Jose Marti, but only Fidel Castro convincingly succeeded on the task. [Brown 2009]

A short Cuba's timeline is presented:

1898- Cuba is ceded to the US which defeated Spain in war.

1902- Cuba becomes independent under the protection of the US.

1933- Sergeant Fulgencio Batista seizes power in a coup.

1959- Fidel Castro leads a guerrilla army into Havana, forcing Batista to flee.

1961- The US breaks off diplomatic relations in response to the nationalization of US-owned properties, and later imposes a complete commercial embargo.

1961- Cuban exiles backed by the US try to invade Cuba at the Bay of Pigs, but are defeated.

1962- The US and the Soviet Union have a showdown that almost touches off war after the US discovers Soviet nuclear missiles on Cuba. The confrontation ends with the Soviets removing the missiles and the US

1975- Castro sends troops to Angola to help fight rebels backed by South Africa. It is the start of 15 years of war in which 300,000 Cubans will fight.

1991- The Soviet Union, Cuba's biggest benefactor, collapses, touching off an economic crisis.

In 1959 the value of U.S. Investments in Cuba – in sugar, mining, utilities, banking, and manufacturing exceeded that in every other Latin American country except Venezuela. The United States also took about two-thirds of Cuban exports and supplied about three-quarters of its imports. [Bethell 1993]

Fidel Castro, the 26 of July Movement, which he led, and other revolutionary forces that had participated in the revolutionary war, sought to affirm Cuban nationalism. [Bethell 1993]

The Revolution in Power

In January 1959 the old regime collapsed in Cuba and a revolution came to power. The fall of the old regime required that new norms, rules, and institutions be devised to replace those that had collapsed or been overthrown. In 1960, the revolution moved toward a Marxist-Leninist political system. A new leadership consolidated centralized and authoritarian rule. Non-communists and anti-communists were eliminated from the coalition. The Federacion de Mujeres Cubanas (FMC) and the Comites de Defensa de la Revolucion (CDR) were founded in August and September 1960. [Bethell 1993]

By the end of 1960, the Cuban state controlled the primary means of economic production on the island. Cuban capitalism had come to an end and its ties with the communist world were expanding. Nikita Khrushchev, the Soviet leader, expressed a willingness to defend Cuba from 'unprovoked aggression.' [Staten 2005]

The Cuban government socialized most of the means of production during its confrontation with the United States. That confrontation need not have affected Cuban-owned business, but on October 1960, 382 locally owned firms, including all the sugar mills, banks, large industries, and the largest wholesale and retail enterprises, were socialized. [Bethell 1993]

Economy

The Cuban economy performed quite well in 1959 and 1960. It grew at almost 10 percent a year and the sugar output of 6.2 million tons per year was greater than the average for the years 1950 through 1958. Housing and roads in rural areas were improved. [Staten 2005]

In June 1963, Prime Minister Castro announced a new strategy which once again emphasized sugar production and slowed down the efforts toward industrialization. [Bethell 1993]

Money, prices, and credit should operate only in dealing with Cuban consumers or foreign countries. The market law of supply and demand could and ought to be eliminated to move rapidly toward communism. Central planning was the key. All enterprises would be branches of central ministries. All financing would occur through the central budget by means of non-repayable interest-free grants. All enterprise deficits would be covered by the state. The money would be a unit of accounting but would not be used to assess profitability. [Bethell 1993]

By the end of 1963, the state-owned 70 percent of all land, and only small farms remained in the private sector. In the spring of 1968, consumer service shops, restaurants and bars, repair outfits, handicrafts shops, street food outlets, and even street vendors passed to state ownership and management. Although an illegal black market developed, for vegetables as well as for plumbing services, the government had put the economy in a straitjacket. [Bethell 1993]

Paradoxically, as the economy became thoroughly centralized, the means for central planning and control were abandoned. In the late 1960s, there were neither real year-to-year national plans nor any medium-term planning. From late 1966 onwards only sectoral planning occurred. A central budget was also abandoned, not to reappear until a decade later. [Bethell 1993]

Cuba sought development through rapid industrialization. Cuba's overwhelming dependence on the sugar industry was seen as a sign of under-development. 'There can be no vanguard country that has not developed its industry. The industry is the future.' Said, Che Guevara. [Bethell 1993]

The Cuban government could not have survived in power without Soviet support, which had increased since the late 1960s. Payments of interest and principal were postponed, Soviet credits were granted free of interest, Soviet subsidies were granted. [Bethell 1993]

Enterprises were given greater authority to hire and fire workers, to use some of their profits to pay bonuses to outstanding workers, to purchase inputs from the private sector on the island and to hire workers on a piecemeal basis. The state also began to sell goods locally on a supply and demand basis. State-run stores with rationed goods and subsidized prices were still maintained to provide a social safety net for the poor. [Staten 2005]

In 1972, Cuba joined the Council for Mutual Economic Assistance COMECON) to expand his trading ties with Eastern Europe and the Soviet Union. Between 1971 and 1975, the value of industrial output increased by 35 percent and the economy grew at an annual rate of 10 to 14 percent compared to 3.9 percent from 1966 to 1970. [Staten 2005]

Castro moved further to liberalize the economy by relaxing the regulations of foreign investment by allowing foreigners to have up to 49 percent ownership in the local business. [Staten 2005]

The revolutionary government's poor performance in housing construction resulted from insufficient production, inefficiency, and disorganization in the construction and construction materials industries. The government did not give high priority in the allocation of construction resources to meet the housing needs of the population. Its principal goals in this area included the building of hospitals, schools and military installations and deployment of the best construction teams overseas. [Bethell 1993]

Soldiers returning from abroad were put to work on farms run by the state, while officers with technical expertise were put to work to find alternatives to the island's dependence on imported fertilizers. The FAR was given the authority to create economic enterprises to begin to meet some of its own budgetary needs. Gaviota is a joint venture in the growing tourist industry of Cuba. [Staten 2005]

Ironically, at the same time, Castro was criticizing Cubans for acting like individualists and capitalists, he was encouraging Western investors and the promotion of joint investment ventures in electronics, mechanical engineering, petrochemicals, pharmaceuticals, textiles, and tourism. [Staten 2005]

At the beginning of 1992, Cuba's future remained uncertain. Only one thing seemed clear: living standards, at least in the short term, would fall for most ordinary citizens no matter who governed their country under whatever kind of regime. [Bethell 1993]

The dollar was legalized in August 1993. More than $400 million in U.S. currency per year was brought into the country via Cuban exiles living in the United States. These dollars fed the black market and served as an underground currency. Given that the government needed U.S. dollars to pay its debts and to purchase imports, the decision to legalize the dollar allowed the government to capture this needed foreign exchange. It could pay its debts and purchase products on the world market. [Staten 2005]

The Cuban government also began to allow self-employment in many different trades such as chauffeurs, hair stylists, shoemakers, photographers, carpenters and auto and bicycle repair. Those individuals who are self-employed are taxed by the state. Those home restaurants (paladares), legalized in 1993, are now common throughout the island and must be licensed by the state and pay taxes. [Staten 2005]

State-run enterprises were now being asked to function on a for-profit basis. Many state-run enterprises were also given the ability to import the necessary equipment and items without state permission. In order to improve its fiscal situation, the government levied a tax on some consumer goods. [Staten 2005]

Foreign investments

By 1994 tourism generated more income (foreign exchange) for Cuba than sugar. The decision was made to encourage the growth of tourism on the island. Reforms made it easier to invest in the production of citrus, tobacco, vegetables, and rice. By the middle of 1994, Spain was investing in the production of tobacco and Israel in the production of citrus. Joint Cuban-Israeli enterprise in Jaguey Grande produces 36 percent of the island's total citrus production today. [Staten 2005]

In September 1995, the Cuban government dramatically changed the law concerning foreign investments on the island. Both joint ventures (a business owned in part by Cuba and in part by foreign investors) and complete foreign ownership of companies were legalized. Most investment capital comes from Spain, Venezuela, Canada, Italy, Mexico, Holland, and the United Kingdom, although more than fifty other countries have investments on the island. [Staten 2005]

In order to attract more investment from abroad, the government created three free trade zones in Havana and Mariel. Goods brought into these Foreign Trade Zones from within Cuba or from abroad are not subject to taxes. Manufacturers receive up to a twelve-year tax holiday to invest and enjoy the benefits of a highly educated workforce and a controlled labor environment. There are more than 290 companies conducting business in the FTZs. [Staten 2005]

Agrarian Reform
On May 17, 1959, the cabinet passed the First Agrarian Reform Law. It placed a 1,000 acre limit on land holdings. All land beyond the limit was claimed by the government and controlled by the INRA (Instituto Nacional de Reforma Agraria). Expropriated land was either turned into cooperatives to be run by the INRA or distributed to individuals in sixty-seven-acre plots. [Staten 2005]

The Agrarian Reform Law, moderate in many respects, was also strongly nationalistic. The Instituto Nacional de Reforma Agraria (INRA) was more willing to intervene in labor-management conflicts when farms were foreign-owned, and to suspend the strict application of the law in these cases to expropriate foreign-owned land. [Bethell 1993]

Reforms on agriculture included the setting aside of land on all state farms and cooperatives for the production of food for local consumption. State farms and cooperatives began developing livestock for consumption by their workers and members. By 1993, individual farmers were also beginning to grow food locally to provide for themselves and their workers; it helped to ensure the labor supply in the agricultural sector. [Staten 2005]

These reforms, which decentralized agricultural production and moved to a more market basis for operation, led to a 17.3 percent growth in agricultural production by 1996. In October 1994, the government legalized, once again, the farmer's markets, where surplus crops could be sold for a profit. As a result, black market sales declined, the availability of food at the markets increased and food prices dropped. [Staten 2005]

Relations with the Soviet Union
The question of communism also mattered for the slowly evolving links with the Soviet Union. The Soviet deputy Anastas Mikoyan visited Cuba in February 1960 to sign the first important bilateral economic agreement between the two countries and to promote other relations. [Bethell 1993]

The end of the Cold War and the Special Period dramatically affected the Cuban Revolutionary Armed Forces (Fuerzas Armadas Revolucionarias; FAR). All military assistance, weapons and supplies deliveries came to an end. Spare parts for military vehicles, ships and aircraft became difficult to find. Training exercises were reduced. The FAR's highly successful internationalist mission came to an end in 1992. The last Russian troops left the island in 1993. [Staten 2005]

The Soviet Union did not support Castro's efforts to wage revolutionary wars in Latin America. The relationship that eventually developed was one of mutual benefit in which each country received support in the pursuit of its own national goals. In the 1970s, Cuba received economic development assistance, technology, preferential trading partners and the means to upgrade its military. [Staten 2005]

Foreign US and Cuban Policies

In the early months of the Revolution, there were three principal themes in Cuban-U.S. relations. First, there was mistrust and anger over U.S. criticism of events in Cuba. The trials against those who served Batista were strongly criticized, in both Cuba and the United States. The second major factor was the Revolution's initial impact on U.S. firms operating in Cuba. The third feature of this period was changing Cuban attitudes to new private foreign investment and official foreign aid. [Bethell 1993]

The Torricelli Act prevents subsidiaries of U.S. companies in other countries from trading with Cuba even if those countries allow trade with the island. President Clinton signed the Helms-Burton Act in March. This act allows American citizens to sue foreign corporations whose trade or investments profit from any properties that were expropriated by the Castro government after 1959. It allows the U.S. government to penalize foreign companies that conduct business in Cuba. [Staten 2005]

Most people understand that the U.S. policy toward the island is largely a function of its domestic politics and is not likely to change dramatically in the next few years. The embargo is a blunt, singular tool of U.S. power. Thus the U.S. is unable to use perhaps its most important weapon: its soft power. This means that Castro will have a much greater say over the future of the island. [Staten 2005]

Appreciable success was registered in improving state-to-state relations in general. The case of Franco's Spain was noteworthy. From 1963 until Franco's death in 1975, Cuba had excellent economic relations with that country. Cuba also retained correct diplomatic relations with the Mexican government. [Bethell 1993]

The most decisive new initiative in foreign policy was the support from 1977 for the Sandinista insurgency against Anastasio Somoza's rule in Nicaragua, the first substantial commitment to promoting insurgency in the Americas in a decade. Cuba also provided political, military and economic support to the insurgents in El Salvador, especially in 1980 and early 1981. Cuban reservists fought courageously against the U.S. troops that invaded Grenada in October 1983 – the first such military clash in a quarter of a century. [Bethell 1993]

A small number of revolutionary leaders concluded well ahead of the rest of the citizenry that it was impossible to conduct a revolution in Cuba without a major confrontation with the United States. U.S.-Cuban relations continued to deteriorate during the second half of 1959. [Bethell 1993]

Relations with the United States began to deteriorate rather quickly. The seizure of the U.S.-owned Cuban Telephone Company in March 1959 became a symbol of defiance and stoked the passions of nationalism among the Cuban people. [Staten 2005]

President Jimmy Carter began making overtures to Castro. In April 1977, the United States and Cuba signed agreements concerning fishing rights and the maritime boundary in the Straights of Florida. Carter created a U.S. Interest Section in Havana in September and removed some of the restrictions on travel to the island by U.S. citizens. [Staten 2005]

Venezuela with its vast oil reserves was a perfect target for an oil-hungry Cuba that was forced to rely on a less than dependable and faraway Soviet Union. Castro began to provide support to revolutionaries and urban terrorists in Venezuela in 1963. [Staten 2005]

Political and Planning System

Cuba was forced to turn to a more pragmatic strategy of development. From 1970 to the mid-1980s, the Cuban revolution moved to adopt a more institutionalized model of socialism somewhat closer to that in the Soviet Union and Eastern Europe. Yet, it was clear that Cuba under Castro could never imitate this model. Castro ruled in such a personal manner that the attempt to institutionalize the Communist Party of Cuba could never be complete. [Staten 2005]

The survival of the Cuban regime is due to a variety of factors. A point which applies generally to communists rule is that these systems – however economically inefficient in many respects and however lacking in democratic accountability – are very effective at maintaining political control by a party elite over an entire society. [Brown 2009]

Cuba was utterly unprepared for a centrally planned economy. It lacked technical personnel as much as statistics. The plans called for the achievement of spectacular growth targets. Instead, the Cuban economy collapsed in 1962. The government froze prices and imposed rationing for most consumer products. The ration card demonstrates the failure to generate economic growth. The Cuban economy fell further in 1963. [Bethell 1993]

Cuba's first socialist constitution was adopted at the First PCC Congress in 1975 and approved through a referendum. It created the Popular Power system in which elected municipal assemblies elected members to the regional assemblies and the National Assembly. [Staten 2005]

Castro commanded the airwaves of radio and television in a country where both were well established by 1959. He moved incessantly throughout the country as a revolutionary prophet touching, moving, educating and steeling his people for combat: to struggle for a new life, a better future, against known and unknown enemies. [Bethell 1993]

The political system concentrated decision-making powers very heavily at the top. Despite some trends towards decentralization in the mid-1970s, Cuba had still a highly centralized political system, where most fundamental decisions were made by a relatively small number of people in Havana, most of whom had held high posts for over twenty years. [Bethell 1993]

Opposition

Arguing that central planning, budgets, financial cost-accounting, and other such tools were essential to building socialism, some opposition was skeptical of mass-mobilization campaigns. They demanded the greater use and institutionalization of party organs and other political organizations, supporting the reintroduction of elections and a Constitution. [Bethell 1993]

The real threat to Castro's political power comes from within the country. In one way, one could argue that he may fall victim to his own successes. By achieving one of the most literate and highly educated citizenries in the world and by achieving a revolutionary social safety net found nowhere else in the developing world, he has created a set of high expectations and desired among his people. [Staten 2005]

Vocal opposition to the perceived growing communist influence over the new government came from President Urrutia, who was forced to renounce in July, and Pedro Diaz Lanz, the head of the Cuban air force and who defected to the United States in June. [Staten 2005]

On October 1959, Huber Matos, military commander of Camaguey province and one of the leading figures of the revolutionary war, resigned along with fourteen officers over the rising influence of communism in the regime. [Bethell 1993]

In 1962, revolutionary power had become consolidated, although the leaders would not realize this for some years. Opponents of the regime took up in arms in the first half of the 1960s, it was especially strong in the Escambray mountain region. Thousands of Cubans died in this renewed civil war (1960-66). They were, however, thoroughly defeated by 1966. With many like-minded Cubans emigrating, the regime, in effect, exported the opposition. [Bethell 1993]

Seeing increased divisions within the leadership of the revolution, fearing the failure of the revolution and expecting U.S. opposition and interference, Castro began to centralize the revolutionary power structure and emphasize loyalty, unity, and survival. [Staten 2005]

By the second half of 1970, the workers had taken enough. They staged a general 'strike.' Although apparently uncoordinated, some 400,000 workers, a fifth of the workforce, stayed away from work in August and September 1970 on any given day. [Bethell 1993]

Gossip

In order to identify enemies of the Revolution, gossip became an arm of state power. The organization of party cells, selection of party members, and all promotions and dismissals had to be cleared through the powerful Organization Secretary Anibal Escalante. [Bethell 1993]

The Committees for Defense of the Revolution (CDR) are social organizations that keep a vigilant eye on potential 'counterrevolutionaries' and are, in effect, a network of government informers. They reflected Castro's hard-line view that 'To be a traitor to the revolution is to be a traitor to the country.' [Brown 2009]

The Party

Membership in the mass organization in the 1980s had become a prerequisite for a successful life in Cuba. Responsible positions were open only to those who were integrated into the revolutionary process by their membership in one or more such organizations. Only those judged to have been vanguard workers had the right to acquire such consumer durable as sewing machines, refrigerators or television sets, and only they had priority access to scarce housing. [Bethell 1993]

The PCC leadership organs (the Political Bureau, the Secretariat, and the Central Committee) that had not functioned in the 1960s began meeting regularly. The Central Committee, which was primarily made up of members from the military and the Ministry of the Interior in the 1960s, came to represent most sectors of Cuban society. The PCC experienced a dramatic increase in membership growing from 55,000 in 1969 to 211,642 in 1975, the year of Cuba's First PCC Congress. [Staten 2005]

The mass organizations and other political and bureaucratic institutions were subordinated to the party, a relationship which is made explicit in the Constitution of 1976. At the same time, Fidel Castro unveiled the first one-hundred-member Central Committee. The principal change in the composition of the Central Committee was the decline in the military's share of the membership, down among full members from 58 percent in 1965 to 17 percent in 1986. [Bethell 1993]

The PCC had little, if any, role in the decisions. It merely approved Castro's policies. The fact that an extremely popular general could be executed also drove home the continuing importance of the personal significance of Castro to the revolution. [Staten 2005]

The Military

A new phase of Soviet-Cuban military co-operation opened with Cuba's decision to send eventually 36,000 troops to support the Popular Movement for the Liberation of Angola (MPLA) in the civil war that broke out in that country in 1975-76. In January 1978, thousands of Cuban troops, supported and led by Soviet and East German officers helped Ethiopians repel the Somali invasion. [Bethell 1993]

In the second half of the 1970s, Cuba had the desire to win wars and perform well overseas in military roles. Cuban troops in Ethiopia, Angola, and Grenada were drawn from the best managers, technicians and workers, contributing to the decline in productivity and efficiency in Cuban sectors. [Bethell 1993]

In late 1975, Cuban troops intervened in the Angolan civil war that had broken out when the Portuguese empire in Africa began to crumble. Cuban troops in support of Mengistu Haile Mariam's Ethiopian government also proved decisive in defeating a Somali invasion of that country in 1977. Cuban support of the Sandinistas during their struggle with Anastasio Somoza dictatorship in Nicaragua was minimal compared to its efforts in Africa. [Staten 2005]

Cuban troops had stopped the South African military invasion of Angola and bloodied the South African armed forces, contributing to the negotiation of South Africa's withdrawal from Angola and the independence of Namibia. However, Angola's political regime changed contrary to Cuba's own preferences; the Angolan government moved to open its economy to markets forces and to open its politics to multiparty competition. [Bethell 1993]

As well as attempting to build and sustain broad popular support, the Cuban leadership has built up a large army and had a fifth of the population bearing arms. They have been ready to resort to guerrilla warfare, if need be, thus raising the cost of a hostile foreign intervention. [Brown 2009]

In 1980, Castro announced a change in its military policy. He created a militia made up of nonmilitary personnel that numbered almost 1.5 million people. It was done largely to mobilize and reinvigorate popular support for the revolution. [Staten 2005]

Highlights for Chapter 7

- The evolution of Cuba toward communism was gradual, and it reflected the evolution in the thinking of the foremost leader of the revolution, Fidel Castro.
- In 1960, the revolution moved toward a Marxist-Leninist political system. A new leadership consolidated centralized and authoritarian rule.
- The Cuban government socialized most of the means of production during its confrontation with the United States.
- The Cuban economy performed quite well in 1959 and 1960. It grew at almost 10 percent a year.
- By the end of 1963, the state-owned 70 percent of all land, and only small farms remained in the private sector.
- The Cuban government could not have survived in power without Soviet support, which had increased since the late 1960s.
- Between 1971 and 1975, the value of industrial output increased by 35 percent and the economy grew at an annual rate of 10 to 14 percent.
- Castro moved further to liberalize the economy by relaxing the regulations of foreign investment by allowing foreigners to have up to 49 percent ownership in a local business.
- Soldiers returning from abroad were put to work on farms run by the state.
- Castro was encouraging Western investors and the promotion of of joint investment ventures.

- State-run enterprises were now being asked to function on a for-profit basis.
- By 1994 tourism generated more income (foreign exchange) for Cuba than sugar.
- By 1995, both joint ventures (a business owned in part by Cuba and in part by foreign investors) and complete foreign ownership of companies were legalized.
- Reforms on agriculture included the setting aside of land on all state farms and cooperatives for the production of food for local consumption.
- The end of the Cold War brought all military assistance, weapons and supplies deliveries to an end.
- The Soviet Union did not support Castro's efforts to wage revolutionary wars in Latin America.
- The embargo is a blunt, singular tool of U.S. power. Thus the U.S. is unable to use perhaps its most important weapon: its soft power.
- Appreciable success was registered in improving state-to-state relations in general. The case of Franco's Spain was noteworthy.
- Relations with the United States began to deteriorate rather quickly at the beginning of the revolution.
- Castro ruled in such a personal manner that the attempt to institutionalize the Communist Party of Cuba could never be complete.
- Communists rule – however economically inefficient in many respects and however lacking in democratic accountability – is very effective at maintaining political control by a party elite over an entire society.
- Castro moved incessantly throughout the country as a revolutionary prophet touching, moving, educating and steeling his people for combat.
- The real threat to Castro's political power comes from within the country.
- In order to identify enemies of the Revolution, gossip became an arm of state power.
- The Committees for Defense of the Revolution (CDR) are social organizations that keep a vigilant eye on potential 'counterrevolutionaries.'

- The mass organizations and other political and bureaucratic institutions were subordinated to the party, a relationship which is made explicit in the Constitution of 1976.
- In the second half of the 1970s, Cuba had the desire to win wars and perform well overseas in military roles.
- Cuban troops had stopped the South African military invasion of Angola and bloodied the South African armed forces.
- Castro created a militia made up of nonmilitary personnel that numbered almost 1.5 million people.

Chapter 8: Africa

Africa has always been known as the "Dark Continent." At the beginning of 2001, only fourteen out of Africa's fifty-four countries were democracies. One-third of the world's 21 million refugees were in Africa. Because of war, famine, and civil strife, there were a further 30 million displaced people within individual African countries. The security forces within thirty-three African countries regularly used torture on their citizens, and in twenty-seven African countries people were regularly incarcerated without charge or trial and left to rot in prison. [Freeth 2011]

So why doesn't it work? Why are there so many hungry people in a continent where there is the potential, over much of it, to get double the annual grain yields per hectare of the best farms in Europe? A continent that has more agricultural land, more mineral wealth and other natural resources than any other? A continent where, only a half century ago, before "liberation," there were food surpluses and almost every country was self-sufficient in grain? [Freeth 2011]

The answer is simple. Every country, every institution, every enterprise is made up of individuals. And it's the individuals within each business or organization, or government, or country that make them tick – or stop ticking. The problem in Africa lies with individuals and, more specifically, the spiritual forces within or behind those individuals. [Freeth 2011]

Three words come to mind when people try to explain the failure of Africa's first generation after independence: leadership, tribalism, and resources. Imagining a 'tribal' Europe gives you some idea of what African citizenship is like. The European Union has only 23 languages. Africa has at least 2000, and between 6000 and 10,000 political or social entities, each of which once had its own governance and legal system, its leadership and customs and culture. Africans played no part in the creation of their nation states. Their boundaries were drawn on maps in Europe by Europeans who had never even been to Africa, with no regard for existing political systems and boundaries. [Dowden 2009]

Before the Europeans arrived, slavery was already the norm in most of Africa. Most societies seem to have kept a group in slavery without the rights of property and family that regular members enjoyed. West and Central Africa were vulnerable to the trans-Saharan trade in slaves. Slaves were also traded along the coast and between kingdoms. But the colonization of America, North and South, created an astronomical new demand for slaves. [Dowden 2009]

Independence officially restored power in Africa to Africans, but the countries created and the systems that the European imposed on Africa as they left were not rooted in African culture or experience and not strong enough to contain social and ethnic pressures that lay immediately beneath the surface. European influence – indirect and sometimes direct – remained strong in Africa, and the Europeans were joined by Russia and America, who wanted to ensure "stability' by propping up dictators in the new states to serve their strategic interests and protect their economic stakes in Africa. [Dowden 2009]

When it came to economists Africa's rulers were mostly either socialist idealists or greedy dictators. Men like Kaunda and Nyerere had been deeply influenced by Christian socialists missionaries, who had strong feelings about how the fruits of the earth should be shared but little idea about how economic systems worked. [Dowden 2009]

At independence in 1966, Botswana, a land-locked country with 70 percent of its surface covered by the Kalahari Desert, was one of the poorest countries in Africa, with a GDP per capita of about US$70. From being the third poorest in mainland Africa, Botswana is now the second richest in terms of per capita income. It has achieved an average annual growth rate of about 9 percent with a GDP (purchasing power parity) per capita of about US$14,800. [Freeth 2011]

When African countries became independent, most of their leaders believed the next stage in nation-building should be government ownership of the economy. The new rulers argued that political independence would not be complete without economic independence. They saw themselves as liberating Africa from colonial rule and wanted to gain control of their production as well as their governance. In country after country mines, land and businesses were nationalized. It was seen as Africa reclaiming its inheritance. Nationalization policies received substantial support from the World Bank and donors. [Dowden 2009]

In the 1990s thirty-one African countries, three-quarters of the nations of mainland Africa suffered wars or violent social upheaval. In Sierra Leone, Liberia, Sudan, Angola and Congo, rulers and rebels had become like competing warlords, seizing as much of the economy as they could to further their war aims. Whatever the motive for starting the war, the pursuit of resources – diamonds and other minerals and timber – sometimes became an end itself. [Dowden 2009]

Here are four ways in which governments in the rest of the world could help Africa without paying a penny in aid. First, agricultural export subsidies that undercut African farmers and prevent them from earning their living as equal producers in the world. Second, the West should recognize that aspects of globalization damage countries with weak economies. Third, Western countries could manage migration better by balancing their marginal need to recruit the world's brightest and best-educated talent with Africa's desperate need to retain its most talented people. Fourth, Africa's stolen money is often passed through the international banking system without question. Those who stole it are allowed to travel the world unhindered. Corruption kills as surely as terrorism or drug dealing, and the same obligations should be imposed on banks to watch the funding of all three. [Dowden 2009]

British Colonies
Zimbabwe

It is believed that to a greater extent than most people understand, it's the malevolent spirits of the dark underworld, represented by the bird and the crocodile, that have allowed the leaders of Zimbabwe to cause much of the people's suffering. People's minds have been deceived and clouded by their fear of these spirits. Meanwhile, the world outside has little or no knowledge of the spiritual forces that are at play in the hearts and minds of the people of Africa, or of the evil influence that the spirit world has on the interplay between the corrupt authorities and ordinary men and women. [Freeth 2011]

Nearly forty years ago Ian Smith, the Prime Minister of Rhodesia, became the first and only white colonial ruler to break away from the British Crown. In 1965 Smith declared independence. Although Rhodesia in 1965 was home to just over 200,000 whites and four million blacks, Smith shared Rhodesia's belief that black majority rule would occur "never in a thousand years."

Smith was of course wrong. In 1980, after a civil war that cost 30,000 lives, the black majority took charge of the country, which was renamed Zimbabwe. Robert Mugabe—the nationalist leader whom Smith had branded a "Marxist terrorist" and jailed for more than a decade, became President.

A recent timeline for Zimbabwe follows:

1965- Prime Minister Ian Smith unilaterally declares independence from Britain under white-minority rule, leading to international isolation.

1980- Independence following the lengthy guerrilla war. Zanu party wins elections and Robert Mugabe becomes prime minister.

1983-87- Gukurahundi campaign, in which 20,000 are thought to have been killed in Matabeleland by Mugabe's Fifth Brigade. The violence ends following a unity accord when the Zanu party is absorbed into the renamed governing Zanu-PF party.

1998-2002- Zimbabwe intervenes in the civil war in DR Congo.

2000s- Land redistribution: White farmers forced off the land.

In the 1980s, Mugabe became prime minister. He maintained all the repressive laws that Smith had enacted to bolster his dictatorship, and even when he dropped the State of Emergency in 1990 he kept legislation like the Law and Order Maintenance Act which prevented people meeting and discussing politics without government permission. Mugabe wanted a one-party state and, steadily accumulating powers to the presidency, step by step he tried to create one. [Dowden 2009]

Mugabe's main target in the 1990s was not the whites. It was the Ndebele. Like all but two African countries, Zimbabwe is ethnically divided. The Shona live in the center, east and north and makeup 80 percent of the population. The Ndebele live in the south-west and makeup 20 percent. They speak different languages and have different cultures. They also have a history of enmity. In a speech in parliament in 1982, he threatened to take 'two eyes for an eye and two teeth for a tooth.' War was declared against the Ndebele's ZAPU and Mugabe's Shona ZANU won. [Dowden 2009]

Although Zimbabwe was not important in economic terms, it became part of the British political battleground along with fox hunting and public schools. The right was pro-white, the left and most liberals supported black majority rule. Those who supported Rhodesia and white rule feel vindicated by the treatment of the white farmers when their land was taken. And for its old liberal and left supporters, Zimbabwe has become the ultimate symbol of the failure of leadership and governance in Africa – a bitterly disillusioning experience. [Dowden 2009]

Mrs. Thatcher was persuaded to visit Africa to sell the new British policy, and in 1989 she flew to Zimbabwe to visit the British army training camp at Nyanga in the eastern highlands with Mugabe and President

Chissano of Mozambique. None of this convinced Mugabe. British duplicity seemed to irk him more and more. When he found that Britain did not respect him – perhaps love him as he psychologically needed – he felt betrayed and sought revenge. White farmers were the obvious target. [Dowden 2009]

Zimbabwe is broken. On average, Zimbabweans born at independence could be expected to live for fifty-seven years. In 2006 that had plummeted to thirty-seven for men and thirty-four for women, the lowest in the world. The country's GDP had shrunk to a fraction of what it once was and inflation, 160,000 percent in early 2008, made money meaningless. Zimbabweans fled in their millions – more than 4 million at the last count. [Dowden 2009]

Sudan

Every African country has its own colonial legacy, residues of alien rule. In many, it is shocking to find how much remains, how things are still done in the old colonial way. [Dowden 2009]

Sudan is no exception. Today Sudan, Africa's biggest country by area, is ruled as an empire as it was 100 years ago when the British ruled and the Ottomans before that. The word Sudan means 'the land of black people,' but it has always been ruled by an Arabic-speaking, Muslim elite. [Dowden 2009]

Some 134 languages are spoken in Sudan but among its ruling elite, you will find only one – Arabic. Ask most members of the government if they are African and you will get an ambiguous reply. Ask them if they are Arab and they will say of course. They are in Africa but of Africa. [Dowden 2009]

A short timeline for Sudan follows:

1820-21- Ottoman Empire conquers the northern part of the country.

1899-1955- Sudan is under joint British-Egyptian rule.

1955 -Prior to Sudan's independence, conflict breaks out between Muslim Arabs in the north and Christian/Animist Africans in the south.

January 1, 1956 -Sudan gains its independence after an agreement between the United Kingdom and Egypt.

1972 -Seventeen years of civil war ended with the signing of the Addis Ababa Agreement between the north and the south.

1977 -Oil is discovered in southwestern Sudan. The civil war in the 1980s and 1990s prevents much exploration or development of the oil deposits.

1983- President Numeiri introduces Sharia Islamic law.

2003- Start of conflict in the Darfur region.

2009- International Criminal Court issues an arrest warrant for President Omar Bashir on charges of war crimes and crimes against humanity relating to the drawn-out conflict in Darfur.

2011- South Sudan gains independence following years of war with the central government in Khartoum.

Looking north, not south, they see themselves – and Sudan – as Arab and Islamic. If they look south it is in the spirit of Islamizing or 'civilizing' the blacks who live there. Southerners are as physically and culturally different from northerners as Chinese and Norwegians. Black African, with a huge diversity of ethnicities and languages, the southerners have always felt neglected and exploited by the north. [Dowden 2009]

Most of the south was first conquered under the Ottomans, then taken over by the self-proclaimed Mahdi, the charismatic military-religious leader, in the 1880s before his state was finally conquered by the British. The British motive for taking over Sudan had little to do with Sudan and everything to do with India. Protecting the Suez Canal and the Nile waters to ensure ships to sail from Britain to India. [Dowden 2009]

The British ruled the north and south as separate entities. The British made no attempt to forge a single nation-state. So at independence, much of the south was nominally Christian while the north remained solidly Muslin. Sudan did not grow out of a common identity. [Dowden 2009]

South Africa

South Africa was different from other African countries. Self-governing from 1902 to 1961, it was a white colony which recognized the sovereignty of imperial Britain. In 1948 the Afrikaner Nationalist Party, many of whose leaders were Nazi sympathizers who had been locked up during the Second World War, came to power and formalized racial separation in law. In 1961 the apartheid government broke the last constitutional links with Britain and declared South Africa a republic. Did white South Africans really believe that they would stay in control for ever? [Dowden 2009]

Whites made up 14 percent of the population and owned almost all of the wealth, including the best land. Some were British, others French, and Portuguese driven out of Algeria, Angola, and Mozambique in the wars for independence. The majority, however, were of Dutch origin: Afrikaners. Their families had been there for 400 years, they spoke a language that was distinct from Dutch and they had no other home in the world. [Dowden 2009]

A brief timeline for South Africa follows:

1910 - Formation of Union of South Africa by former British colonies of the Cape and Natal, and the Boer republics of Transvaal, and Orange Free State.

1912 - Native National Congress founded, later renamed the African National Congress (ANC).

1948 - Policy of apartheid (separateness) is adopted when National Party (NP) takes power.

1960 - Seventy black demonstrators killed at Sharpeville. ANC banned.

1976 - More than 600 killed in clashes between black protesters and security forces during the uprising which starts in Soweto. The challenge to white rule escalates over the years.

1991-1994 – A negotiated end to apartheid leads to first non-racial elections and formation of a Government of National Unity under Nelson Mandela.

From a white viewpoint, apartheid was only what the word meant: separateness, a way of reserving certain areas for themselves. A common white reaction to questions about apartheid was, 'They have their own areas and if they aren't as nice as ours, it's because the blacks are dirty and lazy.' Whites never went to see Soweto or Winterveld or New Brighton. They had no conception of what life was like in these officially created slums. These places were what blacks experienced as apartheid. Systematically dispossessed of land, homes and the opportunity to work, to have a family and a future, they were a slave class whose sole purpose was to provide cheap labor for whites. Above all, apartheid stripped them of their rights as citizens and their dignity as human beings. [Dowden 2009]

Under apartheid, South Africans were divided by race, under Botha's plan South Africans would be kept apart by class and economics. Tough immigration laws would keep the unskilled poor away from urban wealth-making centers. [Dowden 2009]

September 1979 was the turning point. First, a ceasefire and the restoration of British rule in Rhodesia, then an election that ended white rule and brought independence the following year. That made South

Africa and its colony, the occupied territory of Namibia, the last white-ruled countries in Africa. [Dowden 2009]

The second event took place when Venda was declared an independent homeland, removing South African citizenship from another half million blacks. Botha's plan was to create a 'constellation of states' that included these nominally independent homelands. [Dowden 2009]

The third and most dramatic event turned out to be the least significant. On 22 September an American reconnaissance plane picked up a bright flash in the Indian Ocean south of South Africa. The conclusion was grim: apartheid had nuclear weapons. Israel was behind the development. [Dowden 2009]

The final event took place in October. Chief Gatsha Buthelezi, a Zulu prince, accepted the role of chief minister of KwaZulu 'homeland,' a post created and paid by the apartheid government. He refused to accept KwaZulu 'independence' or to implement aspects of the system. He claimed to be fighting apartheid from within by using its structures to build a black power base. An 'African tribal warfare' started, killing thousands of people. The implication was that this would be the fate of the whole of South Africa if there was a democracy. Buthelezi was allowed to win the election on its own territory in KwaZulu. Buthelezi became minister for home affairs in Mandela's first government. [Dowden 2009]

Black South Africans have already waited fifteen years for real change. Another generation finding promises unfulfilled may be less patient. At the moment South Africa needed a manager who could deliver on those promises, the ANC elected a populist 'man of the people' with a mixed record as a well-organized supervisor. [Dowden 2009]

South Africa is not just another African country, its extraordinary transition – conducted by face to face negotiations without intermediaries – was a miracle. Mandela, constantly building bridges, exuding hope at every turn, became the guiding spirit of the country and the continent. In its transition from being the last Nazi-inspired political system of the twentieth century, South Africa produced the most humanistic constitution the world had ever seen, guaranteeing personal freedoms but also protecting minority rights and the weak and vulnerable. [Dowden 2009]

The wave of enthusiasm produced by the 1994 election did not bring foreign investment in its wake. In 1996 the government produced a strategy to develop a 'competitive, fast-growing economy' through tight fiscal and monetary discipline and increased foreign and domestic investment, and by opening the economy to international competition. [Dowden 2009]

Although the economy did begin to pick up, the hoped-for foreign investment did not flow in and the price of gold began to slide. The Finance Ministry declared, 'South Africa remains one of the most unequal countries in the world, with the poorest 40 percent of households still living below the minimum household subsistence level.' In 2001, 65 percent of South Africans were living below the poverty line. Of these, 46 percent – 19 million people – were 'trapped in poverty.' [Dowden 2009]

In 2003 Mbeki introduced Black Economic Empowerment, a code that forced all companies to give a share of ownership to blacks, give a percentage of contracts to black-owned companies and employ a proportion of black workers at specified grades. [Dowden 2009]

But what if economic growth in South Africa simply does not create jobs? In 2007 real unemployment was estimated to be around 43 percent and there had been a 12 percent drop in manufacturing jobs since 1994. The problems lie deeper than racial redistribution. South Africa's education system is not producing sufficient numbers of skilled people, especially black skilled people. [Dowden 2009]

But the most serious economic factor is the failure of the energy supply. In early January 2008, the lights went out. Power cuts had become a regular feature of South African life, sometimes lasting for eight hours. No new power stations were built. By 2008, while other middle-income countries in Asia and South America were enjoying the benefits of a mining boom, South Africa, which contains some of the biggest reserves of the most valuable minerals in the world, was stagnating. [Dowden 2009]

Kenya

To outsiders, until 2008, Kenya was the African success story, the tourist destination with stunning beaches on the Indian Ocean where happy smiling Africans wait on you and teach you to say Jambo and Karibu. So when Kenya exploded in January 2008 after a rigged election, everyone was shocked that such terrible murder and mayhem could happen there. 'But Kenya is such a peaceful, stable country,' as if Kenya had somehow been immune from the political ills that have plagued Africa for the past fifty years. [Dowden 2009]

A short timeline for Kenya follows:

1895- Formation of British East African Protectorate, which becomes the crown colony of Kenya - administered by a British governor - in 1920.

1944- Kenyan African Union (KAU) formed to campaign for African independence. First African appointment to the legislative council.

1963- Kenya gains independence. Opposition groups are stifled and the country survives ethnic tensions and a coup attempt. Multiparty elections are allowed in 1991.

1998- Al-Qaeda operatives bomb the US embassy in Nairobi, killing 224 people and injuring thousands.

2007- Disputed general elections are followed by deadly violence.

It is true that Kenya has never had a successful coup, though one nearly succeeded in 1982 to depose President Daniel Arap Moi. Unlike other African countries where political unrest caused the educated middle class to flee, Kenya has civil servants, lawyers, businessmen and other professionals who can make things work. But, cursed by poisonous and rapacious politicians since independence in 1963, Kenya could hardly be called peaceful. [Dowden 2009]

Unsurprisingly Kenyans boil over from time to time. In 1990 there was a rally in favor of multi-party democracy. Politicians called on people to come to Kamakunji, a big open field near the center of Nairobi. Suddenly two police Land Rovers roared onto the field and fired tear gas at the group in the middle. They also appeared to shoot at the crowd around the side which responded with a hail of stones. Within seconds the peaceful but tense demonstrations exploded in mayhem. The rioting lasted three days in Nairobi and spread to other cities. More than twenty people were killed and hundreds injured. [Dowden 2009]

The roots of that violent discontent go a long way back. Kenya was nearly White Man's country, like Algeria, South Africa, and Southern Rhodesia. After the Second World War a Kikuyu rebellion began, Mau Mau, aimed at reclaiming the land. Only thirty-two white settlers were killed but 3000 African police and soldiers, 12,000 alleged Mau Mau supporters and 1800 African civilians died. It took twelve battalions of the British army and a squadron of Royal Air Force bombers to defeat it. During the rebellion, Britain hanged more than 1000 Kenyans – more than the total number of people executed throughout the rest of the retreating British Empire. [Dowden 2009]

The movement for independence was unstoppable. The Luo, then the second largest ethnic group in Kenya, led by the fiery communist, Oginga

Odinga, joined KANU. The alliance of Kikuyu and Luo spelled the end for British rule and, fearing the firebrand Odinga, the British finally released Kenyata from jail to lead the country to independence. [Dowden 2009]

Vice-President Odinga was trying to push Kenya towards the Soviet camp and socialism. In 1966 Odinga was sacked and locked up. Daniel Arap Moi became the new Vice-President. Britain had been forced to concede independence but had retained control. Kenya has been a solid pro-Western ally ever since, making its ports available to Western navies and providing training grounds for Western armies. [Dowden 2009]

Kenya's economy grew at around 5 percent a year during the Kibaki years largely because the government got out of the way and Kenyans worked hard. But in 2005 a poll found that more than half of Kenyans thought the economy was doing badly. Despite the economic turnaround, half the population was living in what the UN defines as poverty – less than a dollar a day. The most important issue for most Kenyans was equality, in terms of both opportunity and availability of resources. [Dowden 2009]

The only distinction between Kenya's politicians was between those who were in and those who were out. No policy or ideology divided them. It was all about personal preferment based on ethnic support. By election time in December 2007, Kenya was facing the perfect political storm. The margin of victory was too thin. In the Luo town of Kisumu on Lake Victoria, an angry mob started attacking Kikuyus and their businesses. In retaliation organized gangs of Kikuyu youths in the Nairobi slums launched attacks into Luo areas. Before long some 1500 Kenyans were dead, scores injured and 600,000 made homeless. [Dowden 2009]

Nigeria

Nigeria has been described as a failed state that works. By any law of political or social science, it should have collapsed or disintegrated years ago. Some people are living fabulously wealthy lives amid the ruins. And others survive and get by. How? It's a mystery. The secret lies in the layers of millions upon millions of networks, personal ties, family links, ethnic loyalties, school fraternities, Church connections and scores of other unrecorded, informally organized bonds of trust that make things happen. [Dowden 2009]

Europeans and Americans, coming from lands where spontaneous offers of help are rare, are often enchanted by the warm welcome they receive in Africa. With smiles wider than their faces men offer to sort out customs and immigration for you, carry your bags or find you a taxi. Unsuspected visitors who have accepted have been robbed, kidnapped and even murdered. Officials in uniform, often the biggest hyenas of all, tell you, 'You are in big trouble. Come with me,' and lead you to a side room to explain how the 'problem' can be solved. [Dowden 2009]

A timeline for Nigeria follows:

1850s- Britain establishes a presence around Lagos, which it consolidates over the next 70 years as the Colony and Protectorate of Nigeria. In 1922, part of former German colony Kamerun is added under League of Nations mandate.

1960- Independence, with Prime Minister Sir Abubakar Tafawa Balewa leading a coalition government. He is killed in a coup in 1966.

1967- Three eastern states secede as the Republic of Biafra, sparking a bloody civil war.

1983- Major-General Muhammadu Buhari seizes power in a bloodless coup, ushering in a period of 16 years of government overthrows and political instability, capped by the 1999 presidential and parliamentary elections.

2000- Adoption of Islamic, or Sharia, law by several northern states in the face of opposition from Christians.

2009- The Boko Haram Islamist movement launches a campaign of violence which drags on for years and spreads to neighboring countries. One high-profile incident involves the kidnapping of 200 school girls in 2014.

The north of Nigeria is dominated by Hausa-speaking Muslims, the south-east by the Igbos and the south-west by Yorubas. The two latter groups are mostly Christian or follow traditional religions, though there are many Yoruba Muslims too. The British got on well with the aristocratic Muslim rulers of northern Nigeria. They reminded them of the Indian princes and Sultans with whom Britain had ruled India for so long. [Dowden 2009]

Religion reinforces some of Nigeria's political divisions but it is not the cause of the division. Nigerians are deeply religious, the vast majority Christian or Muslim. When religion overlays ethnicity and culture, it is easy to claim God or Allah backs your cause. The ethnic stereotyping is countered by the southerners' proposal that the presidency should rotate between religions. The assumption – spelled out shamelessly at political rallies – is that each group may suffer for a while but every decade it will also 'eat' meaning gobble up the national resources. In other words, the elite of each region of Nigeria will take it in turns to loot the country. Faced with these alternatives no wonder the military has been allowed to rule for so long in Nigeria. Everyone fears that political breakdown will lead to strife: a bare-fisted, free-for-all fight to the death. [Dowden 2009]

In the 1970s Obasanjo deployed a team of old cronies with no idea how to create a modern economy. But in his second term, at the urging of Western countries, Obasanjo appointed a technocratic team to run the economy. Buoyed by oil price rise, the Nigerian economy began to pick up. Obasanjo was well placed to create a new deal for the Delta. He began by trying to suppress revolt there by sending in the army. There were attacks on oil companies and the kidnapping of foreign oil workers. The violence was controlled by Strong Men and military chiefs. Internationally Britain and America did not put pressure on Obasanjo. They needed a powerful ally in Africa and Obasanjo provided that, siding with Britain rather than South Africa over Zimbabwe and promoting free-market reforms that Western countries urged on the continent. [Dowden 2009]

But what Obasanjo's rule did allow was freedom for a new, younger, entrepreneurial professional class. They are developing businesses in the non-oil sector that had until recently been a desert created by oil. [Dowden 2009]

Obasanjo's last chance was to leave office gracefully and organize a free and fair election to choose his successor. He picked Umaru Yar'Adua, a Muslim northerner from an old aristocratic family with a relatively clean reputation. The ruling party, the army, local government, the police, and secret police collaborated in what must go down as one of the most blatantly stolen elections in the history of democracy. They set about it with brazen vigor, stealing and stuffing ballot boxes, intimidating opposition voters, buying votes and bribing officials. The reports are so similar that it is hard not to believe that the rigging exercise was centrally controlled with Obasanjo's approval. [Dowden 2009]

Portuguese Colonies

The end of the Belgian, Spanish and Portuguese empires in Africa felt more like expulsion. The Portuguese had been in Africa longest and had the most colonies there. They declared Angola, Mozambique, and Guinea Bissau to be part of the Portuguese state, not colonies and refused to abide by the United Nations decolonization resolutions. They did not leave until 1975, they fled in bitter defeat. [Dowden 2009]

Angola

The Portuguese imperial venture had been more thoroughgoing than the British or French. Of all European imperial powers, the Portuguese were in Africa longest and penetrated it most deeply. Because they were trader-settlers, rejected by their own country of birth, they created a class of people in Africa, white, mixed-race and black, who had been de-Africanized, spoke no African language and who were, culturally, European. In Angola, they were not the colonists, they became the liberationists, or at least claimed to be, formed into a Marxist liberation movement, their credentials approved by the communists of Moscow and Havana. [Dowden 2009]

The fundamental difference between the Portuguese adventurers who settled and married in Africa and the majority of British, Dutch and French traders was that the Portuguese depended for their physical survival on local kings and chiefs while the other Europeans maintained close links with their trading companies in Europe and demanded protection by their national navies. [Dowden 2009]

In Portuguese territories, Euro-African intermediaries had ruled like kings, but after the Second World War, they were dealt a terrible blow. Their old enemy, the Portuguese government, needing to solve a land shortage in Portugal, encouraged the migration of hundreds of thousands of poor rural Portuguese to Africa. They arrived on the back of a coffee boom and immediately began to take the jobs that had previously been done by the Euro-Africans. [Dowden 2009]

As the Euro-Africans became increasingly marginalized in Angola, these families who had lived on Angolan coast for centuries turned to the only people who would help them: the Portuguese Communist Party. By historical accident, it was the most Stalinist party in Western Europe, closely allied to the Soviet Union. Being also anti-imperialist, it supported these new recruits from Angola and helped construct a Communist Party for them. The old slave-trading families had no problem pretending they represented the working class and the peasants of Africa. They were happy enough to chant slogans about solidarity and liberation if that was the price to pay for retrieving their birthright as the rulers and exploiters of Angola. [Dowden 2009]

A timeline for Angola follows:

1483- Portuguese arrive.

17th and 18th centuries- Angola becomes a major Portuguese trading arena for slaves. Between 1580 and 1680 a million plus are shipped to Brazil.

1885-1930- Portugal consolidates colonial control over Angola, local resistance persists.

1950s-1961- Nationalist movement develops, a guerrilla war begins.

1974- Revolution in Portugal, colonial empire collapses.

1975- Portuguese withdraw from Angola without formally handing power to any movement. MPLA is in control of Luanda and declares itself government of independent Angola. Unita and FNLA set up a rival government in Huambo. Civil war begins, dragging on until 2002.

1979- Jose Eduardo dos Santos becomes country's leader. He steps down 38 years later.

1987- South African forces enter southeast Angola to thwart MPLA and Cuban offensive against Unita. They withdrew the next year.

1991- Government, Unita sign peace accord in Lisbon.

1992- Disputed elections. Fighting flares again.

In the 1960s Angola produced independence movements along the same lines as the rest of Southern Africa, divided between the black nationalist's parties fighting to drive out the colonialists and Marxist parties which wanted an economic transformation as well as an anti-imperial struggle. The MPLA was Marxist, whereas the other two parties, UNITA, and the FNLA were Africanists. [Dowden 2009]

While France and Britain handed their African colonies over to African rulers in 1960, Marcelo Caetano, the Portuguese dictator who succeeded Antonio de Oliveira Salazar in 1968, decided to stay and fight. He claimed that Portuguese possessions were not colonies but part of Portugal. On 25 April 1974, Portuguese generals mounted a coup to overthrew Caetano. Portugal's African colonies were suddenly pushed into ill-prepared and precarious independence. In Mozambique, Cape Verde and Guinea-Bissau, Moskow-backed parties took over uncontested. But in Angola war among the liberation movements took part. [Dowden 2009]

German and Belgian Colonies

Germans colonized some territories in Africa, for example, Togo, Cameroon, Tanzania, and Namibia. Belgium controlled two colonies during its history: the Belgian Congo from 1885 to 1960 and Rwanda-Burundi from 1916 to 1962.

Congo

Congo is not just another African country in a mess. It is the vast, rich, troubled heart of the continent with all its problems and strengths as well as some special ones of its own. Africa cannot succeed if Congo fails. It is a rich country. Its earth contains deposits of minerals that have only been guessed at. Its fertile soils could feed Africa, its huge rivers charge it with energy. But Congo is one of the poorest countries on earth. Its cities are not linked by roads or railways. There is no police force, no civil service, no government. Its people live closer to the Iron Age than the twenty-first century. [Dowden 2009]

A short timeline for Congo follows:

16th -17th centuries - British, Dutch, Portuguese and French merchants engage in slave trade through Kongo intermediaries.

1870s - Belgian King Leopold II sets up a private venture to colonize Kongo.

1908 - Congo Free State placed under Belgian rule following outrage over the treatment of Congolese.

1960 - Independence, followed by civil war and temporary fragmentation of the country.

1965 - Mobutu Sese Seko seizes power.

1997 - Rebels oust Mobutu. Laurent Kabila becomes president.

1997-2003 - Civil war, drawing in several neighboring countries. Dozens of armed groups fight on in the east, requiring a large United Nations military force to try to maintain order.

After the Rwandan genocide in 1994 more than a million Hutus fled Rwanda into Congo to escape retribution from the invading Tutsi army. With them came the defeated government army which camped with more than a million refugees near Goma on the border. The new Rwandan government said the Hutu soldiers were planning to return and continue the genocide. It accused Mobutu, the President of Congo, of supporting them. Suddenly in October 1996 Rwandan troops with their Ugandan allies invaded eastern Congo and drove most of the refugees back into Rwanda. The Rwandan army pursued them to the west, further into Congo. They fought all the way to Kinshasa. Mobutu was forced to flee and the Rwandans installed Laurent Kabila as President. [Dowden 2009]

The Belgians exploited Congo ruthlessly, but they also built roads and a railway and hospitals and schools. That led to social and demographic change but the Belgians blocked any political development, so when Congo was suddenly pitched into independence in 1960, the African elite was tiny, inexperienced and angry. There was chaos. Congo nearly broke up nut out of the chaos emerged Mobutu Sese Seko, one of the more grotesque figures to rule in independent Africa. America and Europe backed him because they saw him as anti-communist, but he turned into Leopold's true successor, treating the country as his own personal possession and looting it. He renamed it Zaire, treated the treasury as his bank account and allowed the powerful and greedy to feed off the state. [Dowden 2009]

Why didn't the Congolese rise up and overthrow Mobutu? One reason was that his rich, powerful network could silence or buy off any discontent. He also had the protection of America, France, and Belgium. Cold War logic led them to send troops on several occasions when Zaire was attacked by rebels based in Angola, then a Soviet ally. Another reason he survived was that most Congolese took a pragmatic view. They may have felt great anger but no institutions existed that could act as a focal point for the opposition. So their rage exploded from time to time but could not be sustained. Discontent was often directed against a rival ethnic group rather than at the government and Mobutu was happy to leave his people fighting among themselves. [Dowden 2009]

Burundi and Rwanda

Rwanda 1994 is what the world now knows about. Genocide. Rwanda, a small landlocked country in east-central Africa, is trying to recover from the ethnic strife that culminated in government-sponsored genocide in the mid-1990s. In the genocide, an estimated 800,000 ethnic Tutsis and moderate Hutus were killed by dominant Hutu forces in 100 days. [Dowden 2009]

The country has struggled with its legacy of ethnic tension associated with the traditionally unequal relationship between the Tutsi minority and the majority Hutus.

Rwanda is striving to rebuild its economy, with coffee and tea production among its main exports. The World Bank has praised Rwanda's "remarkable development successes", which have helped reduce poverty and inequality.

But in Burundi too, politics conspired to create a narrative of racial slaughter and repeat it again and again. The country was ruled by Tutsis since independence in 1962. There were massacres here in 1965, 1969, 1972, 1988, 1991 and now this latest one triggered by the murder of the first ever Hutu President, Melchior Ndadaye, elected in 1992. [Dowden 2009]

Burundi, one of the world's poorest nations, is struggling to emerge from a 12-year, ethnic-based civil war. Since independence in 1962, it has been plagued by tension between the usually-dominant Tutsi minority and the Hutu majority. A civil war sparked off in 1994 made Burundi the scene of one of Africa's most intractable conflicts.

The relationship between Hutus and Tutsis is unique, complex and very difficult for outsiders to comprehend. There are no words in English to describe it. Caste, class, race or tribe do not match the reality. Its origins are hotly disputed. The colonial version was that Batwa pygmy hunter-gatherers were here first. Then came the short, dark, round-headed Hutu farmers, who settled the land. Tutsi were tall, long-faced cattle keepers who wandered down from north-east Africa in the sixteenth and seventeenth centuries and, according to this version, being a superior race, dominated the inferior Hutus and ruled over them. [Dowden 2009]

They formed two powerful kingdoms with similar but different political and social structures: Rwanda and Urundi – as Burundi was called then. The Germans made the kingdom part of German East Africa in 1890 and they set in law what they perceived as the racial hierarchy. The Belgians, who took over the administration of Burundi and Rwanda from Germany after the First World War, classified every citizen as Hutu or Tutsi and selected the 'superior' Tutsis to be educated as teachers, priests, and doctors. [Dowden 2009]

Whatever its origins, the Hutu-Tutsi division still exists in the psychology and culture of Rwanda and Burundi and also in other parts of the Great Lakes region in the Rift Valley. In Uganda, there are Hutu and Tutsi equivalents. In eastern Congo, there are Tutsi equivalents. Despite the efforts of the present Rwanda government, the categories and stereotypes are alive and well. Burundi and Rwanda are organized and administered not village by village but hill by hill and neighbors in every hill know who is Hutu and who is Tutsi. [Dowden 2009]

The complex relationship was based in the past on both inter-dependency and power. Cattle-keeping Tutsis traded milk and meat for

Hutu farmers' grain and vegetable. The Tutsis formed a sort of aristocracy, but it was not clear-cut. In Rwanda, a king, the Mwami, held the balance of power between them. In Burundi, a princely caste, the Ganwa, was the powerful arbiter. On the whole, the Tutsi, about one-sixth of the Hutus in numbers in Rwanda and Burundi, were the bosses. [Dowden 2009]

The Catholic Church, the most powerful institution in the country after the government, backed the Hutu and democracy although most of the educated elite were Tutsi. Tutsi leaders knew that if they waited for democratic elections, they would be destroyed by demographics. In the first years of independence, after months of bloody battles and massacres, the Tutsi-dominated army and gendarmerie seized power in 1964 and executed the entire Hutu political elite. Tutsi rule lasted until August 1993 when, amid a spate of post-Cold War elections across Africa, Ndadaye was elected president. In October he was murdered by Tutsi extremists. His death was followed by the massacre of between 100,000 and 200,000 people in the space of one week as Hutus and Tutsis turned on each other. [Dowden 2009]

French Colonies

France colonized several territories in Africa. Examples of Sub-Saharan countries are Ivory Coast, Benin, Mali, Guinea, Mauritania, Niger, Burkina Faso, and Senegal. Some other examples of countries colonized by France in Africa are Tunisia, Algeria, Madagascar, and Morocco.

In Sub-Saharan French territories, the transition was peaceful. The French remained directly engaged with Africa after their colonies became independent. Three decades after independence there were more French people in the francophone territories than there had been in colonial times. [Dowden 2009]

Senegal

Senegal is one of the oldest European colonies in Africa. It sent deputies to the French parliament in Paris in 1848 and its borders were established in 1890. Apart from its southern province, Casamance, it has been stable since independence, with Abdullai Wade only the third head of state. There has never been a hint of a military coup. Nor have there been bad rulers: Leopold Senghor stood down as President in 1981 and, after nearly two decades in power, his hand-picked successor, Abdou Diouf, lost the 2000 election to Wade and accepted the result. [Dowden 2009]

A timeline for Senegal follows:

1677- French take over the island of Goree from the Dutch, the start of nearly 300 years of French oversight.

1756-63- Seven Years' War: Britain takes over French posts in Senegal, forms the colony of Senegambia. France regains its holdings during American Revolutionary War of 1775-83.

1960- Senegal becomes an independent country.

2000- Opposition leader Abdoulaye Wade wins the second round of presidential elections, ending 40 years of Socialist Party rule.

In 1895 the Senegalese Islamic mystic and poet Cheikh Amadu Bamba Mbacke founded a global African trading company based on Islamic principles. Those who work for it are known as Mourides. Mourides are scattered all over the globe from Paris to Los Angeles, from Hong Kong to Dubai. They possess in great abundance a commodity that much of Africa lacks: trust. [Dowden 2009]

The movement Amadu Bamba founded is based on three rules: God, work and provoke no-one. He believed that prayer, study, and work would protect people from the corrupting and dehumanizing influence of France and French culture. Among his followers, he promoted the values of humility, endurance, and sharing. He required them to attach themselves to a Sheikh and obey every command. Later his followers founded dahiras, prayer circles where they could meet, socialize and read the Koran and Amadu Bamba's poems. [Dowden 2009]

For rural people arriving in town for the first time, the dahira provides a base and a network. A pay subscription helps fellow members in trouble and contribute to the expenses of the whole movement and its leader. The money from subscriptions enables new members to find accommodation and work. If one of their members dies, it gives money to bring the body home for burial. The Mouride brotherhood offers a secure bridge from rural to urban, from ancient to modern. The wealth gathered from all its members provides a welfare system. Richer members also provide capital for fellow Mourides to start up trading enterprises. [Dowden 2009]

Touba is a city of more than a million people 100 miles east of Senegal's capital Dakar, where Amadu Bamba chose to base his movement. Touba is a state within a state. As you come into town, there is no checkpoint, no security men checking your papers, because there are no policemen. And no taxmen, local officials or courts either. Banks are not necessary. If a trader here wants to buy, he can call up a fellow Mouride anywhere in the world and ask for goods to be sent. The money is paid here in Touba to the traders family. Trust is the key to the Mourides. [Dowden 2009]

About one-third of Senegal population – and all the leading artists, musicians, and businessmen – are Mourides. They put into a religious institution all the trust and taxes, obedience and commitment given by citizens to the nation-state in most countries. And the religious organization fulfills many of the functions and services a welfare state as well as channeling its followers' commercial energies. They also willingly give the Mouride movement a hefty 'tax' on all their dealings. [Dowden 2009]

In Senegal, there is justice, a police force, and a tax system. But not even Senegal seems to inspire civic national commitment. A third of its citizens choose to invest their loyalty and future in a religious body, not their relatively stable and trustworthy nation-state. [Dowden 2009]

In spite of this unique bond of trust that facilitated an entrepreneurial spirit among Senegalese at home and overseas, between 1975 and 1995 the country's economy grew at 2.2 percent, slower than its population growth, 2.8 percent. Between 1986 and 1996 economic growth slowed to 1.9 percent. In the next decade, 1996 to 2006, growth picked up to 5 percent, but it now seems to be falling back again. [Dowden 2009]

Highlights for Chapter 8

- At the beginning of 2001, only fourteen out of Africa's fifty-four countries were democracies.
- The problem in Africa lies with individuals and, more specifically, the spiritual forces within or behind those individuals.
- Three words come to mind when people try to explain the failure of Africa's first generation after independence: leadership, tribalism, and resources.
- Africa has at least 2000 languages, and between 6000 and 10,000 political or social entities.
- When it came to economists Africa's rulers were mostly either socialist idealists or greedy dictators.
- The new African rulers argued that political independence would not be complete without economic independence.
- In the 1990s thirty-one African countries, three-quarters of the nations of mainland Africa, suffered wars or violent social upheaval.

- Robert Mugabe—the nationalist leader whom Smith had branded a "Marxist terrorist" and jailed for more than a decade, became President of Zimbabwe.
- Mugabe wanted a one-party state and, steadily accumulating powers to the presidency, step by step he tried to create one.
- Like all but two African countries, Zimbabwe is ethnically divided.
- The country's GDP had shrunk to a fraction of what it once was and inflation, 160,000 percent in early 2008, made money meaningless.
- Today Sudan, Africa's biggest country by area, is ruled as an empire 100 years ago when the British ruled and the Ottomans before that.
- Some 134 languages are spoken in Sudan but among its ruling elite, you will find only one – Arabic.
- Looking north, not south, they see themselves – and Sudan – as Arab and Islamic.
- The south was nominally Christian while the north remained solidly Muslin. Sudan did not grow out of a common identity.
- Whites made up 14 percent of the population and owned almost all of the wealth, including the best land.
- Under apartheid, South Africans were divided by race. Under Botha's plan, South Africans would be kept apart by class and economics.
- South Africa needed a manager who could deliver on those promises, the ANC elected a populist 'man of the people'
- Mandela, constantly building bridges, exuding hope at every turn, became the guiding spirit of the country and the continent.
- In 2007, South Africa's education system was not producing sufficient numbers of skilled people, especially black skilled people.
- But the most serious economic factor is the failure of the energy supply.
- By 2008, South Africa, which contains some of the biggest reserves of the most valuable minerals in the world, was stagnating.

Chapter 9: Venezuela

Venezuela is a country located at the northern tip of South America. It occupies a roughly triangular area that is larger than the combined areas of France and Germany. Venezuela is bounded by the Caribbean Sea and the Atlantic Ocean to the north, Guyana to the east, Brazil to the south, and Colombia to the southwest and west. The national capital, Caracas, is Venezuela's primary center of industry, commerce, education, and tourism.

Venezuela was a democracy during 40 years (1958-1998) until Hugo Chavez, a camouflaged military putschist, won the 1998 elections and started a poisoned democracy using parliamentary partisans. He started by changing the constitution in 1999 and making his own interpretations of the law using the Justice Supreme Court.

Today, Venezuela, the country with the largest proven oil reserves in the world, is suffering a humanitarian crisis. Bordering Colombia and Brazil in South America, the mountainous country with white-sand beaches and the highest waterfall in the world has been engulfed in a political, economic, and social struggle for most of the 21st century.

In these 20 years of misgovernment, Venezuela tried to imitate the Cuban approach to socialism-communism, but in fact produced a disaster that compares only to failed or collapsed countries in Africa. The performance of the economy has been the worst in the world; lack of food, medicines and health services have made people suffer as much as war or post-war situations. Venezuela has not suffered a war but the country is governed under the equivalent of martial law.

<u>Dictatorship and Democracy</u>

Marcos Perez Jimenez was in power since the end of the 1940s until the end of the 1950s. Using oil income, the government built impressive infrastructure including government buildings and roads. National security was tight and many opponents suffered torture and death.

Admiral Wolfgang Larrazabal and a temporary alliance took power after a coup against Marcos Perez Jimenez in 1958; next, moderate leftist Romulo Betancourt of the Democratic Action Party (AD) won the presidential election.

During the years of democracy, which started in 1958, Venezuela benefited from the oil boom and its currency reached a peak against the

US dollar; oil and steel industries were nationalized. 1973 was a year of high income for the country.

Each five years, Democratic elections brought in new governments, every five years the two main parties shared power; AD and COPEY were both considered social democratic parties. Carlos Andres Perez (AD) elected president amid economic depression, launched austerity programs with IMF loans in 1989. Riots, martial law and general strike followed, with hundreds killed in street violence.

Colonel Hugo Chavez entered the scene; he and his supporters made two coup attempts in 1992. Some 120 people were killed in the suppression of the coups. Colonel Chavez was jailed for two years before being pardoned by president Rafael Caldera.

President Perez was impeached on corruption charges during the period of 1993-95; he was funding campaigns in nearby democratic countries. Compared with the level of corruption of the Chavez-Maduro government, his misdemeanor was peanuts.

Venezuela is highly vulnerable to external shocks due to its heavy dependence on oil revenues. Oil accounts for about 95 percent of Venezuela's export earnings and 25 percent of its gross domestic product (GDP). The state-run petroleum company, Petroleos de Venezuela, S.A. (PDVSA), controls all the country's oil exploration, production, and exportation.

Gustavo R. Coronel has published some material about the problems in Venezuela in the following links:

https://www.armyupress.army.mil/Journals/Military-Review/English-Edition-Archives/March-April-2017/ART-005/

Chavez 'Democratic-oriented' Dictatorship

People were tired of political parties, therefore, in the 1998 elections, they decided to try a newcomer in politics, Hugo Chavez. He had no political experience but people supported his presidency, expecting a strong hand to combat crime and corruption; neither one or the other were fought.

Hugo Chavez, once elected, launched new processes that brought in a new constitution, he started socialist and populist economic measures and social policies funded by high oil prices, and he became increasingly vocal in his anti-US foreign policy.

In April 2002, amid huge protests that left several deaths, a civil coup was perpetrated. Civilian forces rebelled over the violent stand-off between the government and Petroleos de Venezuela (PDVSA) state oil monopoly managers and unions after the appointment of the new board. Chavez was taken into military custody, but the interim government of business federation leader Pedro Carmona collapsed and Chavez was returned to office. Chavez dismissed 18,000 workers from the state oil company, leaving it acephalous; most technicians and managers were fired for political reasons. The company has never recovered from such a monstrous blow and PDVSA is today a total disaster.

President Chavez won a referendum in 2004 to serve out remaining two-and-a-half years of his term. People who participated in the referendum against Chavez were blackmailed and discriminated by their employers. The people who signed against Chavez were persecuted in their work environment diminishing their right to a decent job. At the time, Chavez started talking about 'Bolivarian Revolution.'

Parties loyal to President Chavez dominated parliament after opposition parties boycotted 2005 elections because the Electoral Committee was fraudulent. Hugo Chavez won a third term in the 2006 presidential elections with 63% of the vote, the largest margin since the 1998 election.

President Chavez suffered his first defeat at the ballot box in 2007 when a referendum narrowly rejected proposals to increase government control over the Central Bank, communalization of society and the power to expropriate more properties.

Chavez remained popular among the country's poor throughout his presidency, expanding social services including food and housing subsidies, health care, and educational programs. The country's poverty's fell from roughly 50 percent in 1998, the year before he was elected, to 30 percent in 2012, the year before his death.

The opposition made gains in 2008 regional elections and won Caracas mayoral poll. President Chavez's allies retained control of 17 out of 22 governorships. Voters in a 2009 referendum approved plans to abolish limits on the number of terms in office for elected officials. This allowed President Chavez to stand again when his term expired in 2012.

In the parliamentary 2010 elections, the opposition made significant gains. In 2012, President Chavez won a fourth term in office, with 54% of the vote on an official turnout at about 81%. Opposition leader Henrique Capriles conceded.

The ruling Socialist Party and allies won 2013 local elections by a margin of 10% in a poll widely seen as a test of the government's handling of the continuing economic crisis.

President Hugo Chavez died in 2013 at age 58 after a battle with cancer. Nicolas Maduro, his chosen successor, was elected president in 2013 by a narrow margin. The opposition contested the result. Maduro pledged to continue his former boss's socialist revolution. "I am ensuring the legacy of my commander, Chavez, the eternal father," he said after the vote.

Opposition Democratic Unity coalition won the two-thirds majority in 2015 parliamentary elections, the National Assembly ended 16 years of Socialist Party control.

The opposition held an unofficial referendum in 2017, in which a reported seven million people rejected President Maduro's proposal to convene a new constituent assembly. The governmental election of the controversial constituent assembly took place in the face of an opposition boycott and international condemnation. The constituent assembly would have sweeping authority to rewrite the country's laws and constitution. Supporters of Maduro won all 545 seats, an outcome disputed by the opposition and independent observers.

Maduro's Socialist Party won 17 of 23 gubernatorial elections in October 2017 and nearly 90 percent of mayoral elections held two months later. The polls were condemned as "neither free nor fair" by the U.S. State Department and boycotted by the three main opposition parties over allegations of electoral fraud. In retribution, Maduro banned the dissident parties from participating in the 2018 presidential race. In January 2018, Maduro announced he would run for a second six-year term.

Maduro's consolidation of power threatened to delegitimize the results of the upcoming presidential election, which was set for May 2018. In February, former state Governor Henri Falcon of the Progressive Advance Party announced he would compete against Maduro, defying his own coalition's boycott of the election and earning him expulsion from the MUD. According to a February survey, more than 60 percent of Venezuelans consider neither Falcon nor Maduro a desirable presidential candidate.

President Maduro won another term in the May 2018 election. The election was not constitutionally valid, and it was supported by the controversial constituent assembly.

Chavez's Land Reform, Nationalization and Expropriations

In 2001 President Chavez, manipulating public opinion and demonstrating his ego, used enabling act to pass 49 laws aimed at redistributing land and wealth. Concern grew in business and some labor circles that he was trying to concentrate economic and political power in the state, along Cuban lines.

In January 2005, President Chavez signed a decree on land reform to eliminate Venezuela's large estates and benefit rural poor. Ranchers said the move was an attack on private property. Expropriated land never became productive again, peasants abandoned the land or turned over their rights to unproductive workers.

Experts said that widespread expropriations had further diminished productivity. Transparency International, which ranks Venezuela 166 out of 176 on its perceived corruption index, reported that the government controlled more than five hundred companies, most of which were operating at a loss. (By comparison, Brazil, which is more than six times as populous as Venezuela, had 130 state-run companies.)

The government did not want to be criticized. By March 2005, new media regulations provided stiff fines and prison terms for slandering public figures.

By January 2007, nationalization began. President Chavez announced key energy and telecommunications companies will be nationalized under the 18-month enabling act approved by parliament. In May 2007, television networks got their blow. Government's refused to renew the terrestrial broadcasting license of RCTV channel, which was critical of President Chavez, prompting mass protests for and against and strong international condemnation.

By June 2007, international oil companies got expropriated. Two leading US oil companies, Exxon Mobil and Conoco Philips, refused to hand over majority control of their operations in the Orinoco Belt to the Venezuelan government, which then expropriated them. In August 2008, it was the bank system which was affected. President Chavez announced his plans to nationalize one of the country's largest private banks, the Spanish-owned Bank of Venezuela.

In November 2013, with inflation running at more than 50% a year, the National Assembly gave President Maduro emergency powers for a year, prompting protests by opposition supporters. Mr. Maduro used the powers to limit private companies profit margins.

Venezuela - Cuba Relations

Over the past 20 years, Venezuela and Cuba have become close allies both economically and politically. Cuba and Venezuela's mutually dependent relationship, seen in trade and investment, security and diplomacy, is notably asymmetrical. Venezuela provides critical oil supplies on subsidized terms in return for Cuban doctors, teachers, sports trainers, and military advisers.

Since his election in 1998, President Chavez was more leftist and very anti-US, as reflected in many of his administration's policies. Some believed Chavez aspired to be the leader of Latin America's radical left and that he was determined to unite the region against the U.S. and the democratic processes and free-market systems that the US supports.

Chavez was said to have aspired to succeed Fidel Castro as the ideological figurehead of Latin America. He relied heavily on Castro's advice, particularly during domestic crises. Chavez appeared psychologically dependent on Castro. The Venezuelan Government had demonstrated a terrific affinity for the Cuban Government. They had a good relationship. Venezuela provided oil on favorable terms. The Cuban Government provided doctors. Many Venezuelans did not like this intervention of a foreign state and they were concerned that Venezuela was going the way of Cuba. Venezuela was unique in its attitudes toward the regime of Fidel Castro.

Venezuela provided oil to Cuba at prices well below commercial value, apparently in order to strengthen this relationship and get Cuban support in several areas. Venezuela provided close to 100,000 barrels per day of oil to Cuba in exchange for a host of services including doctors that staff free health clinics in slums and rural areas. Cuba produces about 50,000 barrels per day of oil, and consumes about 185,000 barrels per day, importing a net of 135,000 barrels per day, mostly from Venezuela.

The ties between President Hugo Chávez and Cuba's communist leaders were plain enough: Cuba has thousands of doctors in Venezuela, not to mention a smaller number of advisers who help on a breadth of issues, like agricultural, engineering, military and even training Olympic athletes.

The economic cost of Venezuela's support to Cuba became an increasingly important constraint on the Maduro administration. Instability in Venezuela reminds the Cuban government of the risks associated with their interdependence on the current regime in Caracas. The ongoing economic and political crisis in Venezuela reinforced the negative aspects of their interdependence.

There are too many Cubans working in Venezuela, including hundreds of Cuban "volunteers" recruited by Chavez to provide literacy and health care programs for the poor. Despite the high cost of the program (salaries are well above Venezuelan averages and are paid in US dollars), Cuban doctors practicing without local licenses, supply shortages, mismanagement of funds (at the municipal level) and mediocre vaccination rates, those who use Barrio Adentro, according to a Datanalysis poll, are highly satisfied with it.

According to the Ministry of Finance, from 2003 to 2006, President Chavez had spent US$12.9 billion to create 24 "missions" - government-funded social programs - in a variety of areas. Mission Robinson I (2003), a literacy program, and Robinson II (2003), a primary education program, reportedly had more enrollees than any other mission. Both benefited from extensive Cuban advice and were based on Cuban literacy campaigns. Perhaps the most visible mission internationally was Barrio Adentro (BA), a network of primary health care modules staffed by over 20,000 Cuban medical personnel.

The 'Alo Presidente' program was notable for Chavez' return to his early remarks about a Cuban-Venezuelan confederation. He used to assert that Cuba and Venezuela each had two presidents and were moving towards a "Bolivarian Confederation," implying other states would also be subsequently included. This is an assertion Chavez had made in the past, and there were even walls painted with joined Cuban and Venezuelan flags in both countries.

Venezuelan opposition presidential candidate Henrique Capriles on 18 March 2013 vowed to end the OPEC nation's shipments of subsidized oil to communist-run Cuba, slamming acting President Nicolas Maduro as a puppet of Havana. "The giveaways to other countries are going to end. Not another drop of oil will go toward financing the government of the Castros," Capriles said, referring to Cuba's present and past leaders, Raul and Fidel Castro. "Nicolas is the candidate of Raul Castro; I'm the candidate of the Venezuelan people," Capriles said during a speech to university students in the oil-rich state of Zulia.

Ties to Cuba were likely to remain a central part of the campaigns. Capriles for months accused authorities of compromising the country's sovereignty by letting Chavez govern for two months from a Havana hospital. Supporters say it had helped expand access to health care, while critics call it a mere subsidy to the Castro government. Maduro's frequent visits to the island during Chavez's two-month convalescence there led opposition leaders to joke that he had picked up a Cuban accent.

As the crisis in Venezuela worsened, Cuba continued to throw its support behind the government in Caracas. Cuba, too, is dependent upon Venezuela's vast petroleum resources. In return for subsidized oil - 40,000 barrels a day - Havana sends doctors, intelligence officials and diplomats to Caracas. President Maduro's bodyguards are also from Cuba. How much influence does Havana hold over President Nicolas Maduro?

But the quiet expansion of Cuba's military role in Venezuela has raised particular concern among critics of Mr. Chávez, who maintain that the military is being retooled — with Cuba's help — into an institution that can be used to quell any domestic challenge to the president.

In a rare public critique, a former aide to Mr. Chavez has lambasted the role of Cuban advisers in delicate areas that he said include military intelligence, weapons training, strategic planning and the logistics of Mr. Chavez himself, who often travels on a Cuban plane. "We are at the mercy of meddling in areas of national security by a Cuban regime, which wants Chavez to remain in power because Chavez gives them oil," the former aide, Antonio Rivero, a brigadier general who retired this year, said in an interview. "The Cuban advisers are there to exert pressure," he added, "and they often claim to speak on the president's behalf as if they were his emissaries."

Some changes in military strategy in Venezuela have already reflected the Cuban model, including an emphasis on preparing for an eventual invasion by the United States; the growth of the Bolivarian militia, an armed civilian force similar to Cuba's Territorial Militia; and a focus on forging military policy within the Bolivarian Alliance for the Americas, the regional political group led by Venezuela and Cuba.

Chavez's supporters describe the ties with Cuba as a natural extension of their compatible ideologies. "The revolutionary government of Cuba applies a concept of national defense with a prolonged and successful track record." And Pedro Carreño, a former interior minister under Mr. Chavez, wrote in a column in the newspaper El Nacional. "Not having military exchanges with Cuba could be grounds for treason of the homeland."

Chavez had also made it clear that any rumbling within the military, over Cuban advisers or other issues, would have consequences. He rarely loses a chance to remind other military branches of the growing might of the militia, which has some 300,000 reservists and is designed to operate at his command. At a recent parade of reservists, Mr. Chavez called on them to "sweep away the bourgeoisie" if he were assassinated.

"No one knows better than Chavez himself that Venezuelan history is sprinkled with one military conspiracy after another," said Fernando Ochoa Antich, who was defense minister when Mr. Chavez attempted his own coup in 1992. "His dependence on Cuba is an effort to improve intelligence controls to prevent a conspiracy from prospering."

US Sanctions

"The middle-class is gone, it isn't protesting anymore," has been claimed. It has been predicted that the demonstrations will wither out. "The people are exhausted, they have to organize their everyday lives," people say. "And not everyone is against Maduro. Those who still get help from the government don't want to lose it."

The US imposed financial sanctions on President Nicolas Maduro after an election giving the ruling party virtually unlimited powers. The measures bar Americans doing business with the South American leader. All of Maduro's assets subject to US jurisdiction have been frozen and Americans are barred from doing business with him, the US Treasury Department's Office of Foreign Assets Control said. The imposition of sanctions on a head of state is an infrequent measure and can be symbolically powerful; other countries may decide to take similar action.

President Donald Trump's national security adviser H.R. McMaster said that the election to form a constituent assembly to rewrite the constitution was an "outrageous seizure of absolute power."

"By sanctioning Maduro, the US makes clear our opposition to the policies of his regime and our support for the people of Venezuela who seek to return their country to full and prosperous democracy," Treasury Secretary Steven Mnuchin said in a statement. "Maduro is a dictator who disregards the will of the Venezuelan people," Mnuchin said. "Anyone who participates in this illegitimate (constituent assembly) could be exposed to future US sanctions for their role in undermining democratic processes and institutions in Venezuela," Mnuchin said.

The US imposed sanctions on several Venezuelan officials, including the chief judge and seven other members of Venezuela's pro-Maduro Supreme Court after they ruled to annul Congress earlier this year.

The National newspaper, sympathetic to the opposition, is sarcastic in its description of Venezuela's socialist head of state Nicolas Maduro: The people in power are concerned above all with their personal well-being, it says, adding that this makes it even sadder that many Venezuelans are still convinced people in these circles are genuinely pursuing a socialist project to renew the country. This idea, says the paper, is simply wrong.

Maduro is doing little to deescalate the situation. In an interview with the Russian broadcaster Russia Today, he accused the United States of colluding with the opposition in trying to topple him. The country, he claimed, was determined to defend itself: "If Venezuela is divided, if the socialist revolution is forced to take up arms, we will fight again under a common flag beyond our national borders." Maduro has already armed 500,000 militiamen.

Ties with Russia

In 2006, President Chavez signed a $3bn (£1.6bn) arms deal with Russia, including an agreement to buy fighter jets and helicopters, marking a re-orientation away from US arms supplies. Venezuela and Russia signed an oil and gas cooperation accord in 2008. Russian warplanes visit Venezuela, with Russian warships heading there for November joint exercises – the first return of Russian navy to the Americas since Cold War. Russia and Venezuela signed accord on joint civilian nuclear cooperation.

Venezuela has sought significant ties with Russia in recent years. Before oil prices fell in 2014, Venezuela was set to become the largest importer of Russian military equipment by 2025. Moscow is becoming Caracas's "lender of last resort" in exchange for increasing amounts of crude oil. In August 2017, the Russian state oil company Rosneft was reselling approximately 225,000 barrels of PDVSA oil per day or 13 percent of total Venezuelan exports. A bilateral agreement struck in November to restructure more than $3 billion of Venezuela's debt to Russia reaffirmed Moscow's support.

Venezuela's Economic problems

President Chavez devalued the bolivar in 2010, by 17% against the US dollar for "priority" imports and by 50% for items considered nonessential, to boost revenue from oil exports after the economy shrank 5.8% in last quarter of 2009.

In December 2010, Parliament granted President Chavez special powers to deal with devastating floods, prompting opposition fears of greater authoritarianism. Government extended price controls on more basic goods in the battle against inflation in 2012. President Chavez threatened to expropriate companies that did not comply with the price controls.

Opposition TV channel Globovision paid a $2.1M fine to avoid having its assets seized in 2012. The media regulator imposed the fine in October over Globovision coverage of a prison riot.

Another policy contributing to the country's economic problems is foreign currency control, first introduced by Chavez in 2003 to curb capital flight. By selling U.S. dollars at different rates, the government effectively created a black market and increased opportunities for corruption. A business that is authorized to buy dollars at preferential rates to purchase priority goods like food or medicine could instead sell those dollars for a significant profit to third parties. In December 2017, the official exchange rate was ten bolivars to the dollar while the black market rate was more than nine thousand bolivars to the dollar.

Imports reportedly felt to $18 billion in 2016, down from $66 billion in 2012, as foreign-made goods became increasingly expensive. Many consumers are faced with the choice of waiting for hours in line for basic goods or paying exorbitant prices to so-called bachaqueros, or black market traffickers.

The government announced cuts in public spending as oil prices reach a four-year low in 2014. In 2016 President Maduro announced measures aimed at fighting the economic crisis, including currency devaluation and first gas price rise in 20 years.

As global oil prices fell from $111 per barrel in 2014 to a low of $27 per barrel in 2016, Venezuela's already shaky economy went into free fall. That year, GDP dropped 10 to 15 percent and inflation soared to an all-time high of 800 percent. By late 2017, revenue had dropped by $100 billion and the country owed some $150 billion to foreign creditors while it held just under $10 billion in reserves.

In 2018 Venezuela slashes five zeros from its old currency, renaming it the Sovereign Bolivar and tying it to a state-backed 'petro' cryptocurrency in a bid to tackle rampant hyperinflation. 2018 inflation attains over one million percent.

Many critics signaled the Chavez government for squandering years of record oil income and accused PDVSA of gross mismanagement and cronyism. In 2017, more than fifty employees associated with the national oil industry had been arrested on charges of corruption and embezzlement. In November of that year, Maduro appointed military general and loyalist Manuel Quevedo to the helm of both PDVSA and the oil ministry, prompting accusations of undemocratic consolidation of power.

In 2013, A massive power cut leaves 70% of Venezuela, including parts of Caracas, without electricity. President Maduro blames "right-wing saboteurs".

Venezuela's economic crisis is marked by soaring inflation and shortages of food, medical supplies, and staples like toilet paper and soap. Experts say the government's strict price controls, which were meant to keep basic goods affordable for the country's poor, are partly to blame. Many manufacturers in the country cut production due to limits on what they could charge for their goods.

Venezuela's Military

Since Hugo Chávez first took office in 1998, civilian-military relations have seen a fusion rather than separation, with both a strong military presence in government with a motive of shaping the political values of the armed forces. The Venezuelan Constitution clearly establishes the military as a non-partisan entity. According to Articles 328 and 330, active service members "have a right to vote," but they cannot participate in "acts of propaganda or political partisanship, and they cannot proselytize."

In a stunning ruling, the nation's highest court re-wrote the constitution to allow the military to actively participate in rallies and gatherings supporting a political party: the government's. The ruling dramatically erodes what is left of democracy, bringing Venezuela back to its nineteenth-century roots when warlords ruled the land. This, apparently, is not clear enough for Venezuela's highest court. In complete opposition to the text, the court ruled that active military participation in partisan acts "is a high water-mark for democratic participation." The ruling goes on to hail the use of the military in partisan activities as "a progressive act geared toward the consolidation of the civilian-military union."

President Chavez inducted active–duty and retired military officers to staff political and bureaucratic positions. The loyal officers were well positioned in Legislative Commissions, Judicial Police Corps (CTPJ), Internal Affairs Ministry, Sports National Institute (IND), National Budgetary Office(OCEPRE) and Agriculture Ministry. By June 2001, as many as 176 active duty military officers had retained senior ministerial and administrative positions in the government.

The position of the President and the Vice-President of Petróleos de Venezuela (PDVSA) which is a state-owned oil company and the Chief Executive Officer of the US subsidiary, CITGO was handed over to military officials.

After Chavez's death in 2013, Nicolás Maduro, the current President of Venezuela is seeking to prolong ideological rule and civilian-military fusion, repeatedly referring to Hugo Chavez. The civil-military status quo will be maintained as this apparent change in personnel would be unlikely to challenge subjective control.

One of the prominent aspects inherent in the new Organic Law was the official creation of the National Bolivarian Militia, earlier known as the General Command for the Reserve and National Mobilization. The militia was initially created as a volunteer civilian reserve force in February 2006. The 2006 Organic Law of the Armed Forces not only gave formal reorganization to the militia but also placed it on an equal footing with the traditional armed forces and was under the direct authority and supervision of the President.

Political Problems

In 2014, Venezuela's chief prosecutor formally charges leading opposition figure Maria Corina Machado with conspiracy to assassinate President Maduro.

In 2014, Protests over poor security in the western states of Tachira and Merida spread to Caracas, where they win the backing of opposition parties and turn into anti-government rallies. The government accuses the opposition of seeking to launch a coup and breaks up the protests. At least 28 people die in the violence.

Antonio Ledezma, the opposition mayor of Caracas, was charged with plotting a coup with US support in 2015. He denies this, accusing the government of stifling criticism.

Three Democratic Unity deputies resign in 2016 from the National Assembly parliament under Supreme Court pressure, depriving coalition of the clear two-thirds majority that would have allowed it to block legislation proposed by President Maduro.

In 2016, Hundreds of thousands of people take part in a protest in Caracas calling for the removal of President Maduro, accusing him of responsibility for the economic crisis. Amid the crisis, the Maduro administration has become increasingly autocratic. In 2016, opposition lawmakers, under the Democratic Unity Roundtable (MUD) coalition, took the majority in the National Assembly for the first time in sixteen years, but Maduro took several steps to ultimately dissolve them.

In September 2016, Venezuela's electoral authority ordered the opposition to suspend a campaign to recall the president. The following month, the Supreme Court stripped the National Assembly of powers to oversee the economy and prevented the release of eighty political prisoners, including opposition leader Leopoldo Lopez.

In March 2017, the judicial branch briefly dissolved the National Assembly. The court revised its order days later following an international outcry but kept the legislature in contempt. A week later the government barred opposition politician Henrique Capriles, who narrowly lost to Maduro in the 2013 presidential election, from running for office for fifteen years.

In April-June 2017, Several people die in clashes with security forces during mass protests demanding early presidential elections and the revoking of a planned constituent assembly to replace the National Assembly. More than 130 people were killed and 4,800 arrested in clashes between police and demonstrators. In response, the government issued an indefinite ban on all protests. Government security forces have attacked, detained, or expelled journalists, according to the Committee to Protect Journalists. That year, Venezuela became one of two countries in the Western Hemisphere, along with Cuba, to be rated as "not free" by Freedom House.

Chief prosecutor Luisa Ortega goes into exile in 2017, saying she was sacked because the government wanted to stop her investigations into alleged corruption and human rights abuses.

In August 2018, Venezuelan officials say two explosive-laden drones were detonated near to President Maduro during a live, televised speech. Mr. Maduro accuses Colombia and elements within the US of a "right-wing plot" to kill him, but provided no evidence for the claim.

A Humanitarian Crisis

Observers have characterized the situation in Venezuela as a humanitarian crisis. In 2016, the Venezuelan Pharmaceutical Federation estimated that 85 percent of basic medicines were unavailable or difficult to obtain. Hospitals lack supplies like antibiotics, gauze, and soap. Infant mortality in 2016 increased 30 percent and maternal mortality 65 percent over two years prior, according to government figures. Diseases like diphtheria and malaria, previously eliminated from the country, have reemerged.

Poverty has also spiked. In 2016, a local university study found that more than 87 percent of the population said it did not have enough money to buy the necessary food. Another study found that 30 percent of school-aged children were malnourished. According to a 2016 report from Human Rights Watch, the Maduro administration "has vehemently denied the extent of the need for help and has blocked an effort by the opposition-led National Assembly to seek international assistance."

Poverty and lack of opportunity are exacerbating Venezuela's high rates of violence. In 2016 Venezuela experienced its highest ever homicide rate at 91.8 homicides per 100,000 residents, according to the Venezuelan Violence Observatory, an independent monitoring group. (The U.S. rate, by comparison, is 5 per 100,000.) Maduro's administration has deployed the military to combat street crime, but rights groups and foreign media have reported widespread abuses, including extrajudicial killings.

The humanitarian crisis has spilled across Venezuela's borders, with as many as five hundred thousand fleeing in the past two years. Many have crossed into neighboring Colombia and Brasil, while others have left by boat to the nearby island of Curacao.

The UN warns of a migration "crisis", estimating that economic woes and food and medical shortages have caused more than two million Venezuelans to leave their country since 2014. Most are settling in nearby Peru, Ecuador, Colombia, and Brazil, leading to tensions in the region.

International Tensions

The Colombian government and the US signed a long-trailed deal on the use of Colombia's military bases in 2009. President Chavez orders 15,000 troops to the Colombian border, citing increased violence by Colombian paramilitary groups.

After a six-year wait, in 2012, Venezuela becomes a full member of a regional economic and political bloc Mercosur and is given four years to comply with the bloc's trading regulations.

Mercosur, comprising Argentina, Brazil, Paraguay, Uruguay, and Venezuela, suspended Venezuela in 2016. In March 2017, the secretary-general of the Organization of the American States (OAS) recommended suspending Venezuela from the bloc unless the Maduro administration moved to hold elections. Venezuela announced its withdrawal from OAS the following month.

The Donald J. Trump administration imposed sanctions on Vice President Tareck El Aissami and eight members of the Supreme Court in the first half of 2017, and days before the July election it added to that list more than a dozen current and former officials. After the vote, Trump sanctioned President Maduro, making him just the fourth foreign leader to receive such a penalty. In August, the administration imposed the most robust sanctions yet, which effectively block U.S. financial institutions from investing in new Venezuelan or PDVSA bonds. The measures, coupled with Maduro's refusal to seek help from the International Monetary Fund, led the government to announce in November that it would restructure and refinance all foreign debt. Venezuela officially defaulted on $200 million in debt interest payments later that month. Despite tensions between Washington and Caracas, the United States remains Venezuela's largest trading partner.

Meanwhile, the Maduro administration retains the support of allies in Bolivia, Ecuador, and several Caribbean nations. China has lent Venezuela more than $60 billion since 2001 and is the South American country's largest creditor. The Chinese Foreign Ministry issued a vote of confidence in November 2017, stating that "Venezuela's government and people have the ability to properly handle their debt issue."

Highlights for Chapter 9
- Venezuela was a democracy during 40 years (1958-1998) until Hugo Chavez, a camouflaged military putschist, won the 1998 elections and started a poisoned democracy with parliamentary partisans.
- In these 20 years of misgovernment, Venezuela tried to imitate the Cuban approach to socialism-communism, but in fact, produced a disaster that compares only to collapsed countries in Africa.

- Colonel Hugo Chavez entered the scene; he and his supporters made two coup attempts in 1992.
- Hugo Chavez, once elected, launched new processes that brought in a new constitution.
- In April 2002, amid huge protests that left several deaths, a civil coup was perpetrated. The coup collapsed and Chavez was returned to office.
- Parties loyal to President Chavez dominated parliament after opposition parties boycotted 2005 elections.
- Chavez remained popular among the country's poor throughout his presidency, expanding social services including food and housing subsidies, health care, and educational programs.
- President Hugo Chavez died in 2013 at age 58 after a battle with cancer. Nicolas Maduro, his chosen successor, was elected president in 2013.
- Opposition Democratic Unity coalition won the two-thirds majority in 2015 parliamentary elections, the National Assembly ended 16 years of Socialist Party control.
- The governmental election of the controversial constituent assembly in 2017 took place in the face of an opposition boycott and international condemnation.
- President Maduro won another term in the May 2018 election. The election was not constitutionally valid, and it was supported by the controversial constituent assembly.
- In January 2005, President Chavez signed a decree on land reform to eliminate Venezuela's large estates and benefit rural poor.
- By January 2007, nationalization began. President Chavez announced key energy and telecommunications companies will be nationalized under the 18-month enabling act approved by parliament.
- In May 2007, television networks got their blow.
- By June 2007, international oil companies got expropriated.
- In August 2008, it was the bank system which was affected.
- Over the past 20 years, Venezuela and Cuba have become close allies both economically and politically.
- Venezuela provides critical oil supplies on subsidized terms in return for Cuban doctors, teachers, sports trainers, and military advisors.

- There are too many Cubans working in Venezuela, including hundreds of Cuban "volunteers" recruited by Chavez to provide literacy and health care programs for the poor.
- Cuba's military role in Venezuela has raised particular concern among critics of Mr. Chávez.
- "We are at the mercy of meddling in areas of national security by a Cuban regime, which wants Chávez to remain in power because Chávez gives them oil."
- "No one knows better than Chavez himself that Venezuelan history is sprinkled with one military conspiracy after another."
- The US imposed financial sanctions on President Nicolas Maduro after an election giving the ruling party virtually unlimited powers.
- H.R. McMaster said that the election to form a constituent assembly to rewrite the constitution was an "outrageous seizure of absolute power."
- "Anyone who participates in this illegitimate (constituent assembly) could be exposed to future US sanctions."
- "If Venezuela is divided, if the socialist revolution is forced to take up arms, we will fight again under a common flag beyond our national borders," Maduro exclaimed.
- In 2006, President Chavez signed a $3bn (£1.6bn) arms deal with Russia, including an agreement to buy fighter jets and helicopters.
- Venezuela was set to become the largest importer of Russian military equipment by 2025.
- President Chavez devalues the bolivar in 2010, by 17% against the US dollar.
- Government extended price controls on more basic goods in the battle against inflation in 2012. President Chavez threatened to expropriate companies that did not comply with the price controls.
- Another policy contributing to the country's economic problems is foreign currency control, first introduced by Chavez in 2003 to curb capital flight.
- In 2016 President Maduro announced measures aimed at fighting economic crisis, including currency devaluation and first gas price rise in 20 years.
- As global oil prices fell from $111 per barrel in 2014 to a low of $27 per barrel in 2016, Venezuela's already shaky economy went into free fall.

- In 2016, the GDP dropped 10 to 15 percent and inflation soared to an all-time high of 800 percent.
- In 2013, A massive power cut leaves 70% of Venezuela, including parts of Caracas, without electricity. President Maduro blames "right-wing saboteurs".
- Since Hugo Chávez first took office in 1998, civilian-military relations have seen a fusion rather than separation, with both a strong military presence in government with a motive of shaping the political values of the armed forces.
- In a stunning ruling, the nation's highest court re-wrote the constitution to allow the military to actively participate in rallies and gatherings supporting a political party: the government's.
- The position of the President and the Vice-President of Petróleos de Venezuela (PDVSA) and the US subsidiary, CITGO, were handed over to military officials.
- With Maduro, the civilian-military status quo will be maintained.
- In 2014, Protests over poor security in the western states of Tachira and Merida spread to Caracas.
- Amid the crisis, the Maduro administration has become increasingly autocratic.
- In April-June 2017, Several people die in clashes with security forces during mass protests demanding early presidential elections.
- Since 2016, Observers have characterized the situation in Venezuela as a humanitarian crisis.
- In 2016 Venezuela experienced its highest ever homicide rate at 91.8 homicides per 100,000 residents.
- China has lent Venezuela more than $60 billion since 2001 and is the South American country's largest creditor.

Chapter 10: The Political System

The first defining feature of a communist system is the monopoly of power of the Communist party. There were other important institutions within a communist state besides the ruling party, among them government ministries, the military, and the security police. All institutions were overseen by the organs of the communist party, which had a higher authority than any other body. [Brown 2009]

The second defining feature of a communist system is the concept of democratic centralism. In theory, it means that there could be a discussion of issues – the 'democratic' component – until a decision had been reached, but thereafter the decision of higher party organs was binding and had to be implemented in a strictly disciplined manner throughout the party and society. [Brown 2009]

<u>Constitutional Legality</u>

The constitutions of some communist countries illustrate the 'leading role of the party.' In the Soviet constitution it is written, 'The leading and guiding force of Soviet society and the nucleus of its political system, of all state organizations and public organizations, is the Communist Party of the Soviet Union.' [Brown 2009]

The Soviet Union constitution held out the promise of autonomy to the member republics but also created a powerfully centralized state in which regional concerns would be subordinated to the plans and policies of the party and its leaders in the capital of Russia. Aside from Russia, the union originally included Byelorussia, Transcaucasia, and Ukraine. [Streissguth 2002]

In the Mongolian People's Republic constitution reads, 'In the M.P.R., the guiding and directing force of society and of the state is the Mongolian People's Revolutionary Party, which is guided in its activities by the all-conquering theory of Marxism-Leninism.' In the case of Vietnam's constitution, 'The Communist Party of Vietnam, the vanguard and general staff of the Vietnamese working class, armed with Marxism-Leninism, is the only force leading the state and society, and the main factor determining all successes of the Vietnamese revolution. [Brown 2009]

The relationship between the individual top leader (the General Secretary) and the politburo varied greatly over time and from one country to another. In other words, while oligarchical rule has been the norm in a majority of communist countries at most times, the power of the top leader has been such that the system became essentially autocratic – a personal dictatorship rather than collective rule by an oligarchy. Some examples are Stalin in the Soviet Union, Mao Zedong in China, and Kim Il Sung and his son Kim Song Il and grandson Kim Jong-un in North Korea. [Brown 2009]

Democracy

Authoritarian regimes flourish in communist societies. In a society which depends on central planning, control cannot be made dependent on a majority's being able to agree; it will often be necessary that the will of a small minority be imposed upon the people. Because this minority will be the largest group able to agree among themselves on the question at issue. [Hayek 1994]

Democracy is essentially a means, a utilitarian device for safeguarding internal peace and individual freedom. As such it is by no means infallible or certain. Our point is that planning leads to dictatorship because dictatorship is the most effective instrument of coercion and the enforcement of ideas and, as such, essential if central planning on a large scale is to be possible. [Hayek 1994]

Democracy is based on a balance of forces to attain an agreement. Therefore, a directed economy must run on more or less dictatorial lines. The complex system of interrelated activities, if it is to be consciously directed at all, must be directed by a single staff of experts, and that ultimate responsibility and power must rest in the hands of a commander-in-chief whose actions must not be fettered by democratic procedure. [Hayek 1994]

The Totalitarians in Our Midst

Many socialists have more sympathy with the Conservatives than with the Liberals. The increasing veneration for the state, the admiration of power, and of bigness for bigness' sake, the enthusiasm for "organization" of everything (we now call it "planning"), and that "inability to leave anything to the simple power of organic growth." [Hayek 1994]

Power without profit in the state promotes authoritarian rulers and is against capitalism and individualism. Lord Keynes, describing in 1915 a typical German author, "Even in peace industrial life must remain mobilized. This is the 'militarization of our industrial life.' Individualism must come to an end absolutely. A system of regulations must be set up, the object of which is not the greater happiness of the individual, but the strengthening of the organized unity of the state. In the new Germany of the twentieth-century, Power without consideration of Profit is to make an end of that system of Capitalism." [Hayek 1994]

Realism is against individualism. Professor Carr explains a realist is one "who makes morality a function of politics" and who "cannot logically accept any standard of value save that of fact." This 'realism' is contrasted, in German fashion, with the 'utopian' thought of 'individualism.' [Hayek 1994]

International capitalism had to intervene to save the world. Professor Carr expressed, "The victors lost the peace, and Soviet Russia and Germany won it because the former continued to preach the right of nations and laissez-faire capitalism, whereas the latter were striving to build up the world in larger units under centralized planning and control." [Hayek 1994]

Monopolies are not healthy in capitalism or communism. Support of the monopolistic organization of industry is the great immediate danger because it leads to totalitarianism. The capitalistic organizers of monopolies aim at a sort of corporative society, however, they are as shortsighted as were their German colleagues in believing that they will be allowed not only to create but also for any length of time to run such a system. [Hayek 1994]

Strong states promoting monopolies are against consumption. Even if railways, road and air transport, or the supply of gas and electricity were all inevitably monopolies, the consumer is questionable in a much stronger position so long as they remain separate monopolies than when they are "co-ordinated" by central control. A state monopoly is always a state-protected monopoly – protected against both potential competition and effective criticism. [Hayek 1994]

The recent growth of monopoly is largely the result of a deliberate collaboration of organized capital and organized labor where the privileged groups of labor share in the monopoly profits at the expense of the community and particularly at the expense of the poorest, those employed in the less-well-organized industries and the unemployed. [Hayek 1994]

Unions use to be accomplices of the state in detriment of individuals. The labor leaders who now proclaim so loudly that they have "done once and for all with the mad competitive system" are proclaiming the doom of the freedom of the individual. [Hayek 1994]

A planned society and freedom do not mix. Twenty-five years ago there was perhaps still some excuse for holding the naïve belief that "a planned society can be a far more free society than the competitive laissez-faire order it has come to replace." [Hayek 1994]

<u>The Party</u>

The party imposes its way of thinking using its immense power over individuals through authoritarianism. Nevertheless, the transformation went on speedily in all facets of party life and in many of its principles, such as ties with the masses, organizational structure, modus operandi, social composition, ways of ruling, and style of life. [Streissguth 2002]

The evolution of the power of the party was in the hands of the leaders. Lenin's 'The State and Revolution' has often been hailed as evidence of a libertarian or democratic Lenin and contrasted with the Lenin of 'What is to be Done?' With its emphasis on hierarchy and discipline within the revolutionary party. It has been used in support of the contention that he was a 'revolutionary humanist' and by those who wish to distance him from the way the Soviet system developed after his death. [Brown 2009]

The vanguard party elevated the inevitability of communism to gain support. Part of the attraction of communism for many – and it was an especial comfort for members of the smaller parties – was the emphasis in the doctrine on inevitability. If all history was a history of class struggles in which the penultimate stage – before the establishment of socialism and its higher phase, classless communism – was the assured victory of the proletariat, led by its vanguard party, then it was possible to look to the future with optimism. [Brown 2009]

Communist regimes have been often described as party-states, and the description makes sense, so closely intertwined were party institutions and governmental structures. Yet official communist doctrine was generally misleading or ambiguous about this. On the one hand, the party was accorded a monopoly of political power, exercised as the 'dictatorship of the proletariat' or, later, playing what was more modestly described as the 'leading role' within the system. On the other hand, it was also in official theory a public (or social) organization rather than an organ of state power. [Brown 2009]

In the Soviet Union, dramatic changes occurred in the party in 1917. It grew in size to perhaps more than 250,000 members, and it operated as a democratic political party, under strong authoritative leadership. If his colleagues accepted Lenin's line, it was mostly after lively debates and having sounded out the moods and opinions of the rank and file. [Streissguth 2002]

In conditions of war, the party was transformed into a struggling machine. Once the party was in power, in conditions of a civil war, another, deep transformation took place: the party became militarized and highly centralized, in a state of almost permanent mobilization and disciplined action. [Streissguth 2002]

In the Soviet Union, toward the spring of 1921, party statistics showed that 90 percent of the membership was now of Civil War vintage. Prerevolutionary cadres, even those who joined in 1917, were drowned in a mass of new entrants, many of them active participants in military and security operations and, quite naturally, imbued with a military, if not militaristic, political culture. [Streissguth 2002]

Provided support to the political cause, the party accepted any type of membership. One significant aspect of party membership is the extent to which communism attracted recruits from long-settled indigenous populations or from recent immigrants. Ethnicity as a factor was played down in communist doctrine. What mattered was the class origin and class solidarity. In a study of the Hebrew University of Jerusalem, Jews in particular 'at various times and in various places were disproportionately represented in the communist movement (be it in the total membership, the apparatus, or the leadership). [Streissguth 2002]

Bolshevik propaganda, Spying, and Censorship

The Bolsheviks, of course, did not invent propaganda. The Bolshevik innovation consisted in assigning propaganda a central place in national life: previously employed to touch up or distort reality, in Communist Russia propaganda became a surrogate reality. Communist propaganda created a fictitious world side by side with that of everyday experience and in stark contradiction to it. [Streissguth 2002]

Alert and suspicious, the working-class of the city constituted itself a vast spy system, through the servants prying into bourgeois households, and reporting all information to the Military Revolutionary Committee, which struck with an iron hand, unceasing. [Streissguth 2002]

With the establishment of a central censorship office, all publications were henceforth subject to preventive censorship. Russians quickly learned the art of self-censorship, submitting only material that experience had taught them might have a chance of obtaining a license. [Streissguth 2002]

In a country in which much of the population could neither read nor write, the printed word reached few. Given their interest in influencing the masses, the Bolsheviks preferred other means of spreading their ideas. Of these, the most effective proved to be the theater and the cinema, art forms in which they encouraged experimentation. [Streissguth 2002]

Enemies of the Regime

Great stress was placed on the threat posed by external enemies, and the regime's domestic critics were portrayed as being in thrall to the malign West. Western military alliances discouraged further communist expansion, but it also helped communist leaders to maintain their power and, in some countries, to win quite broad popular acceptance. [Brown 2009]

All the Asian communist states have, to varying degrees, likewise viewed the United States as a major enemy. Three of the four – North Korea, Vietnam, and Laos – were at various times subjected to American military attack. The Indochina War left communists in charge of Laos also and gave them the possibility of making anti-Americanism a rallying cry. [Brown 2009]

North Korea is a case apart. It remains the most totalitarian of communist states. It, too, has the United States as past and prospective enemy. But it has a deadly rival much closer to home than the USA – South Korea. To have on its borders a Korean state which is much more prosperous and incomparably more democratic is a clear threat to the future existence of North Korea. The communist system in the northern part of the Korean peninsula was mainly the work of the Soviet Union, however, North Korea went to establish a foreign policy independent of both the USSR and China. [Brown 2009]

Nationalism

Cuba is an especially interesting case related to nationalism. The United States policy towards Cuba has played an enormous part in preserving the Cuban communist system in aspic. The American economic embargo, the ban on US passport-holders from visiting the island has achieved precisely the opposite effect from that intended. It has increased anti-Americanism, strengthened the standing of the Castro leadership, bolstered the communist system, and kept the majority of the Cuban people poorer than they otherwise would have been. [Brown 2009]

Apart from the appeal of nationalism and the utility of having an enemy to denounce and hold responsible for current difficulties, it is clearly to the advantage of communist systems if they can deliver adequate social services and fast economic growth. Cuban success in training doctors and providing a reasonable standard of health care, in spite of the country's economic backwardness, is an example. [Brown 2009]

<u>Highlights for Chapter 10</u>

- The first defining feature of a communist system is the monopoly of power of the communist party.
- The second defining feature of a communist system was the concept of democratic centralism.
- The constitutions of some communist countries illustrate the 'leading role of the party.'
- Planning and competition can be combined only by planning for competition but not by planning against competition.
- The price system will fulfill its function only if competition prevails.
- In a society which depends on central planning, it will often be necessary that the will of a small minority be imposed upon the people.
- Planning leads to dictatorship because dictatorship is the most effective instrument of coercion and the enforcement of ideals.
- To increase opportunity is almost precisely the opposite of the "planning" which is generally advocated and practiced in communist countries.
- A system of regulations must be set up, the object of which is not the greater happiness of the individual, but the strengthening of the organized unity of the state.
- Organized capital and organized labor share in the monopoly profits at the expense of the community.
- Excuses, only excuses, for holding the naïve belief that "a planned society can be a far more free society than the competitive laissez-faire order."

- The party with its ties with the masses, organizational structure, modus operandi, social composition, ways of ruling, and style of life.
- Communist regimes have often been described as party-states, so closely intertwined were party institutions and governmental structures.
- Communist party membership attracted recruits from long-settled indigenous populations or from recent immigrants.
- The Bolshevik innovation consisted in assigning propaganda a central place in national life.
- Alert and suspicious, the working-class of the city constituted itself a vast spy system.
- With the establishment of a central censorship office, all publications were henceforth subject to preventive censorship.
- Great stress was placed on the threat posed by external enemies.
- All the Asian communist states have, to varying degrees, likewise viewed the United States as a major enemy.
- North Korea has a deadly rival much closer to home than the USA – South Korea.
- The United States policy towards Cuba has played an enormous part in preserving the Cuban communist system in aspic.

Chapter 11: The Economic System

The third defining feature of a consolidated communist system is non-capitalist ownership of the means of production, and linked to this is the fourth feature – the dominance of a command economy, as distinct from a market economy. Even in established communists systems, some private economic activity continued, whether on a legal or illegal basis – or quite commonly, as a mixture of both. [Brown 2009]

Lenin realized that neither the workers nor the peasants were really interested in Marxism or in revolution; they simply wanted to improve their own material situation. Lenin's devoted elite party would, therefore, become the 'vanguard of the working class' and would strive to teach the workers that their true interest lay in the revolution, not just in wage increases and better working conditions. [Streissguth 2002]

The Soviet revolution was started in Petrograd and was more of a coup than a revolution. In March 1917 bread rationing was introduced in the capital, and badly organized. There were strikes and then street demonstrations, followed by riots and bigger strikes and demonstrations. In all, there were about a thousand serious casualties in March in Petrograd, but little blood was shed elsewhere. [Streissguth 2002]

Lenin and the Bolsheviks instituted the policy of War Communism to cope with the drastic needs of the civil war. But the expropriations of food and the seizures of private business and factories had their effects: Russian industry was all but destroyed, a terrible famine raged in the countryside, and the country had to rely on foreign aid to fend off mass starvation. [Streissguth 2002]

During the Soviet revolution, there were changes in the way crops were distributed. The peasants were now required to give only a part of their produce to the state and were allowed to keep or sell the rest. They were, however, required to pay a tax which was somewhat higher than it had been in the tsarist period. [Streissguth 2002]

The fundamental difference between a command economy and a free-market economy was that decisions about what should be produced and in what quantities, and at what prices that output should be sold, were the result of a hierarchical, top-down process culminating in instructions to all producers. Produces were concerned above all to meet targets set by planners. The absence of private ownership and a market economy meant that the state had control over the career possibilities of all its citizens. [Brown 2009]

The first preoccupation of any individual is to make ends meet. Survival is considered supreme. Strictly speaking, there is no "economic motive" but only economic factors conditioning our striving for other ends. What in ordinary language is misleadingly called the "economic motive" means merely the desire for general opportunity, the desire for power to achieve unspecified ends. If we strive for money, it is because it offers us the widest choice in enjoying the fruits of our efforts. [Hayek 1994]

Economic values are less important to us than many other things precisely because in economic matters we are free to decide what to us is more, and what less, important. Or, as we might say, because in the present society it is we who have to solve the economic problems of our lives. To be controlled in our economic pursuits means to be always controlled unless we declare our specific purpose. [Hayek 1994]

Economic control is not merely control of a sector of human life which can be separated from the rest; it is the control of the means for all our ends. And whoever has sole control of the means must also determine which ends are to be served, which values are to be rated higher and which lower – in short, what men should believe and strive for. [Hayek 1994]

Our freedom of choice in a competitive society rests on the fact that, if one person refuses to satisfy our wishes, we can turn to another. But if we face a monopolist we are at his mercy. And an authority directing the whole economic system would be the most powerful monopolist conceivable. It would have complete power to decide what we are to be given and on what terms. It would not only decide what commodities and services were to be available and in what quantities; it would be able to direct their distribution between districts and groups and could, if it wished, discriminate between persons to any degree it liked. [Hayek 1994]

Planning and competition can be combined only by planning for competition but not by planning against competition. An effective competitive system needs an intelligently designed and continuously adjusted legal framework as much as any other. Even the most essential prerequisite of its proper functioning, the prevention of fraud and deception (including exploitation of ignorance), provides a great and by no means yet fully accomplished object of legislative activity. [Hayek 1994]

A non-market based economic system does not consider the dynamics of financial systems. The price system enables entrepreneurs, by watching the movement of comparatively few prices, as an engineer watches the hands of a few dials, to adjust their activities to those of their fellows. The important point here is that the price system will fulfill this function only if competition prevails, that is, if the individual producer has to adapt himself to price changes and cannot control them. [Hayek 1994]

The power conferred by the control of production and prices is almost unlimited. In a competitive society the prices we have to pay for a thing, the rate at which we can get one thing for another, depending on the quantities of other things of which by taking one, we deprive the other members of society. This price is not determined by the conscious will of anybody. And if one way of achieving our ends proves too expensive for us, we are free to try other ways. [Hayek 1994]

The younger generation of today has grown up in a world in which in school and press the spirit of commercial enterprise has been represented as disreputable and the making of profit as immoral, where to employ a hundred people is represented as exploitation but to command the same number as honorable. [Hayek 1994]

If the resources of different nations are treated as exclusive properties of these nations as wholes, if international economic relations, instead of being relations between individuals, become increasingly relations between whole nations organized as trading bodies, they inevitably become the source of friction and envy between whole nations. Economic transactions between national bodies who are at the same time the supreme judges of their own behavior, who bow to no superior law, and whose representatives cannot be bound by any considerations but the immediate interest of their respective nations, must end in clashes of power. [Hayek 1994]

An international authority can be very just and contribute enormously to economic prosperity if it merely keeps order and creates conditions in which the people can develop their own life; but it is impossible to be just or to let people live their own life if the central authority doles out raw materials and allocates markets, if every spontaneous effort has to be "approved" and nothing can be done without the sanction of the central authority. [Hayek 1994]

Public versus Private Property

So long as the property is divided among many owners, none of them acting independently has exclusive power to determine the income and position of particular people – nobody is tied to any one property owner except by the fact that he may offer better terms than anybody else. [Hayek 1994]

Socialism is directed towards a strong state that controls every individual economic movement. The ideal of justice of most socialists would be satisfied if merely private income from property were abolished and there were no major differences between the earned incomes of different people. What they forget is that, in transferring all property in the means of production to the state, they put the state in a position whereby its action must in effect decide all other incomes. [Hayek 1994]

Communist use the class struggle to justify its policies. Mao's simple solution to the problem of making Marxism work in an overwhelmingly agricultural society was to turn China's greatest weakness, the rural poor, into its ultimate strength. "This means that the Chinese revolution is essentially a peasant revolution," wrote Mao. [Schell 2013]

Communist policies are against innovation, pushing the population to hunger. Collectivization did not encourage new investments in agricultural equipment; the annual Soviet grain harvests continued to decline, and the country still had to import grain from the United States. Workers grew apathetic, and bureaucratic managers of state enterprises grew corrupt. [Streissguth 2002]

Many injustices have been effected in the name of the public property. Many productive entrepreneurs have been robbed by the state in the name of justice. Their properties given away to unscrupulous workers or peasants that abandoned them after propaganda was not necessary. Where boundaries are moved and there is no respect for private property, hunger will result. History has shown this to be the case over and over again. Where property rights are respected and people are allowed to develop in peace and security, there has never been hunger. [Freeth 2011]

Regarding the public and private sectors, even during the initial Lenin years in Russia, there were contradictions on how to keep egalitarian policies. A private sector and a public sector were allowed, workers could choose where to give their contribution. The labor legislation on the New Economic Policy (NEP) modified the policy of war communism: forcible labor conscription was abolished. Workers could freely sell their labor in either the private sector or the state sector of the economy. The regime abandoned its early egalitarian policies. Skilled workers now received much better wages than the unskilled. [Streissguth 2002]

In the Soviet Union improvising was the norm, including the possibility of changing the economic model. The Supreme Economic Council [SEC] was made responsible for large industry and was given authority commensurate with the responsibility. Each segment of the industry was placed under the direct management of a trust which was run by a committee somewhat like a board of directors. The number of such trusts finally reached 486. Each trust was required to submit plans and reports to the SEC for approval, and 50 percent of the profits of every trust was assigned to the state. Legally, however, each trust was an independent enterprise which was to be operated for profit, and which was free to buy or sell to state organizations (including other trusts) or to private businessmen. It was a complex and complicated system, which was not very efficient, but which worked. [Streissguth 2002]

In the Soviet Union, state and private control were ubiquitous, the property changed hands continuously. Between 91 and 92 percent of all the industrial concerns in Russia were given over to co-operative or private or combined state and private control. But the 8.5 percent of the industries which continued to belong to the government employed almost 85 percent of all industrial workers. The government, in other words, kept the larger share. It also tightened rather than loosened its controls. All banking and credit facilities, all transportation, all foreign trade, most large-scale domestic trade, and all large-scale industry remained in the hands of Lenin's organizations. So did the machinery of government. These things were held more tightly than ever before. [Streissguth 2002]

Command Planning

Marx and his followers believed that running an efficient economy could best be done from a single place. The centrally planned economy would eliminate waste by using the talents of experts and planners, who would allocate resources and production wherever they were most needed. [Streissguth 2002]

The application of the engineering technique to a whole nation – and this is what planning means - "raises problems of discipline which are hard to solve." There should be a place from which workers can be drawn, and when a worker is fired he should vanish from the job and from the payroll. The powers the manager of any plant will have to be given will still be considerable. A mistake he "ought" to have avoided is not his own affair; it is a crime against the community and must be treated as such. [Hayek 1994]

Planning without defining other general strategies was an automatic characteristic of communist states. The effect of the people's agreeing that there must be central planning, without agreeing on the ends, will be rather as if a group of people was to commit themselves to take a journey together without agreeing where they want to go: with the result that they may all have to make a journey which most of them do not want at all. [Hayek 1994]

Running the economy of a country is not a trivial task. There need be little difficulty in planning the economic life of a family, comparatively little in a small community. But, as the scale increases, the amount of agreement on the order of ends decreases and the necessity to rely on force and compulsion grows. [Hayek 1994]

The order of planning activities regarding "planning to equalize standards of life" must of necessity begin by fixing an order of priorities of the different claims. They must be ranked according to merits, some must be given precedence over others that must wait their turn – even though those whose interests are thus relegated may be convinced, not only of their better right but also of their ability to reach their goal sooner if they were only given freedom to act on their own devices. [Hayek 1994]

Once a central plan is put into execution, all the resources of the planned area must serve that plan – there can be no exemption for those who feel they could do better for themselves. Once their claim has been given a lower rank, they will have to work for the prior satisfaction of the needs of those who have been given preference. [Hayek 1994]

It is a fallacy that economic planning is merely a technical task which can be solved in a strictly objective manner by experts and that the really vital things would still be left in the hands of the political authorities. Any international economic authority, not subject to a superior political power, even if strictly confined to a particular field, could easily exercise the most tyrannical and irresponsible power imaginable. [Hayek 1994]

Central planning does not allow alternatives nor dynamism. Once a plan with such a level of detail is developed, nobody would be able to change it. People get affected personally, they are attached irremediably to a fix way of living for the next several years. Freedom in choosing our work is, probably, even more, important for our happiness than the freedom to spend our income during the hours of leisure. What matters is that we have some choice, that we are not absolutely tied to a particular job which has been chosen for us. [Hayek 1994]

To increase opportunity is almost precisely the opposite of the "planning approach" which is generally advocated and practiced. The state can do a great deal to help the spreading of knowledge and information to assist in improvement and mobility. Most planners, it is true, promise that in the new planned world free choice of occupation will be scrupulously preserved or even increased. But there they promise more than they can possibly fulfill. If they want to plan, they must control the entry into the different trades and occupations, or the terms of remuneration, or both. [Hayek 1994]

Central planning is a tool that handcuffs human possibilities because of its inflexibility. We shall no longer be free to be rational or efficient only when and where we think it worthwhile; we shall all have to conform to the standards which the planning authority must fix in order to simplify its task. To make this immense task manageable, it will have to reduce the diversity of human capacities and inclinations to a few categories of readily interchangeable units and deliberately to disregard minor personal differences. [Hayek 1994]

With central planning human beings would become objects without desires of innovation, their life becomes predefined. Although the professed aim of planning would be that man should cease to be a mere means, in fact – since it would be impossible to take account in the plan of individual likes and dislikes – the individual would more than ever become a mere means, to be used by the authority in the service of such abstractions as the "social welfare" or the "good of the community." [Hayek 1994]

It is indisputable that if we want to secure a distribution of wealth which conforms to some predetermined standard and if we want consciously to decide who is to have what, we must plan the whole economic system. But the question remains whether the price we should have to pay for the realization of somebody's idea of justice is not bound to be more discontent and more oppression than was ever caused by the much-abused free play of economic forces. [Hayek 1994]

Offer and demand are not well handled in central planning. The power of the planner over our private lives does not need to exercise it by direct control of consumption. The planner would probably employ rationing or similar devices, however, the source of his power would be its control over production. [Hayek 1994]

During the liberal era, the progressive division of labor has created a situation where almost every one of our activities is part of a social process. We are now for almost every part of our lives dependent on somebody else's economic activities. [Hayek 1994]

The Soviet Union

Survival in the Soviet Union meant making deals outside the law and the plan, and a black market in machinery, raw materials, and consumer goods grew several times faster than the official, legal economy. Education, health care, infrastructure, and social services went into decline. The rigidity of the centrally planned economy proved ill-suited to an era of rapid change and open global trade, which rewarded innovation and adaptability above all. [Streissguth 2002]

One of the greatest failures of communist economic systems was in creating new technology. Among the reasons for the poor performance were the meagreness of the rewards for success and the weakness of the penalties for failure. High efficiency and speedy technological development did not bring any special advantages; continuing to produce the same old product did not count as a failure. Shortfalls and waste, arising in part from technological inertia, were 'automatically excused in retrospect by the soft budget constraint.' [Brown 2009]

Yet in many ways, the Soviet Union was still operating as it had in the 1920s. Gosplan was still drawing up its Five-Year Plans and the central government still had control over the allocation of natural resources. Collectivization did not encourage new investments in agricultural equipment; the annual Soviet grain harvests continued to decline, and the country still had to import grain from the United States. Workers grew apathetic, and bureaucratic managers of state enterprises grew corrupt. [Streissguth 2002]

In their effort to rebuild the economy the Bolsheviks returned to the principles of capitalism. After accepting private ownership, they showed considerable flexibility and were willing to use heterodox methods to bring about national recovery. Lenin offered concessions to attract foreign capital, promising foreigners the possibility of unhindered exploitation of the country's natural resources. [Streissguth 2002]

The Soviet government was not entirely responsible for the hyperinflation. The depreciation of the currency began when the imperial government decided to cover war expenditures by printing more money; the revolution and the civil war greatly exacerbated the problem. [Streissguth 2002]

In the middle of 1922, it was more difficult to reconstruct industry than agriculture: famine had been alleviated, but industry remained extremely inefficient, with low productivity and a high cost of production. [Streissguth 2002]

After the first two or three years of the new economic system, the government had reasons to be pleased with the results. Life was gradually returning to normal. Private enterprises dominated the economy, producing more than 50 percent of the national income. Agriculture was almost entirely in private hands; state farms and collective farms occupied less than 2 percent of the land under cultivation. The small-scale industry was private, while large-scale heavy industry was state-owned. The government retained control over the mines, the banking system, and foreign trade, and thus had a decisive influence in running the economy. [Streissguth 2002]

The rate of recovery was uneven in different sectors of the economy. Agriculture was first to catch up with pre-war production standards. Light industry (factories that produced consumer goods) was next to improve, and heavy industry was slowest to recover. Foreign trade revived, though it remained far below what it had been before the war. The mixed economy and the one-party state created a society profoundly different both from what had existed before the revolution and what was to come as a result of Stalinist industrialization. [Streissguth 2002]

The revolution and its immediate aftermath brought about a great social leveling. In the new economic system, however, differentiation once again emerged. NEP spawned a new social phenomenon, the NEPman. They took advantage of the economic opportunities offered by the regime. The new class was a heterogeneous one. Its members came from different social backgrounds: enterprising peasants, descendants of the pre-war petty-bourgeoisie, and even some former members of the aristocracy now tried to make a living in unaccustomed circumstances. The newly rich were visible: conspicuous consumption in the midst of poverty. For most Bolsheviks, the NEPman represented everything they disliked: the petty bourgeois desire for property and profit, lack of ideological interests, and a middle-class life-style. [Streissguth 2002]

From the point of view of the working class, the results of the great revolution were ambiguous. In theory, Soviet Russia was a state of workers and peasants, and the Bolshevik party, in particular, claimed to represent the workers. It may be that many workers derived psychological benefits from living in a political system that was described as the "dictatorship of the proletariat." [Streissguth 2002]

The workers did also have some tangible gains. The state was building a bureaucracy. There was a constant need for functionaries, and the party, on the basis of its ideology, trusted the workers more than others and whenever possible attempted to promote them. The possibility of making a career in the new system was open to all intelligent and ambitious workers. [Streissguth 2002]

The most severe problem was unemployment. Even after the economy recovered, in the second half of the 1920s, unemployment did not diminish but worsened. Since the countryside was tremendously overpopulated, once conditions in the cities became bearable the peasants flocked into the industry, just as before the war. Both private industry and state enterprises were cost conscious and conservative in hiring workers. Older, skilled and experienced workers were less likely to suffer than young workers and women. [Streissguth 2002]

Although NEP may have helped Soviet Russia recover, it also placed a large proportion of the Russian economy out of the Bolsheviks' control – a result that the new government, founded on the basis of total centralization and regimentation, would not tolerate for long. [Streissguth 2002]

In 1928 Stalin abandoned NEP, and set out to construct an economic system which would guarantee the Communist Party monopoly of political power, and enable him to impose his development goals on the economy. Thanks to the vast natural and human resources of the USSR, Stalin's industrialization strategy turned the USSR into the world's second-largest economy. But Soviet citizens saw precious few of the benefits. [Streissguth 2002]

During the Brezhnev era (1964-82) the annual growth rate slowly declined, from 6.5 percent to 2 percent a year – but was still positive. Thus consumers saw their living standards roughly double. Most families acquired a television and refrigerator, although only 1 in 20 owned a car. Everyone was guaranteed a job, minimal subsistence income, and rudimentary housing. [Streissguth 2002]

The economic stability of the USSR during the Brezhnev years was misleading. The crunch came in the late 1970s, with crises in agriculture, transport, and energy. There was probably zero overall growth between 1980 and 1985. After 1978 rationing of key food items was introduced in many outlying regions. [Streissguth 2002]

By 1986 the USSR occupied first place in the world league table only in the production of oil, steel, iron ore, potatoes, and sugar. They occupied sixth place in the production of radios (just behind Singapore), and of passenger cars (behind Italy and France). Given what is known about poor product quality and false statistics, the real situation was even worse. [Streissguth 2002]

The system of central planning which Stalin imposed in the 1930s at tremendous human cost ground on for five decades and transformed the economy of USSR in all its aspects: geography, institutions, social structure, and psychology. The many decades of iron-fisted central planning had left Gorbachev and Yeltsin with a "house built on sand," a terminal economic illness rooted in inefficiency, corruption, and the sheer illogic of running a modern industrial economy through the diagrams of central planning. After 1985, the old system started to break down. The power of central planners steadily eroded, with enterprises and republics behaving in an increasingly independent manner. [Streissguth 2002]

The centrally planned economy, or CPE, was a highly distinctive form of economic organization, in which the conventional laws of supply and demand, taken for granted in the West, did not apply. CPE was the result of a political struggle where all assets (stores, workshops, farms, tools, factories) became the property of the state. It was clear, however, that the Soviet economy was not merely suffering from poor political leadership, nor a cyclical crisis. The economy was declining in productive efficiency, the product of contradictions within the central planning system itself. Despite these chronic economic problems, the key political and economic elites were interested in preserving the status quo. It was impossible to build a coalition in favor of market reform. [Streissguth 2002]

The Gosplan, State Planning Committee, drew up a grid chart matching the flow of available inputs (labor, capital, and raw materials) with the set of desired outputs. Beneath Gosplan were some 60 economic ministries, supervising 120,000 factories, farm and other units in industry, construction, commerce, and agriculture. [Streissguth 2002]

The party tried to use its monopoly of political authority to lay down priorities – such as saving energy or building a pipeline. Unfortunately, there were so many 'priorities' in force that the center lost the ability to make much of an impact. The biggest headache facing Soviet managers on a daily basis was the unreliability of supplies. The Soviet economy seemed to operate under conditions of permanent shortage. Plans were so 'taut' that even the smallest interruption in deliveries could threaten plan fulfillment, and in response, managers hoarded stocks or traded on informal networks to procure the supplies they needed. [Streissguth 2002]

A striking feature of the CPE was the passive role played by money and prices. Planning took place in physical terms, and money flows were only calculated after the basic plan was constructed. Prices bore scant relation to production costs – retail prices covered only about one-third of the cost of producing food, for example. Managers worried about meeting output targets and did not care whether or not they made a profit. They knew that at the end of the year their ministry would always cover their losses. [Streissguth 2002]

The CPE suited some economic sectors better than others. The system had been designed to maximize the growth of the military-industrial sector, which accounted for at least 25 percent of the Soviet industry. Mining and heavy industry also did fairly well, but agriculture, construction, and consumer goods and services were all severely deformed. [Streissguth 2002]

In Cuba, as the 1980s opened, farmers were allowed to sell the surplus to their state quotas in markets where prices were unregulated and transactions were between private persons. Enterprises were allowed to retain some profits to distribute to managers and workers at the end of the year and to improve the enterprise and working conditions. [Bethell 1993]

Highlights for Chapter 11

- The third defining feature of a consolidated communist system is non-capitalist ownership of the means of production.
- The fourth defining feature – the dominance of a command economy, as distinct from a market economy.
- Economic control is not merely control of a sector of human life which can be separated from the rest; it is the control of the means for all our ends.
- One of the greatest failures of communist economic systems was in creating new technology.

- Collectivization did not encourage new investments in agricultural equipment.
- Survival meant making deals outside the law and the plan, and a black market in machinery, raw materials, and consumer goods.
- Lenin realized that neither the workers nor the peasants were really interested in Marxism or in revolution; they simply wanted to improve their own material situation.
- In March 1917 bread rationing was introduced in the capital, and badly organized.
- In their effort to rebuild the economy the Bolsheviks returned to the principles of capitalism.
- After the first two or three years of the new economic system, the government had reasons to be pleased with the results.
- Agriculture was first to catch up with pre-war production standards. Light industry (factories that produced consumer goods) was next to improve, and heavy industry was slowest to recover.
- It may be that many workers derived psychological benefits from living in a political system that was described as the "dictatorship of the proletariat."
- The workers did also have some tangible gains. The state was building a bureaucracy.
- The expropriations of food and the seizures of private business and factories had their effects: Russian industry was all but destroyed, a terrible famine raged in the countryside, and the country had to rely on foreign aid to fend off mass starvation.
- The peasants were now required to give only a part of their produce to the state and were allowed to keep or sell the rest.
- Stalin's industrialization strategy turned the USSR into the world's second-largest economy. But Soviet citizens saw precious few of the benefits.
- By 1986 the USSR occupied first place in the world league table only in the production of oil, steel, iron ore, potatoes, and sugar.
- There need be little difficulty in planning the economic life of a family, comparatively little in a small community. But, as the scale increases, the amount of agreement on the order of ends decreases and the necessity to rely on force and compulsion grows.

- Once a plan is put into execution, all the resources of the planned area must serve that plan – there can be no exemption for those who feel they could do better for themselves.
- It is a fallacy that economic planning is merely a technical task which can be solved in a strictly objective manner by experts.
- The system of central planning which Stalin imposed in the 1930s represented a tremendous human cost.
- The economy was declining in productive efficiency, the product of contradictions within the central planning system itself.
- The party tried to use its monopoly of political authority to lay down priorities – such as saving energy or building a pipeline.
- A striking feature of the CPE was the passive role played by money and prices.
- The CPE had been designed to maximize the growth of the military-industrial sector, which accounted for at least 25 percent of Soviet industry.
- In Cuba, as the 1980s opened, farmers were allowed to sell the surplus to their state quotas in free-markets.

Chapter 12: The Ideological Sphere

The fifth feature of a communist system is the declared aim of building communism as the ultimate, legitimizing goal. It had an important place in the official ideology and motivational and inspirational significance for a substantial number of party activists. [Brown 2009]

The final goal was the justification for all the toil and hardship that might be encountered along the way. Once that goal was abandoned, communist regimes were in danger of being judged on the basis of their capacity to deliver more immediate results. Without the goal of communism, the 'leading role' of the party would become far harder to legitimize. [Brown 2009]

The sixth defining feature of communism was the existence of, and sense of belonging to, an international communist movement. The existence of that movement was of great ideological significance. It was the supposed internationalism of communism which attracted many of its adherents. For individual members of communist parties, the consciousness of belonging to a great international movement was of huge importance. [Brown 2009]

Rafael Samuel testifies the significance of internationalism for true communist believers, 'The communism of my childhood was universalist. We no longer advocated World Revolution, but we believed that socialism was a cosmic process, we thought of the transition from capitalism to socialism as being 'identical' in content anywhere.' [Brown 2009]

Many communist governments owed their existence to Soviet support, but it involved accepting Soviet leadership (and at times crude domination) of the international communist movement. For communist parties which had made their own revolutions – as was the case, for example, with Albania, China, and Yugoslavia – it was much more difficult to accommodate themselves to Soviet hegemony. [Brown 2009]

The need is for an international political authority which, without power to direct the different people what they must do, must be able to restrain them from action which will damage others. [Hayek 1994]

Liberalism and socialism are completely different. Liberals' political notions of "freedom" and "civil rights," of constitutionalism and parliamentarianism, are derived from the individualistic conception of the world. Socialism must present a conscious and determined opposition to individualism. [Hayek 1994]

Material Conditions and Ideal Ends

Freedom is one of the main ideals of any society. After the creation of the Soviet Union and China communists systems, the world was worried about its future. If in the first attempt to create a world of free men we have failed, we must try again. The guiding principle that a policy of freedom for the individual is the only truly progressive policy remains as true today as it was in the nineteenth century. [Hayek 1994]

Ideals are principles to be aimed at and by themselves, they are not bad. However, when the ideals are invented by theoretical minds without practical support the danger affects up to the level of individuals. A complex civilization as like ours is necessarily based on the individual's adjusting himself to changes whose cause and nature he cannot understand: why he should have more or less, why he should have to move to another occupation, why some things he wants should become more difficult to get than others, will always be connected with such a multitude of circumstances that no single mind will be able to grasp them; or, even worse, those affected will put all the blame on an obvious immediate and avoidable cause, while the more complex interrelationships which determine the change remain inevitably hidden to them. [Hayek 1994]

The society has not progressed at the same speed as the technology. Those who argue that we have to an astounding degree learned to master the forces of nature but are sadly behind in making use of the possibilities of social collaboration are quite right so far as this statement goes. But they are mistaken when they carry the comparison further and argue that we must learn to master the forces of society in the same manner in which we have learned to master the forces of nature. [Hayek 1994]

Communist systems are against freedom. Individual freedom cannot be reconciled with the supremacy of one single purpose to which the whole society must be entirely and permanently subordinated. The only exception to the rule that a free society must not be subject to a single purpose is war and other temporary disasters. It is sensible temporarily to sacrifice freedom in order to make it more secure in the future. [Hayek 1994]

Communists use to apply measures that go against the productivity of a country, most socialist countries are not able to produce food, goods, and services to feed their people. Vague but popular phrases like "full employment" may well lead to extremely shortsighted measures, and where the categorical and irresponsible "it must be done at all cost" of the single-minded idealist is likely to do the great harm. [Hayek 1994]

Society must work in a dynamic environment where decisions are not indefinite. Economic measures must take into consideration all variables and be ready to improve. If trade unions successfully resist any lowering of the wages, there will be only two alternatives open: either coercion will have to be used (i.e., certain individuals will have to be selected for compulsory transfer to other and relatively less well-paid positions) or those who can no longer be employed at the relatively high wages must be allowed to remain unemployed until they are willing to accept work at a relatively lower wage. A socialist society would certainly use coercion in this position. [Hayek 1994]

Artificial means should be avoided, productivity must be measured. To aim at the maximum of employment achievable by monetary means is a policy which is certain in the end to defeat its own purposes. It tends to lower the productivity of labor and thereby increases the proportion of the working population by artificial means. [Hayek 1994]

It may sound noble to say, "Damn economics, let us build up a decent world" - but it is, in fact, merely irresponsible. The only chance of building a decent world is that we can continue to improve the general level of wealth. [Hayek 1994]

Collectivism has been eliminated in all communist countries, there must be a valid reason for that. It is more than doubtful whether a fifty years' approach toward collectivism has raised our moral standards, or whether the change has not rather been in the opposite direction. [Hayek 1994]

Collectivism has nothing to put in their place, and in so far as it has destroyed them it has left a void filled by nothing but the demand for obedience and the compulsion of the individual to do what is collectively decided to be good. [Hayek 1994]

Governments must help their people instead of immobilizing them. Instead of fixed policies, let individuals use the suggestions to build on their strength. Responsibility, not to a superior, but to one's conscience, the awareness of a duty not exacted by compulsion, the necessity to decide which of the things one values are to be sacrificed to others, and to bear the consequences of one's own decisions, are the very essence of any morals which deserve the name. [Hayek 1994]

Diversity produces opportunities, uniformity produces poverty. The virtues which are less esteemed and practiced now – independence, self-reliance, and the willingness to bear risks, the readiness to back one's conviction against a majority, and the willingness to voluntary cooperation with one's neighbors – are essentially those on which the working of an individualistic society rests. [Hayek 1994]

Socialism and communism work for the benefit of minority groups and usually manipulate public opinion through class struggle, setting people against each other. The fixed poles now are no longer the liberty of the individual, his freedom of movement, and scarcely that of speech. They are the protected standards of this or that group, their "right" to exclude others from providing their fellowmen with what they need. Discrimination between members and nonmembers of closed groups is accepted more and more as a matter of course; injustices inflicted on individuals by government action in the interest of a group are disregarded; and the grossest violations of the most elementary rights of the individual. [Hayek 1994]

Socialism and communism are ideologies that go against Western principles. The virtues of Anglo-Saxons were independence and self-reliance, individual initiative and local responsibility, the successful reliance on voluntary activity, noninterference with one's neighbor and tolerance of the different and queer, respect for custom and tradition, and a healthy suspicion of power and authority. [Hayek 1994]

The End of Truth

Nowadays socialist truth is distorted knowledge, interpretations of socialism abound. Each leader makes its own. The word "truth" itself ceases to have its old meaning to become interpreted truth. Truth no longer describes something to be found, with the individual conscience as the sole arbiter of whether in any particular instance the evidence (or standing of those proclaiming it) warrants a belief; it becomes something to be laid down by authority, something which has to be believed in the interest of the unity of the organized effort and which may have to be altered as the exigencies of this organized effort require it. [Hayek 1994]

People must be free to believe what they decide is acceptable. If the ideals and tastes of the great majority are always fashioned by circumstances which we can control, we ought to use this power deliberately to turn the thoughts of the people in what we think is a desirable direction. Probably it is true enough that the great majority are rarely capable of thinking independently, that on most questions they accept views which they find ready-made, and that they will be equally content if born or coaxed into one set of beliefs or another. It certainly does not justify the presumption of any group of people to claim the right to determine what people ought to think or believe. [Hayek 1994]

The interaction of individuals, possessing different knowledge and different views, is what constitutes the life of thought. The growth of reason is a social process based on the existence of such differences. To "plan" or "organize" the growth of mind, or, for that matter, progress in general, is a contradiction in terms. [Hayek 1994]

Under competition, the probability that a man who started poor will reach great wealth is much smaller than is true of the man who has inherited property. However, the competitive system is the only one where it depends solely on him and not on the favors of the mighty, and where nobody can prevent a man from attempting to achieve wealth. We often overlook the patent fact that in every real sense a badly paid unskilled worker in this country has more freedom to shape his life than many small entrepreneurs in Germany or a better-paid engineer or manager in Russia. [Hayek 1994]

Successful planning requires the creation of a common view on the essential values. The restriction of our freedom with regard to material things touches us directly on our spiritual freedom. Knowledge cannot create new ethical values, no amount of learning will lead people to hold the same views on the moral issues which a conscious ordering of all social relations raises. [Hayek 1994]

It is not a rational conviction but the acceptance of a creed which is required to justify a particular plan. It was in these efforts to produce a mass movement supported by such a single world view that the socialists first created most of the instruments of indoctrination of which Nazis and Fascists have made such effective use. [Hayek 1994]

Socialist theory and socialists tactics, even where they have not been dominated by Marxist dogma, instead of integrating society, have been based everywhere on the idea of a division of society into two classes with common and mutually conflicting interests: capitalists and industrial workers. [Hayek 1994]

The socialist state defines the luck of individuals. Advancing towards socialism it becomes evident that income and general position are determined by the coercive apparatus of the state, that to maintain or improve its position it has to be a member of an organized group capable of influencing or controlling the state machine in its interest. [Hayek 1994]

Economic security is often represented as an indispensable condition of real liberty. Yet the idea of economic security is no less vague and ambiguous than more other terms in this field; the demand for security may become a danger to liberty. [Hayek 1994]

"Control," i.e., limitation of output so that prices will secure an "adequate" return, is the only way in which in a market economy producers can be guaranteed a certain income. But this necessarily involves a reduction of opportunities open to others. The striving for security by these means in the last decades has increased unemployment and insecurity for large sections of the population. [Hayek 1994]

Some security is essential if freedom is to be preserved because most men are willing to bear the risk which freedom inevitably involves only so long as that risk is not too great. It is essential that we should re-learn frankly to face the fact that freedom can be had only at a price and that as individuals we must be prepared to make severe material sacrifices to preserve our liberty. Benjamin Franklin expressed, "Those who would give up essential liberty to purchase a little temporary safety deserve neither liberty nor safety." [Hayek 1994]

Freedom in Commercial and Military Organizations

There are two irreconcilable types of social organization: commercial and military. In the army work and worker alike are allocated by authority and where, if the available means are scanty, everybody is alike put on short-commons. This is the only system in which the individual can be conceded full economic security. This security is, however, inseparable from the restrictions on liberty and the hierarchical order of military life – it is the security of the barracks. Either both the choice and the risk rest with the individual or he is relieved of both. [Hayek 1994]

The military type of organization as we know it, gives us, however, only a very inadequate picture of what it would be like if it were extended to the whole society. So long as only a part of society is organized on military lines, the unfreedom of the members of the military organization is mitigated by the fact that there is still a free sphere to which they can move if the restrictions become too irksome. With every grant of complete security to one group the insecurity of the rest necessarily increases. [Hayek 1994]

The Nazis

One socialist experience, not related to the Soviets or international socialism was Nazism, it was born in Germany as the National Socialist German Worker's Party.

Professor Eduard Heimann, one of the leaders of German religious socialism, writes: "Hitlerism proclaims itself as both true democracy and true socialism, and the terrible truth is that there is a grain of truth for such claims – an infinitesimal grain, to be sure, but at any rate enough to serve as a basis for such fantastic distortion. Hitlerism even goes so far as to claim the role of protector of Christianity, and the terrible truth is that even this gross misinterpretation is able to make some impression." [Hayek 1994]

The doctrines of National Socialism are the culmination of a long evolution of thought, a process in which thinkers who have had great influence far beyond the confines of Germany have taken part. It is simply collectivism freed from all traces of an individualist tradition. [Hayek 1994]

The support which brought Nazism to power came precisely from the socialist camp. It was not certainly through the bourgeoisie, but rather through the absence of a strong bourgeoisie, that they were helped to power. The connection between socialism and nationalism in Germany was close from the beginning. It is significant that the most important ancestors of National Socialism – Fichte, Rodbertus, and Lassalle – are at the same time acknowledged fathers of socialism. The war hysteria of 1914 is the beginning of the modern development which produced National Socialism, and it was largely with the assistance of old socialists that it rose during this period. [Hayek 1994]

The "German idea of the state," as formulated by Fitche, Lassalle, and Rodbertus, is that the state is neither founded nor formed by individuals, nor an aggregate of individuals, nor is its purpose to serve any interest of individuals; the individual has no rights but only duties. Claims of the individual are always an outcome of the commercial spirit. There is a life higher than the individual life, the life of the people and the life of the state, and it is the purpose of the individual to sacrifice himself for that higher life. [Hayek 1994]

Referring to the relationship between socialism and Nazism, as early as 1922 a detached observer could speak of a "peculiar and, on a first glance, surprising phenomenon" then to be observed in Germany: "The fight against the capitalistic order, according to this view, is a continuation of the war against the Entente with the weapons of the spirit and of economic organization, the way which leads to practical socialism, a return of the German people to their best and noblest traditions." [Hayek 1994]

Nationalization was also related to Nazism and socialism. Europe's oldest and most important socialist party, the German Social Democratic Party (SDP), was founded in 1863 by the prominent German intellectual Ferdinand Lasalle as a workers association. It was merged with a Marxist workers party in1875, prohibited in 1878 and legalized again in 1890. SDP's theoreticians followed a radical line, for example, calling for nationalization of major industries. In the election of 1912, the party won nearly 35 percent of the vote, having the influence of such leaders as August Bebel and Karl Kautsky, the greatest political theorist after Engels death. [Fleming 2008]

The Nazi ideology is related to socialism even though they tried to stay away from international socialism pressures. The ideology preaches the 'common good' as one of its principles, accepting political interests as the main priority of the economic organization. Nazism is a form of fascism that show disdain for liberal democracy and parliamentary systems. Most importantly, it incorporates antisemitism and a 'cult of violence,' clearly demonstrated during World War II.

A characteristic of the Nazis was that the state was in charge of 51% of the stake in important enterprises and up to 49% in enterprises not so important for the country. Compared with socialism, that pursues 100% stake in all enterprises, there is a huge difference. The state for the Nazis was very powerful but compared to socialists, with so much intervention in the economy, was half the participation. However, Nazis wanted political intervention on all matters.

Alfred Rosenberg was one of the biggest creators of Nazi ideology. The problem with Rosenberg was that he insisted on enforcing racism into his ideals. We know by now that diversity is preferable than discrimination, a society that only imposes restrictions on people is destined to fail. That is why fascism and racism are against human nature. "Where great cultures rose, it was a sign of Aryan influence. The intermixing of races – race chaos – had led to the downfall of the greater societies. ... Only by a return to racial purity could Germany become strong again." [Wittman 2016]

It is incredible that still today some societies talk badly against immigrants. Usually, societies do not improve in one generation, however, rejecting immigrants is negative for development. Most of the time, immigrants bring positive viewpoints into social issues. What is needed is an open mind, people must treat problems from an independent viewpoint that does not penalize foreigners. It is the idea that must be discussed and dealt with, not the source of the idea, local or foreign.

The Nazi ideology was rooted on annihilation, "National Socialism is an ideology, and that ideology is to be found in Rosenberg's Myth of the Twentieth Century," A party training official said at an indoctrination session for university students in September 1935. "People who do not possess our faith, or cannot possess it on account of their racial inferiority, must be eliminated." [Wittman 2016]

Invading territories with the purpose of taking over resources was a risky business. Hitler's conqueror mentality was against himself. A better approach would have been negotiating product exchanges.

Willing to conquer the world and annihilating the Jews was an epic enterprise that did not convince humanity. Talking about some people questioning the Nazis movement, the founders rejected criticism. Had the very idea of Nazism been wrong from the start? No, no, Rosenberg replied. "A great idea has been misused by small men." The history of humanity would not be able to forget what happened to the Nazis. Hans Frank took the stand, he confessed his guilt in the annihilation of the Jews. "A thousand years will pass and still Germany's guilt will not have been erased." [Wittman 2016]

"We recognize that the death camp was not just a bad thing that happened but an evil that was done. And all the officials were implicated in this evil. As Arendt and Stangneth both point out, the camps were designed not merely to destroy human beings but also to deprive them of their humanity. The inmates were to be treated as things, humiliated, degraded, reduced to a condition of bare, unsupported, and all-consuming need, which would cancel in them the last vestiges of freedom. In other words, the goal included robbing the inmates of their souls. The camps were animated by anti-spirit, and people caught up in them stumbled around as though burdened by a great negation sign." [Scruton 2017]

On the left, Nazism was defined in broadly Marxist terms. Orthodox Marxist thinkers perceived it to be a mass movement manipulated by big business and finance in a last-ditch attempt to defend capitalism from Socialism. [Williamson 2002]

The nationalist school of historians within Germany in 1933, interpreted Hitler's rise to power as a national revolution, which was both anti-Liberal and anti-Marxist. Herman Rauschning argued that Nazism was a 'revolutionary power whose creed was an action for action's sake and whose tactics were the destruction and undermining of all that is in the existing order.' [Williamson 2002]

For West Germans, and increasingly the West as a whole, Nazism was seen as a variant of totalitarianism. According to Carl Friedrich, it had in common with Russian communism 'a total ideology, a single mass party, terrorist secret police, a monopoly of mass communications, a monopoly of weapons, and a centrally directed planned economy.' [Williamson 2002]

In assessing the nature of Nazism, contemporaries raised questions which are still relevant today: was it a version of Fascism or totalitarianism which had more in common with Stalin's Russia than Mussolini's Italy, or was it a unique revolutionary phenomenon? National Socialism was, as Bracher has pointed out, 'a conglomerate of ideas and precepts, hopes and emotions, welded together by a radical political movement in a time of crisis.' A key component was the belief in German racial superiority, the origins of which can be traced back to the potent merging of Nationalism and Romanticism during the Napoleonic Wars at the beginning of the nineteenth century. [Williamson 2002]

Nazi's Organization

Sombart wrote a book about war, it is devoted to the conflict between the "Ideas of 1789," the ideal of freedom, and the "Ideas of 1914," the ideal of organization. It is the struggle for the victory of the new forces born out of the advanced economic life of the nineteenth century: socialism and organization. [Hayek 1994]

The war economy created in Germany in 1914 "is the first realization of a socialist society and its spirit the first active, and not merely demanding, the appearance of a socialist spirit. The needs of the war have established the socialist idea in German economic life, and thus the defense of our nation produced for humanity the idea of 1914, the idea of a German organization, the people's community of national socialism, where state and economic life form a new unity." [Hayek 1994]

Professor Plenge hoped at first to reconcile the ideal of liberty and the ideal of the organization, but soon these traces of liberal ideas disappeared from his writings. "It is high time to recognize the fact that socialism must be power policy because it is to be organized. Socialism has to win power: it must never blindly destroy power." [Hayek 1994]

Talking about the organization, the famous chemist Wilhelm Ostwald stated publicly that "Germany wants to organize Europe which up to now lacks organization. We, or perhaps the German race, have discovered the significance of the organization. While the other nations still live under the regime of individualism, we have already achieved that of the organization." [Hayek 1994]

Mao Zedong's

In 'On people's democratic dictatorship,' published in 1949, Mao Zedong had declared that the dictatorship would be exercised by four classes: at the center would be the working class, followed by the peasants, the bourgeoisie, and finally, on the periphery but nevertheless numbered among the people, the national bourgeoisie. [Roberts 2003]

In 1949, in the atmosphere of the Cold War, Mao declared that China 'must lean either to the side of imperialism or to the side of socialism,' and it meant leaning towards the Soviet Union. In December 1949 Mao made his first foreign visit, traveling to Moscow to negotiate with Stalin the Treaty of Alliance and Mutual Assistance, which he signed in February 1950. [Roberts 2003]

By 1949, it has been said, all CCP leaders had accepted the proposition that 'while only a peasant revolution could bring the Party to power, only an urban industrial revolution could lay the basis for an independent socialist society.' [Roberts 2003]

In 1953, now that the country had largely recovered from the war and an armistice had been signed in Korea, a moderate but important policy shift took place. In August, Mao Zedong announced the general line for the transition to socialism, which he said would be accomplished 'over a fairly long period of time.' The transition would come under centralized planning, following the course taken by the Soviet Union under Stalin. The First Five-Year Plan was initiated. [Roberts 2003]

Soviet's

The emergence of the Soviet Union was sui generis, based on an ideology, the desire to build a society wholly different from all others in history, and it was to be the beginning of a new era, a just and progressive society. It was to be a new beginning in the annals of humankind. [Laqueur 2015]

The 'Lenin's theory of socialist revolution' was not a consistent, synthesized body of theory. Its salient features were: the maximum manipulation of public opinion; the frenzied cultivation of the image of the class enemy, whether the Tsar, the bourgeoisie, the Mensheviks or the liberals; the desintegration of the army and state machine by means of outright rabble-rousing; pushing the state and the regime towards chaos and dislocation; staging a coup at the precise moment when the government was most weakened and compromised; establishing a harsh dictatorship which took away 'bourgeois liberties and rights;' using terror as a means of keeping millions of people in check; unleashing civil war. [Streissguth 2002]

These features were implemented by a disciplined, organized party led by professional revolutionaries like Lenin himself, people capable of issuing an order to reduce rations to the population: 'Let thousands die, but the country will be saved.' Lenin logic was that some should be killed so that others should live. [Streissguth 2002]

The Russian revolution preserved the traditional popular link between mystique and practice. Lenin's dogmas became the mystique, and destruction became the practice. [Streissguth 2002]

The system ideology was not built methodically according to some predefined blueprint. It was, rather, improvised under the pressure of constant emergencies, although ideologies and programs of the previous era did play their role. A distaste for markets and special relationship with the working class, for example. But these ideological preferences produced more than just facts. They also engendered illusions that are best illustrated by the policies subsumed under the term War Communism. [Streissguth 2002]

An "illusion in action" or, to use a better term, "utopia" is a powerful mobilizer, and yet its results can be – and were – quite different from what was hoped for. Although improvised, the key institution of the new system, the party, was created and recreated in the course of the events. Party cadres, during their short history before October 1917, had trained themselves to be leaders in a revolution that was not even supposed to be socialist. [Streissguth 2002]

The doctrine or ideology in Russia has several components: religion (The Orthodox Church, Russia's holy mission, the third Rome, and the

New Jerusalem), patriotism/nationalism (including chauvinism), geopolitics Russian style, Eurasianism, the besieged-fortress feeling, and zapadophobia (fear of the West). Religion, or rather the Orthodox Church, is of great importance to any ideological reorientation. Under communist rule, the church suffered. Churches were closed, churchgoers were harassed, and priests were imprisoned, exiled, and even killed. [Laqueur 2015]

Before the revolution, the church was probably closer to the state than in any other country. However, the Moscow Patriarchate has recently shown a little caution: even while trying to evade conflicts with the state, it has demonstrated that it does not implicitly support every policy mandated by the government. [Laqueur 2015]

There has been a massive shift in the ideology of the Russian regime in the years since the downfall of the Soviet Union. Marxism-Leninism has been replaced by Russian nationalism and the glorification of a strong state. At present, the process of transition from communism to some form of state capitalism under the supervision of the organs of state security is by no means complete, and it is impossible to know where this reorientation, the search for a new Russian idea, will lead. [Laqueur 2015]

It is frequently argued that Russia has become deeply conservative, patriotic, and religious. But sociological investigations so far call for caution, because the fact that the mainline ideology has changed so much does not indicate much about the depth with which these new convictions are held. [Laqueur 2015]

A great majority would like to see their country a major power, a superpower if possible, but are reluctant to make great efforts, especially financial efforts, to achieve this. The great majority are not motivated by ideology; their psychology and ambitions are primarily those of members of a consumer society. [Laqueur 2015]

Contemporary Russia is a traditional society, and the majority of its people are averse to change. But conservative values does not overwhelmingly shape their outlook and behavior. There are apparently no more true conservatives than liberals in contemporary Russia. According to investigations, religion ranges as an actor of paramount importance for 8 percent of the population. Patriotism, with 14 percent, figures somewhat higher. [Laqueur 2015]

Africa's

Mbeki, from South Africa, claimed that he and Mugabe were comrades in the liberation struggle. The ANC in South Africa and ZANU in Zimbabwe had very different origins and philosophies. The opposing philosophies of their liberation movements, Africanist and Marxist, had made them enemies in the past. The ANC was based on Marxism, identifying the poor of Africa as Marx's working class oppressed by a capitalist ruling class. ZANU was pan-Africanist, race, not class, was the ultimate dividing line. [Dowden 2009]

China's Deng

"In dealing with ideology problems we must never use coercion," and "We must firmly put a stop to bad practices such as attacking and trying to silence people who make critical comments." Deng manifested on December 1978. [Schell 2013]

On March 30, 1979, Deng gave another defining speech to a group of ranking officials, this time on the limits to "emancipating the mind." In it he focused on upholding the "Four Cardinal Principles" that were to become the foundation of Deng's future leadership: adherence to socialism, people's democratic dictatorship, party leadership, and Marxist-Leninist-Maoist thought. [Schell 2013]

North Korea's Juche

For North Korea, what matters is the subjective basis on which regime legitimacy is established rather than such objective factors as economic output or material living conditions. [Miller 2004]

In June 2000, Kim Jong Il reportedly said that "we can make a great unified country when South Korea's economic and technological assets become empowered with North Korea's spiritual and ideological achievement." [Miller 2004]

Another strategic policy under Kim Jong Il is ultranationalism. The nationalism of Kim Il Sung had helped solidify power and consolidate the republic. Nationalism helps to protect regime stability and integrate the political system. [Miller 2004]

With little international support outside China and the Soviet Union, the DPRK emphasized its Juche (self-reliance) policy as both a domestic scheme and an independent foreign policy as opposed to any kind of imperialism. Kim Il Sung stressed the importance of the struggle against US hegemony. [Miller 2004]

Juche is based on human self-determination, and Juche also promotes national self-sufficiency. The idea that man is the center of the universe is by no means a new perspective; nor is the doctrine of political sovereignty or self-determination. Furthermore, nothing is new about Juche's emphasis on human consciousness as the determinant of human behavior. For example, North Korea opposes the modern global economy because it makes nations with raw materials and labor dependent on nations with capital and technology. [Miller 2004]

No person should be subjected to another person's capricious control, nor should be submitted to institutional manipulation. Institutions, as in the case of science, are designed to serve human beings rather than be served by them. Even ideologies themselves are regarded as institutional means to human well-being. Another component of human nature is faculty, which makes value judgment possible. Humans are endowed with the natural right and capability to make behavioral choices through free consciousness. [Miller 2004]

These elements of human nature are to be cultivated and developed through socialization and political education. For this reason, ideological education becomes an integral part of human development, and such education should be continuous throughout one's life. The practice of 'education through work' in the form of a factory college should be seen in this vein. [Miller 2004]

The human faculty is viewed as having a series of concomitant properties. They are consciousness (Uisiksong), creativity (Changuisong), and self-determination (Jajusong). Practically all workplaces and schools in North Korea are required to set aside at least one full day each week for study-learning (haksop) in which every citizen participates. [Miller 2004]

Cuba's Marxism-Leninism

On December 1961, Fidel Castro proclaimed that he was Marxist-Leninist and that he would be so until death. The making of a radical revolution in Cuba required a break with the United States and support from the Soviet Union. [Bethell 1993]

When Fidel Castro and his bearded guerrillas triumphantly entered Havana on the evening of January 8, 1959, no one could have predicted the direction of the revolution. Yet, by the middle of April 1961 the defining themes of the revolution were clearly in place. A socialist economy was developed with programs designed specifically to redistribute wealth and address the needs of the poor majority in Cuba. [Staten 2005]

In 1961, Fidel Castro summarized the regime's cultural policies in an ambiguous phrase: 'Within the revolution, everything; against the revolution, nothing.' Material opposed to the revolution was not published; that which was not explicitly critical of the regime but produced by its known opponents was judged unconventional and unacceptable by the government (e.g., actual or rumored homosexual behavior) had an uncertain fate; homosexuals suffered the greatest hostility in the late 1960s and again in 1980. [Bethell 1993]

Castro used his immense popularity and charisma to mobilize the passions and will of the people toward the creation of a 'new socialist man.' The new socialist man was to be committed to an egalitarian society and place the needs of the community before himself. Laborers were to work for the good of society rather than personal gain. They were to work hard out of a moral commitment to the building of a socialist community. [Staten 2005]

In support of this commitment to an egalitarian society, the government provided access to social services free of charge. Healthcare, education, daycare, social security, and much housing were provided free to all Cubans. [Staten 2005]

Revolutionary idealism, spirit, excitement and fervor eventually give way to the realities of everyday life. The 1960s radical experiment was born of idealism as well as the concept of social justice, Fidel Castro's charisma, the challenge and hostility of the United States and the growth of Cuban nationalism. [Staten 2005]

'Socialism didn't arrive here through cloning or through artificial insemination.' The 1960s, in particular, were a time when Castro and his associates took seriously the idea of creating a 'new man' or 'new socialist person' and the building of a 'moral economy' rather than one based on material incentives. [Brown 2009]

In the 1970s there was something of a retreat from the utopian urge to create a 'new socialist person' and more emphasis on consolidating 'socialist' – meaning communist – institutions. The Communist Party as an organization became increasingly central to the Cuban political and economic system. [Brown 2009]

Revolutionary idealism with its emphasis on community rather than private gain was emphasized once again. Imports were cut and wages were reduced except in the case of the poorest workers whose wages were actually increased. [Staten 2005]

Cuban internationalism of this period had another component that received little notice in the Western countries. This component sent thousands of Cuban doctors, teachers, construction workers, agronomists and other development project specialists (in irrigation, mining, fishing, cattle raising and sugar production) to Africa and other parts of the developing world. [Staten 2005]

Venezuela's Absurd (Twenty-First Century) Socialism

Venezuela has many similarities with Nazi's Germany in the form Absurd Socialism seized power. Chavez used the democratic infrastructure to build upon his hidden intentions, to develop another communist system in the Caribbean. Using the word socialism over and over, and without the consent of the population, he was building popular opinion to transform the country toward a new socialist perspective. The constitution of the country does not mention the word socialism in any of its articles.

Chavez wanted to follow a path similar to Cuba, but in fact, he moved closer to African dictators. Power was the main objective, the destruction of the wealthy population was like an avenge and the embezzlement of public funds became the day to day activity for public officials.

Chavez had clear intentions, followed by actions, to destroy private infrastructure. All the land and factories seized by the government ended unproductive on the hands of the people taking charge. These people were incapable of making their new ownership progress, they lacked knowledge and stamina. Chavez was not successful in making the economic progress, he knew how to spend money though.

Chavez was planning to communalize agriculture, industry, and services, building a society where the community was in charge of all their needs. Chavez knew how to spend money coming from the petroleum industry, but he did not know how to produce wealth. He thought the income from the oil industry was enough to feed his people; he was mistaken.

Another clear similarity with Venezuela is Africa dictatorships. In the same way that African countries squandered their oil or mineral income for Strong Men benefits, Venezuela did the same, obeying Chavez dictatorship to maintain collapsed institutions that did not increase the wealth of the population. The damage to the nation can amount to one thousand billion dollars during Chavez and Maduro regimes.

Highlights for Chapter 12

- The fifth feature of a communist system is the declared aim of building communism as the ultimate, legitimizing goal.
- The sixth defining feature of communism was the existence of, and sense of belonging to, an international communist movement.
- "Hitlerism proclaims itself as both true democracy and true socialism, and the terrible truth is that there is a grain of truth for such claims."
- The support which brought Nazism to power came precisely from the socialist camp.
- There is conflict in Nazism between the "Ideas of 1789," the ideal of freedom, and the "Ideas of 1914," the ideal of the organization.
- "People who do not possess our faith, or cannot possess it on account of their racial inferiority, must be eliminated."
- "A thousand years will pass and still Nazi Germany's guilt will not have been erased."
- Nazism had in common with Russian communism 'a total ideology, a single mass party, terrorist secret police.'
- 'While only a peasant revolution could bring the Party to power, only an urban industrial revolution could lay the basis for an independent socialist society.'
- The emergence of the Soviet Union was sui generis, based on an ideology, the desire to build a new society.
- The categorical and irresponsible "it must be done at all cost" of the single-minded idealist is likely to do the great harm.
- Responsibility, not to a superior, but to one's conscience, is the very essence of any morals which deserve the name.
- The interaction of individuals, possessing different knowledge and different views, is what constitutes the life of thought.
- Advancing towards socialism, it becomes evident that income and general position are determined by the coercive apparatus of the state.
- The 'Lenin's theory of socialist revolution' was not a consistent, synthesized body of theory.

- Marxism-Leninism has been replaced by Russian nationalism and the glorification of a strong state.
- "In dealing with ideology problems we must never use coercion," Deng manifested on December 1978.
- For North Korea, what matters is subjective rather than such objective factors as economic output or material living conditions.
- North Korea emphasized its Juche (self-reliance) policy.
- No person should be subjected to another person's capricious control, nor should be submitted to institutional manipulation.
- These elements of human nature are to be cultivated and developed through socialization and political education.
- The human faculty is viewed as having a series of concomitant properties. They are consciousness (Uisiksong), creativity (Changuisong), and self-determination (Jajusong).
- On December 1961, Fidel Castro proclaimed that he was Marxist-Leninist and that he would be so until death.
- Fidel Castro said, 'Within the revolution, everything; against the revolution, nothing.'
- In Cuba, an egalitarian society placed the needs of the community before the individual.
- The Communist Party as an organization became increasingly central to the Cuban political and economic system.
- Cuban internationalism sent thousands of Cuban professionals to different countries.
- Venezuela has many similarities with Nazi's Germany in the way its 'socialism' seized power.
- Chavez wanted to follow a path similar to Cuba, but in fact, he moved closer to African dictators.
- Chavez had clear intentions, followed by actions, to destroy private infrastructure.
- Chavez thought the income from the oil industry was enough to feed his people; he was mistaken.
- The damage to the nation can amount to one thousand billion dollars during the Chavez and Maduro regimes.

Chapter 13: The Strong Man

Africa is the continent that has produced most dictators, and African leaders do not emerge from thin air. They are products of their societies. Many of the first generation leaders were first in their families to receive a Western education, however, their backgrounds varied. Most precolonial African political systems contained strong democratic elements. African kings and states were constrained by checks and balances such as committees of elders or spirit mediums. They made sure the king ruled well and in accordance with custom and religion. If a king ruled badly he could be deposed. [Dowden 2009]

African rulers are not different from rulers anywhere. What makes them different may be that elsewhere rulers are constrained by constitutions, institutions and pressure groups that prevent them from becoming megalomaniac or kleptocratic dictators. African politics are all local and personal. Africa's one-party states increasingly became one-man states – the Strong Man or Big Man syndrome. All tyrants suffer from the same apocalyptic monomania, but in the late twentieth century Africa provided some of the most spectacular examples. [Dowden 2009]

In his book Dispatches from a Fragile Continent, the American journalist Blaine Harden described the classic African President: 'His face in on the money. His photograph hangs in every office in the realm. His ministers wear gold pins with tiny photographs of Him on the lapels of their tailored pinstriped suits. He names streets, football stadiums, hospitals, and universities after himself...' [Dowden 2009]

Nelson Mandela argued that poverty is the cause of Africa's Strong Man syndrome. In a speech at the London School of Economics in 2000, he reminded his audience of the backgrounds of most African rulers: 'Children go to school without any learning aids. Taught in a language which is not theirs, by teachers often not so very qualified... Poor children eating porridge in the morning, porridge at lunch, porridge as their dinner, unable to concentrate...' Mandela begged to understand and asked that Africa's rulers should not be judged by Western standards because they had grown up in poverty. 'When you assess the achievements and failures of Africa you must keep this background in mind.' [Dowden 2009]

With all the powers of statehood at their disposal, doling out jobs, declaring states of emergency, deploying the police, the Strong Man demanded and often got blind obedience. Strong Men identified personally and totally with the power of office. The president became the presidency with no distinction between the self and the office, L'etat c'est moi, the dictum of France's King Louis XIV, was also good if the well-worn joke in Moi's Kenya. [Dowden 2009]

Mobutu Sese Seko, who ruled Zaire, now renamed Congo, was the ultimate Strong Man. He gave himself a string of titles that outdid even Idi Amin. His name means 'The Cock that Covers all the Chickens.' Mobuto promoted authenticité, a return to African values – though there was nothing made in Africa in his palaces, and he began each day with pink champagne. He treated the country as its founder, King Leopold of Belgium, had done: a private state that owned outright, its people his slaves. He stayed in power by leasing out state contracts, offices and positions to other political players. In return they had to pay hum a percentage. All officials, from ministers to soldiers, were allowed to steal whatever they wanted through bribes or theft from the ordinary people. [Dowden 2009]

In the 1970s, the Strong Man often became the Strong Military Man. Africa suffered at least forty military coups in its first two decades of independence. Western diplomats said, 'Of course we don't like military governments, but it is stable, less corrupt and more popular than what was there before.' All of Nigeria's military coups were popular when they happened, though their popularity didn't last long. One that did was in Burkina Faso. Captain Thomas Sankara seized power in 1983 and was genuinely popular. [Dowden 2009]

By the late 1980s, outside Botswana, Senegal and Gambia, Africans lived one-party states, mostly ruled by Presidents for life. African states were simply crumbling away like old colonial mansions that had fallen into desuetude. The elites who seized the instruments and symbols of power from the departing imperial powers had stopped the process of democratization dead. [Dowden 2009]

In most cases, military dictators looted their countries, impoverished their peoples and charmed Western visitors. At the time their people grumbled and occasionally rioted, but rarely were military governments challenged. That applies to most of Africa. Only three times did Africans rise up against military governments in the popular movement. The first was in Sudan in 1985. The second was in Togo in 1991. The third was in Cote d"ivoire in 2001. [Dowden 2009]

For outsiders, the passivity of Africans in the face of appalling oppression was depressing. It was embarrassing that South African blacks, who were physically better off and freer than most of their fellow Africans, were organizing mass resistance while in the rest of Africa, where criticism of the government could mean death and people were is desperate poverty, there was merely resignation. [Dowden 2009]

At the heart of African politics is an attitude to power. Power whether used for good or evil, is widely revered for its own sake. The Big Man is given great respect because he has power. Many African societies traditionally had little sense of equality, and even today you can be shocked to see people prostrate themselves before their superiors. [Dowden 2009]

To avoid adversarial party politics, President of Tanzania Nyerere instituted a one-party state with elections for individual candidates rather than parties. Other African rulers did the same for the more obvious reason that they wanted total power, making themselves 'President for life' at the same time. [Dowden 2009]

Stalin

Josif Vissarionovich Djugashvili was born on 21 December 1879. His mother who doted on her baby son, called him Soso. In later life he was going to take the name Stalin, 'man of steel,' and become one of the evilest tyrants in history. [Evans 2005]

On October 1917, Stalin maneuvered himself into a most advantageous position, although he had played little part in the events. He became Commissar of Nationalities and two years later he joined the Politburo and in 1922, he became the General Secretary of the Communist Party. He used his position to place friends in important positions in local and central government, expecting his patronage to be repaid. [Evans 2005]

During the period immediately after Lenin's death, the Soviet Union was first governed jointly by a triumvirate of Kamenev, Zinoviev and Stalin, whose common aim was to oppose Trotsky. In 1929, Trotsky was banished from the Soviet Union and after spending some time in Turkey and France finally settled in Mexico. All along, Stalin's opponents had underestimated him and their hatred of Trotsky had blinded them to the ambitions of Stalin. One by one the unprincipled schemer dismissed and replaced the leadership with men on whose unquestioning support he could depend. Now Stalin was supreme in Russia, in effect, he was already a dictator. [Evans 2005]

In a conversation with a fellow Georgian in the mid1930s, Stalin said that 'people need a tsar,' i.e., someone to revere and in whose name to live and labor. Stalin himself believed that the extravagant build-up of his 'image' as a charismatic, almost superhuman, leader helped to solidify support for communism and to bestow on it legitimacy. [Brown 2009]

It was Stalin, people believed, who had led them to a great victory. The fact that no alternative standpoint – such as information about Stalin's culpability for the earlier losses – could be aired in the mass media, or published even in the smallest circulation book, naturally reinforced rosy views of Stalin and of the invincibility of the Soviet Union. [Brown 2009]

The view most commonly held is that Stalin had a lust for power and that the Terror was a tool he used deliberately to destroy his rivals and those opposed to his policies and, at the same time, indicate to the Russian people that he would not tolerate any opposition to his rule. [Evans 2005

Of course, millions of Russians already knew the truth about Stalin since they had either been victims or relatives and friends of victims who had suffered under his rule. These, together with the thousands released from the labor camps, reacted strongly against Stalin and Stalinism. [Evans 2005]

In 1956, Nikita Khrushchev accused Stalin of flagrant abuses of power, acts of gross brutality and developing his own cult of personality. Khrushchev detailed the mass arrests of the purges, the unjustified executions and the suffering of those sent yo the labor camps. He accused Stalin of the murder of Kirov and called for the rehabilitation of Trotsky. [Evans 2005]

Hitler

To the end, Rosenberg held fast to the righteousness of the Nazi cause and to Hitler's greatness, for all his flaws. "I venerated him, and I remained loyal to him to the end." "And now Germany's destruction has come with his own. Sometimes hatred rises in me when I think of the millions of Germans who have been murdered and exiled, of the unspeakable misery, the plundering of the little that remained, and the squandering of a thousand-year-old wealth. But then again there rises in me the feeling of pity for a man who also was a victim of fate, and who loved this Germany as ardently as any of us." [Wittman 2016]

The only arbiter between the masses of conflicting agencies which composed the Third Reich was Hitler himself. In theory, Hitler was all-powerful. He combined in his position as Fuhrer 'the functions of a supreme legislator, supreme administrator and supreme judge,' and was also 'the leader of the Party, the Army and the People.' [Williamson 2002]

Hitler hated paper work and delegated as much of it as possible to his subordinates. He disliked the mental effort required to come to a decision and usually preferred to let events take their course rather than intervene. His vague declarations of intent were impossible to translate precisely into clear laws and directives. It was difficult to obtain a decision from him, especially when he was in his remote chalet in the Berghof. [Williamson 2002]

Yet Hitler was no weak dictator. In a negative sense he did control Germany, in that he had broken most potential centers of opposition to the regime. He was interested in foreign policy and rearmament and he was capable of implementing his policies. Perhaps his weakness depended rather on the inherent instability of the regime he had created. [Williamson 2002]

Hitler had no intention of expropriating private industry as long as it was useful to him. There was a concentration of monopoly power by such firms as I.G. Farben, the large chemical combine. Big business remained a partner of the Nazi regime, but it was a partnership that could be terminated by the Nazi Party in the event of a clash of interests. [Williamson 2002]

According to Hitler, the Jews were behind the great political ideals, including communism and capitalism, and Germans were afraid of losing their country to unwanted ideals. "Rosenberg went beyond that: he argued that the Jews, intent on controlling not just the Soviet Union and Germany but the entire world, were controlling both capitalism and communism. This was a great Jewish scam. They were pulling all the strings. They were playing both sides against the middle. On the heels of the brief but bloody 1919 communist uprising in Munich, it was not difficult for Rosenberg's readers and Hitler's listeners to envision apocalyptic consequences should the Reds rule in Germany." [Wittman 2016]

Jews were all over the world, therefore any political ideology had Jewish partisans. To blame Jews for any world ideology was insane, it was a pity that the German people followed Hitler blindly. It was clear since the beginning that Hitler was taking the wrong path to solving society issues. Toward the second half of 1920, Hitler added a significant new element to his speeches. He began using explicit warnings that the Jews who had brought Bolshevism to the Soviet Union now wanted to impose it on Germany.

Hess said he had read Rosenberg's Myth, Hitler Mein Kampf, and Goebbels' newspaper editorial. "For me as an old fanatic of National Socialist, I took it all as fact – just as a Catholic believes in his church dogma," he said. "It was just truth without question; I had no doubt about that. I was absolutely convinced that the Jews were the opposite pole from the German people, and sooner or later there would have to be a showdown." From the books, he said, he learned that though the Jews were a minority, they controlled the press, the radio, the films. So when Himmler told him his duty was to exterminate Jews, "it fitted in with all that had been preached to me for years." [Wittman 2016]

The Jews were blamed of many wrongdoings. The Jews were guilty of anything that did not work well in the country. Not only in Germany but also in the Soviet Union, "In 1920, Rosenberg planted the insidious idea in Hitler's mind that a Global Jewish conspiracy was behind the communist revolution in the Soviet Union, and he repeated the claim over and over. Rosenberg was the preeminent champion of a theory that Hitler used to justify Germany's devastating war against the Soviets two decades on. Not least, Rosenberg laid the groundwork for the holocaust." [Wittman 2016]

Hitler cleverly played on the nation's longing for unity and recovery. He hid his brutal anti-Semitism and his grandiose plans for expansion into eastern Europe. He appealed to the conservative millions of Germany by pledging the new government to 'take under its firm protection Christianity as the basis of our morality and the family as the nucleus of our nation and state.' Hitler's economic plans were vague, but he did promise to save the farmer and to launch 'a massive and comprehensive attack on unemployment.' [Williamson 2002]

Hitler's strength lay not in the originality of his ideas but in the way in which he expressed them and captured the incandescent anger, fear and deep resentment of the middle classes about what was happening to them and their country. National Socialism could certainly exist without Hitler, but it was he who turned it into a major force, first in Bavaria and later in the Reich as a whole, through his ceaseless propaganda and mobilisation of the masses. [Williamson 2002]

Convinced now that he was no longer a 'drummer' but a man of destiny called to save Germany, he systematically defeated all attempts to debate policy or share decision-making and promoted an image of himself as a 'myth person' or 'demi-god' who stood far above the mundane arguments and bitter disagreements that frequently occurred within the party. In that sense the Fuhrer cult helped integrate the disparate groups with conflicting interests, which made up the Nazi Party, into a coherent whole. [Williamson 2002]

Hitler was trying to justify his ideology. The Church, communism, and the Jews were the main targets, "Rosenberg was the Fuhrer's delegate for ideological matters. Adolf Hitler and Alfred Rosenberg had much in common. The major problems of the day: the destructiveness of the churches, the danger of communism, and the menace of the Jews." [Wittman 2016]

Most totalitarian regimes identify who may their enemies be. They need to invent enemies to be blamed for their bad performance. Trying to justify a new view of the world is difficult if you have no enemies. It is easy to confront than to share. Hitler started his confrontational ideology using Rosenberg suggestions.

Mein Kampf, most of which was written in prison, provides the essential key to understanding his first principles, even though it is not a precise blueprint for the future. Page after page Hitler interprets the world as an arena where the supposedly creative forces of the Aryan races clash with the allegedly cunning and evil agents of world Jewry, who operated from their base in Bolshevik Russia. Hitler defined the state in ethnic terms and his whole programme for regenerating Germany depended ultimately on creating a racially pure state, which would be strengthened by the colonization of western Russia. [Williamson 2002]

"Hitler did not have to destroy democracy; he merely took advantage of the decay of democracy and at the crucial moment obtained the support of many to whom, though they detested Hitler, he yet seemed the only man strong enough to get things done." [Hayek 1994]

The party rallies at Nuremberg were more than practical conventions. They were mystical ceremonies designed to demonstrate the strength of the Nazi mass movement and feed the Fuhrer cult. Hitler would stand on the balcony at his hotel, the Deutscher Hof, above a sign reading Hail Hitler in lights on the facade, and salute crowds of Germans who, one reporter recalled, "looked up at him as if he were a Messiah." Was it a wonder that Germans treated Hitler's every word as something akin to the gospel? [Wittman 2016]

Personality cult is typical of authoritarian regimes. All authoritarian regimes venerate one leader, it is probably a cult taken from religious creeds. Even atheists have a bias toward individual leadership. Leaders cannot be blinded by greatness. They are servants of the people, they should not take the role of masters. Insane leaders must be identified as soon as possible, they make irreparable mistakes against humanity.

Mao Zedong

Mao's substantial appeal seems to derive, at least in part, from his ability to project a commanding sense of fearlessness and strength. For better or for worse, he was a leader unafraid to exercise authority. [Schell 2013]

In a letter to his third wife, Jiang Qing, written not long before his death, Mao compared himself to the tiger, a symbol of power, but added that he was also "just a monkey." "I have a tigerish nature as my main characteristic," he continued, "and a monkey nature as my subordinate characteristic." [Schell 2013]

By Mao's own account, from his earliest years he was constantly on guard against the tyranny of his father, who regularly beat him. His father was, said Mao, "a severe taskmaster" and a "hot-tempered man," making the young Mao's home a place for unending antagonism, menace, and violence, where survival depended on the boy's readiness and willingness to struggle. [Schell 2013]

Mao was forced to study the Confucian classics, breeding within him a loathing of the monotonous memorization and recitation process. What he adored, instead, was reading "the romances of old China," as he called them, especially tales of rebellious heroes and bandits, in which his native province, Hunan, historically abounded. Mao found ways to continue his subversive reading, "devouring everything I could find, except the Classics." [Schell 2013]

Adding to the tension, Mao was also in a constant state of rebellion against the other main authority figure in his life, his classics teacher, whom he described as being from "the stern treatment school ... harsh and severe, frequently beating his students." [Schell 2013]

In one occasion, the ten-year-old Mao was so upset of being beaten that he ran away from school and wandered lost for several days, "afraid to return home for fear of receiving another beating there." To his surprise, however, upon finally going home, far from being punished, Mao found that both his father ans his teacher had unexpectedly softened. Perhaps alarmed by the boy's boldness in fleeing, his father was "slightly more considerate," while his teacher became "more inclined to moderation." For Mao, this was an important lesson in the power of defiance. "I learned that when I defended my rights by open rebellion, my father relented, but when I remained meek and submissive, he only cursed and beat me the more." [Schell 2013]

Mao concluded that one way to overcome the kind of "ignorance and darkness" that had brought China "to the brink of destruction" was strong, heroic, willful, sometimes even brutal and violent leadership. [Schell 2013]

Delving into the interrelationship between an individual's physical strength and a nation's collective strength, Mao derided those who "overemphasize knowledge" and have "white and slender hands," "flabby" skin, and "small and frail" bodies. Only "when the body is strong," he proclaimed, can one "advance speedily in knowledge and morality and reap far-reaching advantages." [Schell 2013]

Real strength could only arise, he wrote, through the discipline of endless "drill," which in turn could only be generated by a will that was "savage and rude" and had "nothing to do with delicacy." Physical education was important, he wrote, because it "not only harmonizes the emotions, it also strengthens the will," which he has coming to see as a precursor of those human qualities he most admired – military heroism, courage, dauntlessness, audacity, and perseverance. All were, he declared, "matters of will." [Schell 2013]

"It is said that one man who scorns death will prevail over one hundred men," Mao scribbled. "This is because he fears nothing, because his motive power presses forward in a straight line. Because he cannot be stopped or eliminated, he is the strongest and the most powerful." Here was a clear elucidation of the role that Mao saw evolving for himself. He was born activist and already dreaming of bending Chinese reality to his will. [Schell 2013]

Mao's simple solution to the problem of making Marxism work in an overwhelmingly agricultural society was to turn China's greatest weakness, its rural poor, into its ultimate strength. "This means that the Chinese revolution is essentially a peasant revolution," wrote Mao. [Schell 2013]

Mao never tired of disturbing the established order with his version of "creative destruction." "Trouble-making is the revolution," he pronounced across China just as he was fomenting his last "disorder under heaven," the Great Proletarian Cultural Revolution. Mao saw the institutionalization of a sense of "permanent revolution" as an important way of keeping political zeal at a fever pitch and his adversaries off-balance. [Schell 2013]

Mao suggested that true revolutionaries sometimes needed to be willing to countenance outright killing. "This man Hitler was even more ferocious," Mao told confidants. "The more ferocious the better, don't you think? The more people you kill, the more revolutionary you are." [Schell 2013]

Mao was terminally beguiled by the idea that agricultural production could be increased simply through dynamic leadership, exhortation, and mass mobilization, rather than through expertise, technology, and capital investment. His dream was to industrialize China with verve and panache via a new "high tide" of socialist fervor that would so inspire his fellow peasants to generate the resources needed to finance the country's industrial development. [Schell 2013]

Mao wanted to remake China from the ground up. His new, self-proclaimed slogan was "greater, faster, better, and more economical results." He imagined that "the people" were organizing themselves into "community dining rooms, kindergartens, nurseries, sewing groups, barber shops, public baths, [and] happy homes for the aged." because they knew it would lead them "toward a happier collective life." [Schell 2013]

Precisely those periods of Mao's most uncompromising nihilism finally managed to bring about what no previous reformer or revolutionary had been able to, namely, a forceful enough demolition job on China's "old society" to finally free Chinese from their traditional moorings. Mao's brutal interim was perhaps the essential, but paradoxical, precursor to China's subsequent boom under Deng Xiaoping and his successors. [Schell 2013]

Mao launched the Cultural Revolution to prevent China from "taking the capitalist road," yet ironically his efforts ended up having precisely the opposite effect. [Schell 2013]

Mugabe

Robert Mugabe proclaimed in the 1970s that bullets and power of the barrel were the way forward for Zimbabwe. "We came to power through the barrel of a gun and that is how we intend to keep it." [Freeth 2011]

Mugabe went to Fort Hare, the university for blacks in South Africa, then on to study in Zambia and Ghana. He studied politics fanatically and became a convinced Marxist, but he did not engage in political action until he was thirty-six years old in 1960. [Dowden 2009]

In 1976, during an interview, Mugabe said that he wanted liberation now, by military force, and that he would settle for nothing less than majority rule. He said he was no longer interested in interim measures in Rhodesia, and announced that there were thousands of newly recruited and trained fighters ready to go to war. [Dowden 2009]

Mugabe had begun as a militant, served his time in prison, forced the British to realize there was no alternative, come to power and then settled into a friendly relationship with the former rulers and pursued moderate economic policies. [Dowden 2009]

Mugabe's inflexible, military approach was not popular among African Presidents in the region, who still thought a deal could be worked out persuading the rest of the world to bring justice to Rhodesia, Mugabe opted for resistance and an armed struggle. Mugabe was battling colonists who had settled and invested their life in Rhodesia. [Dowden 2009]

Mugabe thinks Zimbabwe is his because he took it by force – exactly the same mentality as the brutal white colonists who seized it more than a century ago. His aim, he says, is total independence but Zimbabweans will remain dependent on others' charity for the foreseeable future. [Dowden 2009]

Idi Amin Dada

The self-made man does not exist in Africa. If the motto of Europe is individualism: 'I think therefore I am,' Africa's would be communalism: 'I relate, therefore I am.' In Zulu there is a saying: 'One is a person through others,' or, as John Mbiti, the Kenyan theologian, put it: 'I am because we are and, since we are, therefore I am.' Africans know who is family and know where they come in it, both vertically and horizontally. A man without a family is no-one. He is nothing. [Dowden 2009]

In Uganda I first knew the paradox of Africa's beauty and evil. Africa's huge patience and humanity – and its cruelty and violence. Uganda was in the early stages of a catastrophe. Idi Amin ruled for almost a decade, Uganda was to suffer tyranny and civil war. Their dreams shattered, Ugandans were to get hugely poorer. [Dowden 2009]

In 1966, Milton Obote drove out President Mutesa in a coup, making himself Executive President. He gathered all power to himself, made

Uganda a one-party state and planned radical socialism. But in using the army to overthrow the constitution, he had involved the soldiers in politics. It has always been assumed that the British had a hand in the coup that brought Idi Amin to power. In the early hours of 25 January 1971, while Obote was in Singapore, the government was overthrown. Amin immediately reversed Obote's socialist policies, which would have led to the nationalization of some fifty British business in Uganda. [Dowden 2009]

In southern Uganda, Amin's first year in power did not feel like a reign of terror. On the contrary, many people said the country was freer than it had been under Obote. Yet beneath cheerful surface horrible things were happening. Soldiers from Obote's ethnic group, the Langi, and Acholi officers, the backbone of the army, were butchered. They were replaced by people from Amin's area. [Dowden 2009]

Amin became the prototype African military dictator and clown, the jumped-up sergeant who ruled like a profligate king in a wasteland of terror and destitution. His image became the emblem of Africa for decades. On 6 August 1972 Amin announced that all Asians who did not have Uganda citizenship were to be expelled and their businesses were given to Ugandans. The Asians, most of them petty traders, were not liked. They did not mix with Africans and many Asian businessmen exploited them brutally. So when Amin expelled them, many thought that they would be given Asian's businesses, cars and homes and be rich. [Dowden 2009]

Development experts blame Africa's failure on policy: the wrong policies, or the right policies badly implemented. But it was not policies that messed up Africa. It was politics. The deadly combination of internal competition for power and outside interference wrecked Africa. As an individual, Amin was extraordinary. What he did to his country was not. [Dowden 2009]

Fidel Castro

Fidel Castro came from quite a wealthy landowning family. He was much closer to his devoutly Catholic mother than to his strong-willed and irreligious father. [Brown 2009]

Fidel Castro distinguished himself both academically and on the sports field in a leading Jesuit college before entering the law faculty of Havana University. [Brown 2009]

Fulgencio Batista staged a military coup in March 1952. One year later, Castro made his first attempt to bring down the Batista regime. He led a group of radical opponents in an attempt to take over the Moncada Fortress in Santiago de Cuba. Castro and his comrades were defeated. Castro was imprisoned for over a year. [Brown 2009]

After his release from jail, Castro left Cuba for Mexico, where he joined his younger brother Raul. With a group of fellow revolutionaries, he acquired an ancient boat, the Granma, and sailed to Cuba. The group of revolutionaries took to the hills of Sierra Maestra and fought a guerrilla war against the Batista regime over the next two years. [Brown 2009]

Castro was a romantic revolutionary by temperament – his comrade in-arms Che Guevara, even more so – but he was also a much more inspirational leader than any of Cuba's official communists. [Brown 2009]

Fidel Castro, the 26 of July Movement, which he led, and other revolutionary forces that had participated in the revolutionary war, sought to affirm Cuban nationalism. [Bethell 1993]

The Bay of Pigs invasion (Playa Giron) in April 1961 represents the pivotal event in the early years of the Cuban revolution. It allowed Castro to consolidate his power and eliminate virtually all his opposition on the island. All dissidents, both real and imagined, including all bishops, many journalists, the urban underground resistance and most CIA's agents and sympathizers were rounded up and thrown in jail. It was the perfect victory for Castro. His often-predicted invasion by the United States had finally occurred. The Cubans had won a victory against the United States. [Staten 2005]

On December 1961, Fidel Castro proclaimed that he was Marxist-Leninist and that he would be so until death. The making of a radical revolution in Cuba required a break with the United States and support from the Soviet Union. [Bethell 1993]

In October 1962, the USSR installed forty-two medium-range ballistic missiles in Cuba. Kennedy demanded the withdrawal of Soviet 'offensive missiles' from Cuba and imposed a naval 'quarantine' on the island to prevent the additional shipment of Soviet weaponry. [Bethell 1993]

Castro's political style emphasized active engagement as opposed to theoretical pursuits. It also highlighted the power of self-discipline and conscious action. Subjective will was the fundamental resource for revolutionary leaders to overcome objective obstacles in war, politics or economics. [Bethell 1993]

The Cuban people absolutely adored Fidel Castro. This immense popular support gave Castro the power to radicalize the economy and challenge the powerful economic interests on the island, in particular, the sugar industry and major U.S. corporations. [Staten 2005]

Castro is a bundle of contradictions. He is an idealist and a realist. He can be an ideologue and a pragmatist. He is capable of 180-degree shifts in policies. He can be cooperative and obstinate. He can be gentle and ruthless. He generates both love and hatred. He has had tremendous successes and tremendous failures. He has maintained his revolutionary commitments to free education, cradle-to-grave healthcare and social security to all. He is a classical Latin American caudillo. [Staten 2005]

Kim Il Sung

After World War II ended with Japan's surrender in 1945, the Soviets chose Kim Il Sung to become the communist leader of North Korea. According to author Lankov, Kim Il Sung found himself the leader of North Korea almost by accident and was initially frustrated that he was chosen for the political appointment. At the time Kim Il Sung might have preferred a career as a Soviet army officer to the strange and complicated life of a politician. However, in 1946 and even in 1949 he was hardly the real ruler of Korea. The Soviet military authorities and the apparatus of advisers had a decisive influence on the life of the country, and in the first years of the DPRK Kim was only nominally ruler. [Miller 2004]

Kim Il Sung became the President of North Korea in 1972 under the terms of his new 'socialist constitution,' a position he held until his death (July 1994). He was re-elected President in 1982, having named his son Kim Jong Il as his eventual political successor. Kim Il Sung faced the problem of how could a generation, untried in revolution and war, be trusted to maintain the impetus of continuous revolution? Kim Il Sung answer was that the revolution could best be maintained by a leader from a great revolutionary family. [Miller 2004]

Kim Jong Il grew up in privilege from his teenage years, had never served a day in the military until he was named supreme commander of the People's Army in December 1991, wore his hair in an artsy pompadour, and was notably uncomfortable amid the roar of the crowd. North Korea has been aptly described by historian Bruce Cumings as 'a corporate state and a family state.' Family members and in-laws hold a very large number of top leadership posts in the country. Although passage of power from father to eldest son was traditional in Korean dynasties and Confucian families, it was heretical in a nominal 'people's democracy.' [Miller 2004]

Despite recent overtures to the international community, North Korea is still ruled by one of the few remaining Stalinist regimes, one that continues to sequester information about basic social and economic conditions in the country. [Miller 2004]

Hugo Chavez

Having grown up as a poor child in the Venezuelan countryside, Chavez had an organic and intuitive connection with the poor and the working-class citizens which he came to dominate like a champion.

Chavez style was confrontational, disrespectful and self-centered. He would spend countless hours on national TV offending anyone who would dare to disagree with him, and was known for reprimanding and firing cabinet ministers on live TV. Countless hours of the show Alo Presidente were produced.

Chavez came to power, after unsuccessfully attempting a coup, by winning an election in 1998. He won by selling the idea of giving power to the people, and ending the corruption of the traditional political parties that had governed Venezuela for the last forty years. Shortly after coming into office, Chavez began implementing steps to take control of PDVSA, the national oil company, which was then autonomously run. Little by little, he fired its top management and replaced it with cronies. Then in 2002 he fired some 18,000 PDVSA workers — around 40 percent of its workforce — and had them slowly replaced with more of his backers. Apart from ruining PDVSA, it expanded the president's power by giving him an endless source of funds to use for narrow political goals.

Chavez expanded the political power of the presidency as well. He packed the Venezuelan supreme court, took over the CNE (the body that is supposed to oversee elections and ensure their fairness), undermined press freedom by shutting down the opposition's television stations, politicized the military by promoting officers based on loyalty rather than competence, and through a long sequence of constitutional changes transferred most decision making power from the legislature to the presidency.

Chavez's call for revolution expressed a rejection of imperialism that sought to establish democratic socialism for the 21st century (Absurd Socialism). Chavez's plan to accomplish this involved taking control of all branches of power – the executive, legislative, judicial and military. Once in power, Chávez replaced the existing Congress by creating a new National Assembly, which he controlled. He used his new National Assembly to rewrite the constitution to perpetuate himself in power. The new National Assembly also reshaped the Supreme Court. They alleged the existing justices were corrupt, and inserted Chavez followers in their place.

Chavez's authoritarianism extended into the economy. He started a war against the private sector. He nationalized thousands of private companies and industries, to the amazement of his followers and to the astonishment of business owners and consumers who did not see it coming. While he didn't, contrary to popular myth, nationalize the oil industry (it had been government-owned since 1976, and he merely devastated its productivity and output by packing it with cronies and failing to maintain its infrastructure), he did manage to trash most of the non-oil economy. Chavez created an image of an enlightened world leader, selling oil at a discount to many Latin American nations to buy good will. For example, he struck a deal to provided Cuba with deeply discounted oil in exchange for Cuban doctors.

In a country that should be one of the great agricultural exporters of the Americas, he turned farms into a non-viable business by subsidizing consumption and controlling prices, and converted large swathes of commercial-agriculture land back into subsistence-level peasant farms. As a result, his country became heavily reliant on food imports and suffered from serious food shortages.

And the ultimate condemnation of the Chavez approach is: It was all about instant spending, with no consideration to long-term investments. Once the oil stops flowing, there will be nothing left but debt and broken institutions. Chavez was an innovator in how he *spent* money, but he did little to improve how Venezuela actually *makes* money. He paid no attention to diversifying the economy or investing in domestic production outside of the oil sector. The country relies on imports for many of its most basic goods and services, included food and medicines.

President Maduro has tried to imitate Chavez's style, making Chavez an immortal figure, promoting rituals and making his burial place a center of worship and spending lavishly to create a cult centered on the "Eternal Commander." Unfortunately for Maduro, who does not have the charisma or the political instincts of his predecessor, the barrel of oil is now $40 instead of $100. The population is restless with poverty, which did not improve as Chavez promised. Rampant and very public corruption has beleaguered the public sector and armed forces.

Thanks to Chavez's legacy, president Maduro still holds control over the Supreme Court of Justice and the Armed Forces. His followers have organized civilian groups called "colectivos" to mobilize against the opposition. He also has the support of the Militia, a large group of paramilitaries, well-trained and uniformed and unconditional followers of the "eternal commander," Chavez. There is no opportunity in the private sector, since it was destroyed by nationalization, using confiscation or expropriation of private companies. The local currency is totally worthless.

It has never been clearer that Nicolás Maduro – who cynically described its presidential vote as "a triumph of democracy" – is a dictator. Dozens of countries throughout Europe and the Americas warned that the fraudulent presidential elections should not occur and are now refusing to recognize the results. We are not dealing with an authoritarian government that, like Chavez's, still managed to loosely navigate between the lines of democracy and the rule of law. Maduro's is a textbook dictatorship, with assassinations, torture and sexual abuse of political prisoners, violent censorship of the press, and a sociopathic strategy to use the hunger ot its own citizens as a tool for political control.

Now, when many Venezuelans barely have the energy to try to feed themselves, it is very unlikely that a popular uprising will end well. As for a coup, one has to wonder why military forces involved in human rights abuses and drug trafficking would want to depose Maduro – and how that could ever lead to democracy. So, in the face of all this, what can we do to help restore democracy in Venezuela?

The democratic world must recognize the National Assembly as the only legitimate government of Venezuela, and work with it to draw up a plan towards democratic transition. The assembly was elected in December 2015, in a vote that was universally recognized as free and fair, and the opposition controls 67% of seats. Yes, these politicians have made their share of mistakes, and sometimes their internal bickering pushes away Venezuelan voters, but they are still the only legally elected officials in the country

Highlights for Chapter 13
- Africa is the continent that has produced most dictators, and African leaders do not emerge from thin air.

- Africa's one-party states increasingly became one-man states – the Strong Man.
- Nelson Mandela argued that poverty is the cause of Africa's Strong Man syndrome.
- With all the powers of statehood at their disposal, the Strong Men demanded and often got blind obedience.
- Mobutu Sese Seko, who ruled Zaire, now renamed Congo, was the ultimate Strong Man.
- By the late 1980s, outside Botswana, Senegal, and Gambia, Africans lived one-party states, mostly ruled by Presidents for life.
- Africa suffered at least forty military coups in its first two decades of independence.
- But in most cases, military dictators looted their countries, impoverished their peoples and charmed Western visitors.
- For outsiders, the passivity of Africans in the face of appalling oppression was depressing.
- That applies to most of Africa. Only three times did Africans rise up against military governments in the popular movement.
- At the heart of African politics is an attitude to power. Power whether used for good or evil is widely revered for its own sake.
- Stalin said that 'people need a tsar,' i.e., someone to revere and in whose name to live and labor.
- By 1930, after Lenin death, Stalin was supreme in Russia, in effect, he was already a dictator.
- Stalin's 'image' as a charismatic, almost superhuman, leader helped to solidify support for communism and to bestow on its legitimacy.
- It was Stalin, people believed, who had led them to a great victory.
- In 1956, Nikita Khrushchev accused Stalin of flagrant abuses of power, acts of gross brutality and developing his own cult of personality.
- To the end, Rosenberg held fast to the righteousness of the Nazi cause and to Hitler's greatness.
- "I venerated him, and I remained loyal to him to the end," Rosenberg wrote.
- Leaders cannot be blinded by greatness. They are servants of the people, they should not take the role of masters.

- Hitler combined in his position as Fuhrer 'the functions of a supreme legislator, supreme administrator, and supreme judge,' and was also 'the leader of the Party, the Army and the People.'
- Yet Hitler was no weak dictator. In a negative sense, he did control Germany, in that he had broken most potential centers of opposition to the regime.
- According to Hitler, the Jews were behind the great political ideals, including communism and capitalism, and Germans were afraid of losing their country to unwanted ideals.
- The Jews were blamed of many wrongdoings. The Jews were guilty of anything that did not work well in the country.
- Hitler's strength lay not in the originality of his ideas but in the way in which he expressed them.
- Hitler promoted an image of himself as a 'myth person' or 'demi-god' who stood far above the mundane arguments.
- Most totalitarian regimes identify who might their enemies be. They need to invent enemies to be blamed for their bad performance.
- "Hitler did not have to destroy democracy; he merely took advantage of the decay of democracy."
- Crowds of Germans who, one reporter recalled, "looked up at him as if he were a Messiah."
- Personality cult is typical of authoritarian regimes. All authoritarian regimes venerate one leader, it is probably a cult taken from religious creeds.
- Mao's substantial appeal seems to derive, at least in part, from his ability to project a commanding sense of fearlessness and strength.
- Mao to his wife, "I have a tigerish nature as my main characteristic," he continued, "and a monkey nature as my subordinate characteristic."
- Mao said, "I learned that when I defended my rights by open rebellion, my father relented, but when I remained meek and submissive, he only cursed and beat me the more."
- Mao concluded that one way to overcome the kind of "ignorance and darkness" that had brought China "to the brink of destruction" was strong, heroic, willful, sometimes even brutal and violent leadership.

- "This means that the Chinese revolution is essentially a peasant revolution," wrote Mao.
- "Trouble-making is the revolution," Mao pronounced across China.
- Mao told confidants, "The more ferocious the better, don't you think? The more people you kill, the more revolutionary you are."
- Mao launched the Cultural Revolution to prevent China from "taking the capitalist road," yet ironically his efforts ended up having precisely the opposite effect.
- Robert Mugabe proclaimed in the 1970s that bullets and power of the barrel were the way forward for Zimbabwe.
- Mugabe studied politics fanatically and became a convinced Marxist.
- In 1976, Mugabe said that he wanted liberation now, by military force, and that he would settle for nothing less than majority rule.
- Mugabe came to power and then settled into a friendly relationship with the former rulers and pursued moderate economic policies.
- Mugabe was battling colonists who had settled and invested their life in Rhodesia.
- Mugabe thinks Zimbabwe is his because he took it by force – exactly the same mentality as the brutal white colonists who seized it more than a century ago.
- Idi Amin ruled for almost a decade, Uganda was to suffer tyranny and civil war.
- It has always been assumed that the British had a hand in the coup that brought Idi Amin to power.
- In southern Uganda, Amin's first year in power did not feel like a reign of terror. On the contrary, many people said the country was freer than it had been under Obote.
- Amin became the prototype African military dictator and clown, the jumped-up sergeant who ruled like a profligate king in a wasteland of terror and destitution.
- On 6 August 1972 Amin announced that all Asians who did not have Uganda citizenship were to be expelled and their businesses were given to Ugandans.
- Fidel Castro distinguished himself both academically and on the sports field in a leading Jesuit college before entering the law faculty of Havana University.

- A group of revolutionaries took to the hills of Sierra Maestra and fought a guerrilla war against the Batista regime over the next two years.
- Castro was a romantic revolutionary by temperament.
- The Bay of Pigs invasion (Playa Giron) in April 1961 allowed Castro to consolidate his power and eliminate virtually all his opposition on the island.
- In October 1962, the USSR installed forty-two medium-range ballistic missiles in Cuba.
- The Cuban people absolutely adored Fidel Castro.
- Castro is a bundle of contradictions. He is an idealist and a realist. He can be an ideologue and a pragmatist.
- Castro is a classical Latin American caudillo.
- After World War II ended with Japan's surrender in 1945, the Soviets chose Kim Il Sung to become the communist leader of North Korea.
- At the time Kim Il Sung might have preferred a career as a Soviet army officer to the strange and complicated life of a politician.
- Kim Il Sung became the President of North Korea in 1972 under the terms of his new 'socialist constitution,'
- Kim Il Sung answer was that the revolution could best be maintained by a leader from a great revolutionary family.
- Kim Jong Il grew up in privilege from his teenage years and had never served a day in the military.
- Although passage of power from father to eldest son was traditional in Korean dynasties and Confucian families, it was heretical in a nominal 'people's democracy.'
- Despite recent overtures to the international community, North Korea is still ruled by one of the few remaining Stalinist regimes.
- Chavez grew up as a poor child in the Venezuelan countryside, he had an intuitive connection with the poor.
- Chavez style was confrontational, disrespectful and self-centered.
- Chavez came to power, after unsuccessfully attempting a coup, by winning an election in 1998.
- Shortly after coming into office in 1998, Chavez began implementing steps to take control of PDVSA, the national oil company.

- Chavez packed the Venezuelan supreme court, took over the Electoral Council, undermined press freedom and politicized the military.
- Chavez accomplished total control of all branches of power – the executive, legislative, judicial and military.
- Chavez created an image of an enlightened world leader, selling oil at a discount to many Latin American nations to buy good will.
- Chavez's authoritarianism extended into the economy. He nationalized thousands of private companies, industries, and expropriated land.
- Chavez was an innovator in how he *spent* money, but he did little to improve how Venezuela actually *makes* money.
- President Maduro tried to imitate Chavez's style, making Chavez an immortal figure, creating a cult centered on the "Eternal Commander."
- The population is restless with poverty, which did not improve as Chavez promised.
- There is no private sector since it was destroyed by nationalization, using confiscation or expropriation of private companies.
- Thanks to Chavez's legacy, president Maduro still holds control over the Supreme Court of Justice and the Armed Forces.
- It has never been clearer that Nicolás Maduro is a dictator.
- Maduro's is a textbook dictatorship, with assassinations, torture and sexual abuse of political prisoners.
- Now, when many Venezuelans barely have the energy to try to feed themselves, it is very unlikely that a popular uprising will end well.
- The democratic world must recognize the National Assembly as the only legitimate government of Venezuela.

Chapter 14: Human Rights

A simplified version of the United Nations Universal Declaration of Human Rights is presented, it was taken from the following link: https://www.youthforhumanrights.org/what-are-human-rights/universal-declaration-of-human-rights/articles-1-15.html

1. We Are All Born Free & Equal. We are all born free. We all have our own thoughts and ideas. We should all be treated in the same way.

2. Don't Discriminate. These rights belong to everybody, whatever our differences.

3. The Right to Life. We all have the right to life, and to live in freedom and safety.

4. No Slavery. Nobody has any right to make us a slave. We cannot make anyone our slave.

5. No Torture. Nobody has any right to hurt us or to torture us.

6. You Have Rights No Matter Where You Go. I am a person just like you!

7. We're All Equal Before the Law. The law is the same for everyone. It must treat us all fairly.

8. Your Human Rights Are Protected by Law. We can all ask for the law to help us when we are not treated fairly.

9. No Unfair Detainment. Nobody has the right to put us in prison without good reason and keep us there or to send us away from our country.

10. The Right to Trial. If we are put on trial this should be in public. The people who try us should not let anyone tell them what to do.

11. We're Always Innocent Till Proven Guilty. Nobody should be blamed for doing something until it is proven. When people say we did a bad thing we have the right to show it is not true.

12. The Right to Privacy. Nobody should try to harm our good name. Nobody has the right to come into our home, open our letters, or bother us or our family without a good reason.

13. Freedom to Move. We all have the right to go where we want in our own country and to travel as we wish.

14. The Right to Seek a Safe Place to Live. If we are frightened of being badly treated in our own country, we all have the right to run away to another country to be safe.

15. Right to a Nationality. We all have the right to belong to a country.

16. Marriage and Family. Every grown-up has the right to marry and have a family if they want to. Men and women have the same rights when they are married, and when they are separated.

17. The Right to Your Own Things. Everyone has the right to own things or share them. Nobody should take our things from us without a good reason.

18. Freedom of Thought. We all have the right to believe in what we want to believe, to have a religion, or to change it if we want.

19. Freedom of Expression. We all have the right to make up our own minds, to think what we like, to say what we think, and to share our ideas with other people.

20. The Right to Public Assembly. We all have the right to meet our friends and to work together in peace to defend our rights. Nobody can make us join a group if we don't want to.

21. The Right to Democracy. We all have the right to take part in the government of our country. Every grown-up should be allowed to choose their own leaders.

22. Social Security. We all have the right to affordable housing, medicine, education, and childcare, enough money to live on and medical help if we are ill or old.

23. Workers' Rights. Every grown-up has the right to do a job, to a fair wage for their work, and to join a trade union.

24. The Right to Play. We all have the right to rest from work and to relax.

25. Food and Shelter for All. We all have the right to a good life. Mothers and children, people who are old, unemployed or disabled, and all people have the right to be cared for.

26. The Right to Education. Education is a right. Primary school should be free. We should learn about the United Nations and how to get on with others. Our parents can choose what we learn.

27. Copyright. Copyright is a special law that protects one's own artistic creations and writings; others cannot make copies without permission. We all have the right to our own way of life and to enjoy the good things that art, science, and learning bring.

28. A Fair and Free World. There must be proper order so we can all enjoy rights and freedoms in our own country and all over the world.

29. Responsibility. We have a duty to other people, and we should protect their rights and freedoms.

30. No One Can Take Away Your Human Rights.

China

In China, the worst violations of human rights happen in the areas of democracy, freedom of thought and freedom of expression. In Tiananmen, several rights were violated, Right to Life, No Unfair Detainment, Freedom to Move, Freedom of Thought, and The Right to Public Assembly.

Several attempts to promote democratization occurred in China over the years. They were primarily initiatives coming from intellectuals. Among them, a movement of political dissent began in the late fall of 1978. However, instead of exhorting people "never to forget class struggle" or "bombard the headquarters," it called on Chinese leaders to reevaluate the April Fifth Movement, promote democratic thinking, and liberate themselves from the oppression of the "lost decade" of the Cultural Revolution. [Schell 2013]

Freedom of Expression is commonly suppressed in China. Probably supported by the government, there were some demands to deepen political reforms and to silence the voices of democracy. On December 5, 1986, twenty major Chinese cities were soon racked by demonstrations in which students demanded a speed-up of political reforms. Slogans such as "No Democratization, No Modernization" and "Government of the People, by the People, and for the People," were displayed. Deng told party leaders, "This proves that you cannot succeed without recourse to methods of dictatorship." [Schell 2013]

Wei Jingsheng

One of those intellectuals was Wei Jingsheng who wrote a poster on "The Fifth Modernization." He supported the new openness, but he diverged from Deng Xiaopao in his belief that if leadership focused only on seeking to modernize agriculture, industry, science and technology, and defense without including an essential "fifth modernization," namely, democracy, China would never become a truly modern and stable society. [Schell 2013]

Some sources of opposition to Wei, representing the government, came from the press. The state-owned Beijing Daily countered with its own editorial: "The kind of democracy we need is socialist democracy or democracy enjoyed by the overwhelming majority of people. We don't want bourgeois democracy, which enables a handful of people to oppress the majority of people." [Schell 2013]

The democracy movement, said Deng, had now "gone too far" and was no longer in the interest of "stability, unity, and the Four Modernizations." "Can we tolerate this kind of freedom of speech which flagrantly contravenes the principles of our constitution?" he asked. His answer was an emphatic no. "We practice democratic centralism," he declared, reminding everyone of his and the PRC's Leninist roots, "not bourgeois ... individualist democracy." [Schell 2013]

Six months later, Wei was finally brought to trial on October 16, 1979. In his defense, he gave a ringing endorsement of free expression. "The constitution grants citizens the right to criticize their leaders because their leaders are human beings and not gods. It is only through the people's criticism and supervision that those leaders will make few mistakes, and only in this way that the people will avoid the misfortune of having their lords and masters ride roughshod over them." [Schell 2013]

In the end, it didn't really matter how Wei positioned his defense. The party understood the fundamentally antagonistic nature of his critique – that all human beings had an innate right to basic freedoms – and, despite his efforts to give it a patriotic, utilitarian spin, the party was implacably opposed to it. [Schell 2013]

Even though the party had all the power to silence opposition, more and more citizens began pointing to a more fundamental problem – the lack of transparency, accountability, and democracy in the political system. [Schell 2013]

Fang Lizhi

Fang Lizhi, was another human rights voice trying to be heard. He was the country's most famous astrophysicist, born in 1936, emerged in the 1980s as an electrifying champion not just of academic freedom but also of freedom of speech, human rights, and democracy. Fang encouraged students to embrace social concerns and political activism – and to look to the West for new models of intellectual commitment. [Schell 2013]

Fang asked: if "foreigners are no more intelligent than we Chinese, why, then, can't we produce first-rate work?" He answered, "The reasons for our inability to develop our potential lie within our social system." He urged his audience to "be open to different ways of thinking ... and willing to adopt the elements of those cultures that are clearly superior. A great diversity of thought should be allowed in colleges and universities. For if all thought is narrow and simplistic, creativity will die. At present, there are certainly some people in power who still insist on dictating to others according to their own narrow principles ... We must not be afraid to speak openly about these things. In fact, it is our duty." [Schell 2013]

Fang roused a crowd to repeated rounds of applause with his argument that political liberties are universal, innate, and foundational, rather than simply means to an end: "Human rights are fundamental privileges that people have from birth, such as the right to think and be educated, the right to marry, and so on ... But we Chinese consider these rights dangerous." [Schell 2013]

The party repeatedly urged Fang to tone down his political evangelism, but he proved deaf to their entreaties. When asked what he thought of Deng's sacrosanct Four Cardinal Principles, he impishly replied that although they were "articles of faith among the political leadership," he preferred four different principles, namely, "science, democracy, creativity, and independence." [Schell 2013]

Deng Xiaoping had made up his mind about democracy and human rights. Fang Lizhi's vision of a democratic China, with its echoes of Wei Jingsheng's "fifth modernization," was precisely what Deng was convinced the country did not need. [Schell 2013]

As Deng saw it, Fang was cancer that had to be excised from the body politic. "I have read Fang Lizhi's speeches. He doesn't sound like a Communist Party member at all, Why do we keep people like him in the Party? He should be expelled, not just persuaded to quit." Fang was forced to step down as vice president at the University of Science and Technology and unceremoniously expelled from the party. [Schell 2013]

After the mayhem of June 4 in Tiananmen, Fang and his wife, fearing for their lives, sought shelter in the American embassy. Fang hoped his stay would be temporary, but after the White House unexpectedly announced that he had "sought sanctuary," China's Public Security Bureau branded him a "black hand" who had helped to create the "counterrevolutionary rebellion" that had just been suppressed. [Schell 2013]

As the months drifted by, Fang and his wife remained in their strange limbo, while the Chinese government charged the U.S government with harboring criminals and traitors. [Schell 2013]

For a year Fang and his wife remained inside the embassy as the Chinese government pressed its propaganda campaign against him and other dissidents, going so far as to call Fang "scum of the intelligentsia." On June 25, 1990, he and his wife were finally allowed to leave Beijing on humanitarian medical grounds via a U.S Air Force plane sent by President George H. W. Bush. [Schell 2013]

Liu Xiaobo

In 2010, when he won the Noble Peace Prize while still locked in a Chinese prison cell, the writer and activist Liu Xiaobo became a living global symbol for the lineage of Chinese thinkers who have viewed democracy and human rights as a matter of principle, rather than merely as tools in their country's search for renewed greatness. [Schell 2013]

An admirer of nonviolent leaders such as Vaclav Havel, Mohandas Gandhi, and Martin Luther King Jr., Liu prided himself on his intolerance for groupthink and political pandering. "The Chinese love to look up to the famous, thereby saving themselves the trouble of thinking," he wrote before the 1989 demonstrations began. That's why they "rush into things en masse." Upon his arrival at Tiananmen Square, Liu was surprised to find himself truly inspired by what he found: a new sense of "civic consciousness." [Schell 2013]

"Each stage in the expansion and escalation of this student movement and its development into a civic movement has been prompted by the government's political folly," Liu wrote. "We must attempt to change the government's long-standing inability to listen to the voice of the people and its ideology of privilege that denies the people the rights to demonstrate, strike and establish popular organizations." [Schell 2013]

"Chinese society has been living in a vicious cycle of a new emperor replacing an old emperor," Liu and three other activists on a hunger strike proclaimed. "History has proven that the stepping down of some unpopular leader and the assumption of power by some very popular [new] leader cannot solve the essential problems of Chinese politics. What we need is not a perfect savior, but a perfect democratic system." [Schell 2013]

Finally, Liu and his three fellow fasters proclaimed their "Four Basic Slogans:" [Schell 2013]

1. We have no enemy! Don't let hatred and violence poison our wisdom and the process of democratization!

2. We all need to examine ourselves. China's backwardness is everyone's responsibility!
3. We are first and foremost citizens.
4. We are not looking for death, but are seeking a true life!

What gave Liu's writing about the 1989 massacre such resonance was his humanistic perspective, which he had acquired in part from reading China's greatest twentieth-century writer, Lu Xun. "Behind the superficial, arrogant nationalism lies a national ethic that is disconnected from civic values. It is more nearly a primitive jungle ethic of master and slave. In front of the strong, people act like slaves; in front of the weak, like masters." [Schell 2013]

In terms of his basic political philosophy, Liu was very much the heir of Fang Lizhi's vision of democracy and human rights as values that transcend their utilitarian benefit to a country's development. For both men, liberal values were part of a universal humanistic legacy that was just as much Chinese as it was French or American. [Schell 2013]

Liu called on Chinese to adopt the West's tradition of employing a "critical attitude toward everything." China's present condition "needs a challenge, even 'a menace,' from another civilization; it needs a vast and surging, boundless sea to pound it out of its isolation, its solitude, and its narrow-mindedness." As Liu saw it, the party's elite was using the economic boom to keep the intellectual elite "atomized, scattered and isolated." "First they terrorized them with a bloody crackdown, then they seduced them with material rewards," he said. [Schell 2013]

Compelled to live in a society that would not countenance the public expression of dissenting views, Liu wrestled with a dilemma: How could he stay true to his beliefs under such repressive circumstances? He particularly admired former Czech president and playwright Vaclav Havel as one of those rare human beings who, even while living in totalitarian circumstances, had somehow found "the strength in himself to express solidarity with those whom his conscience commands him to support," and who, by stepping beyond "living within the lie," had managed to find a way "to live within the truth." Or, as dissident artist Ai Weiwei described the choices in a 2012 tweet, one can decide "to be true or to lie. To take action, or be brainwashed. To be free, or to be jailed." [Schell 2013]

What Liu found most humiliating was not China's weaknesses, but the embarrassing way its leaders had historically presumed its citizenry to be incapable of participating in the process of self-government. "During the last century of China's history the nation has fallen victim to cycles of self-abasement and self-aggrandizement, and this is because we have never been able to escape the clutches of the demon of nationalism," he wrote in a provocative 2002 essay. "But the primary mindset that guided the probing was neither 'liberation of humanity' or even 'enriching the peoples,' but rather a sense of shame at China's loss of sovereignty and other national humiliations." [Schell 2013]

On December 8, 2008, the police arrived at Liu's apartment, seized his books, papers and computer files and detained him yet again. This time he was accused of using "rumor-mongering and slander to incite subversion of state power and overthrow of the socialist system." In his trial he argued, "Over the past two decades, from 1989 to 2009, I have consistently held that China's political reform should be gradual, peaceful, orderly and under control. I have always opposed the notion of sudden radical leaps, and have opposed violent revolution even more stoutly." [Schell 2013]

Liu stubbornly defended freedom of speech, which, he declared, had disappeared after 1949, when "the entire country fell into a tawdry chorus of enforced uniformity." He reminded the court that "treating speech as a crime not only runs counter to the modern trends in world history but more deeply, abuses humanism and human rights in a fundamental moral sense." "No force can block the thirst for freedom that lies within human nature, and someday China, too, will be a nation of laws where human rights are paramount," expressed Liu. He was sentenced to eleven more years in prison. [Schell 2013]

For Liu, human rights had no class or national character, as prescribed by Marx, Lenin, and Mao. For him, human rights could not be eschewed, even if one wished to do so. They were something everyone just had by dint of being human. "Human rights," said Liu, "are not bestowed by a state." [Schell 2013]

Tiananmen

All that May of 1989, students and sympathetic citizens would occupy the square by staging a nonstop drama of protest. As the days and then weeks passed and people became less and less fearful of a crackdown, an increasingly festive atmosphere took hold. On May 12, student leaders declared a hunger strike until party leaders responded in a meaningful way to their demands, including permission to conduct mass political campaigns, more effective measures to halt official corruption, greater official dialogue between the government and students, and greater freedom of the press. [Schell 2013]

"Seventy years have passed since the May Fourth Movement and still we have no freedom and democracy," proclaimed one speaker. "Hu Yaobangs's death has the potential to start a student movement!" Deng was in no mood for talking, he labeled the students' actions "a planned conspiracy and a turmoil" that jeopardized "the great aspiration of the revitalization of China cherished by the whole nation." [Schell 2013]

The party central finally agreed to engage in direct dialogue with student leaders. Premier Li Peng found himself sitting stiffly opposite a pair of young students. There was no progress in the meeting. Li Peng's report to Deng on the meeting sealed the movement's fate. Deng and his colleagues, except Zhao Ziyang, were so deeply offended that they promptly agreed to declare martial law. Deng removed Zhao from power and locked him up in his home in Beijing until his death in 2005. [Schell 2013]

Deng now moved to crush the democracy movement itself. On May 20 the government declared martial law and dispatched troops to secure the square. But tens of thousands of ordinary people promptly and nonviolently spilled into the streets to block the progress of the People's Liberation Army as they tried to enter the city. As humiliating as this was, for the government, the most painful part of the tragedy was yet to come. [Schell 2013]

On June 2, Deng gave new orders to clear the square, by force if necessary. This time the gun obeyed the command of the party. On June 3, the second wave of armed troops began to close in around the city, starting from various points on the outskirts of Beijing and working inward like a noose closing around the center. [Schell 2013]

In the spring of 1989, Tiananmen Square was roiling with hundreds of thousands of disheveled freethinkers, challenging the leadership of the party that Mao had founded and Deng had so painstakingly rebuilt. When Deng contemplated these "masses," what he saw were not idealistic young patriots bravely exercising their democratic rights, but his worst nightmare: the specter of disorder and instability. Consequently, his eventual decision to order armed PLA soldiers to restore order – even to fire on the people if necessary to clear the square – was almost inevitable. [Schell 2013]

By the time these troops reached Tiananmen Square in the darkness of the early morning on June 4, most of the killing had already taken place in the city's periphery as soldiers had to battle their way through numerous citizen-erected barricades. All that was left was to dislodge the last remaining students, bedraggled and fearful, from their refuge around the Monument to the People's Heroes. [Schell 2013]

In Western scholarship, the demonstrations of spring 1989 loom, like the May Fourth Movement, as a milestone in what was presumed to be China's ineluctable historical path toward greater openness, if not a full-scale multiparty liberal democracy. But for Deng, as for Sun Yat-sen, Chiang Kai-shek, and Mao Zedong, such non-party-sanctioned demonstrations were milestones to nowhere – or, worse, way stations to a poorer and weaker China. [Schell 2013]

Deng instinctually returned to his Leninist roots, blaming the "Western imperialists" and their "rule of international monopoly capital" for destabilizing China, and denouncing the West's imposition of sanctions for human rights violations as an insult to the Chinese nation and the developing world. [Schell 2013]

Deng was also alarmed by the way the geopolitical map of the world was being redrawn after the Chinese Communist Party's near-death experience in Tiananmen Square. In Poland, the non-Communist opposition party Solidarity had – on June 4, 1989, of all days – won national elections. The Berlin Wall fell that November, and soon Communist Party-run and Soviet Union-dominated states were unraveling one after another all across Eastern Europe. Most disturbing was the violent end of Romania's communist dictator, Nicolae Ceausescu, whose three-decade rule was terminated with his unceremonious execution on Christmas Day 1989. [Schell 2013]

On March 10, 2008, the Dalai Lama released a statement on the anniversary of the 1959 Tibetan uprising against Chinese communist rule. "China is emerging as a powerful country due to her great economic progress," he wrote. "This is to be welcomed but ... the world is eagerly waiting to see how the present Chinese leadership will put into effect its avowed concepts of 'harmonious society' and 'peaceful rise.' There must be improvements in observance of the rule of law, transparency, and right to information, as well as freedom of speech." [Schell 2013]

And, sure enough, as inequality increased, so did social instability. The number of officially reported "mass incidents" of local protest rose from thousands to tens of thousands a year until 2006, at which point the government stopped releasing annual statistics. [Schell 2013]

Cuba

Social Security and Workers' Rights were affected by the labor policy in Cuba. The changes in labor policy were dramatic. The phasing out of material incentives was to be coupled with a renewed emphasis on moral incentives: the revolutionary consciousness of the people would guarantee increased productivity and quality and reductions in cost. Workers would be paid the same regardless of variations in effort or quality. [Bethell 1993]

Since moral incentives proved insufficient to stimulate production and productivity the government engaged in mass mobilization for work in the sugar fields and other sectors of the economy. These so-called volunteers – who often lacked the right to refuse – were deployed throughout the country rather ineffectively. They were supplemented by a substantial portion of the personnel of the Cuban armed forces. [Bethell 1993]

Workers were to rise above narrow and temporary interests, such as better wages and better working conditions, to sacrifice themselves for the good of the people. Labor was exhorted to heroic efforts and to respond to moral incentives, voluntary work becoming a euphemism for unpaid overtime work. [Bethell 1993]

The Right to Education in Cuba has always been successful. Cuba's educational transformation was the revolutionary government's most impressive achievement. Illiteracy was down to 12,9 percent in the 1970 census and to 5.6 percent in 1979. The government expropriated all private (including Church-affiliated) schools. Political criteria were among the factors in making decisions on student admissions even to non-political professions such as medicine and despite the fact that the universities and the Academy of Sciences emphasized applied technical research. [Bethell 1993]

The universities were organized on a broad 'industrial model,' to train professional personnel in a hierarchical system. Cuba de-emphasized the development of the liberal arts or the possibility of active intellectual criticism of major political, social, economic or cultural problems. The educational system, however, was inhospitable to political and intellectual dissent; it restricted freedom of expression and repressed many critics. The fruits of education and culture were thus curtailed. For this tragic loss,

Cuba served as a negative example of the uses of government power to limit the full development of human potential. [Bethell 1993]

Social Security in Cuba had some success. Government policies and performance in the area of health care also registered appreciable success. The government quickly established health care as the right of every citizen, expanding the system of free provision that had existed before the Revolution. [Bethell 1993]

We Are All Born Free & Equal in the Cuban Economy. By 1996, it was clear that the economy was growing once again and that Cuba had survived the worst of the Special Period. Yet, the reforms were having some unanticipated outcomes. In particular, the dual existence of the dollar and the peso economies was beginning to bring about a visible gap between the rich or the privileged and the poor. The privileged work in the tourist and service industries that have access to dollars. The poor are those trapped in the peso economy of the ration card and state-run stores. [Staten 2005]

In particular, this places a difficult burden on white-collar professionals who work for the state. Such as doctors, nurses, teachers, engineers, government administrators, and others. Their monthly peso income allows them a basic standard of living but does not allow them to "get ahead." Many professionals have second jobs in the tourist sector as taxi drivers, where they can earn much more in U.S. dollars. [Staten 2005]

Political prisoners in Cuba have their freedom affected. According to the government's official figures, the number of political prisoners fell from about 20,000 in the mid-1960s to 4,000 in the mid-1970s, and to as few as 1,000 in the 1979-80 crisis. [Bethell 1993]

Zimbabwe

The Right to Your Own Things has been violated in Zimbabwe. Property rights – full legal ownership of the land – are a non-negotiable absolute for any country wishing to see its agriculture flourish, its people fed, and its resources developed. [Freeth 2011]

Where boundaries are moved and there is no respect for private property, hunger will result. History has shown this to be the case over and over again. Where property rights are respected and people are allowed to develop in peace and security, there has never been hunger. [Freeth 2011]

Of all the professions, farming is the closest to the laws of nature that God set in place at the beginning of time. If you do not take account those laws, things go wrong very quickly. God created everyone and everything to be loved. All life responds positively to love. Nature – or God's creation – needs to be loved and cared for if it is to thrive. But where the right kind of love and faithfulness are lacking, life begins to ebb away. [Freeth 2011]

The problem with not having ownership lies in the way that human nature works. What a person does not own, he does not look after wholeheartedly. There is a vast difference in the way that people look after and develop the land when they own it – and have an assured future on it – and when they do not. If you do not own the land, you just do not have the same motivation to develop and care for it. [Freeth 2011]

Many people also believe that Mengistu advised Mugabe to create hunger so that he could have complete control over the population of Zimbabwe. Under this strategy, there is only one thing to do to productive farms – destroy them. [Freeth 2011]

The Right to Trial in Zimbabwe has been affected. The rule of law refers to a state of constitutionalism where the law (nor parliament) is supreme and where all governments power is subject to the law. It is the antithesis of authoritarianism, and it provides that individuals' rights may only be interfered with to the extent authorized by law. [Freeth 2011]

Rule by law means the opposite. It refers to a police state in which the government invokes the law (indeed creates law) to "justify" excessive use of government force. Detention without trial laws is a common example of these. When a country is under rule by law dictatorship is complete. [Freeth 2011]

Responsibility right and leaders are needed in Zimbabwe. In normal times, people like to think that they would never bury their principles in a time of crisis. But it's only in those times that a person's true nature is revealed. During a period of tyranny, leaders need to be visionaries, with prophetic voices, who are able to rise above the present crisis and take a principled stand. But nobody in the farming leadership dared to draw a line in the sand and say, "So far and no further!" [Freeth 2011]

The Right to Democracy in Zimbabwe is also affected. But democracy is not only about popular will, we know that through the European experience. The German Government in the 1930s was elected popularly and then they went on to do terrible things. Democracy is not only about what the majority of the people think, it's also about protecting fundamental human rights, making sure that you can't do certain things to the individuals. Cases such as this have resonance not only in the region but across the world. They can set examples and they're important, incrementally, in establishing what the fundamental principles of constitutional democracy are and should be all about. [Freeth 2011]

Soviet Union

Food and Shelter for All and Survival in Russia. People live to survive, nothing else matters, "The putsch! Tanks looked so crazy in the center of Moscow. My parents came into town from the dacha to stock up on groceries in case civil war broke out. That gang! That junta! They thought that all they had to do was call in the tanks and that would be enough. Like people only wanted one thing, food, and as long you gave it to them, they would agree to anything. The masses swept the streets ... The nation awoke ... I suddenly germinated ... My mother is a flighty person, she goes around without a thought in her head. She's completely removed from politics and lives according to the principle that life is short, you have to take everything you can get in the moment. But even she went out to the White House with her umbrella slung over her shoulder ... [Alexievich 2016]

Africa

In Lagos, Nigeria, it is a daily occurrence – several times a day – and it's a growing phenomenon all over Africa, power cuts that shut down the lights and air conditioning and the start-up roar of the generator. Some interpret it like a good sign: the growing demand for power in Africa. The economies are on the move. But did nobody realize that an improvement in economic activity would reveal a shortage of power? Power – or lack of it – is becoming a problem all over the continent. Africa did not plan for success. [Dowden 2009]

North Korea

The North Korean state directs all significant economic activity, and only government-controlled labor unions are permitted in this country of 22 million persons. The industry continues to operate at significantly reduced capacity, reflecting antiquated plants and equipment and severe shortages of inputs. This decline is due in part to the collapse of the former Soviet Union and East European communists governments and the subsequent sharp decline in trade and aid. [Miller 2004]

The Government's human rights record remained poor, and it continued to commit numerous serious abuses. Citizens do not have the right peacefully to change their government. There continue to be reports of extrajudicial killings and disappearances. Citizens are detained arbitrarily, and many are held as political prisoners; prison conditions are harsh. The constitutional provisions for an independent judiciary and fair trials are not implemented in practice. [Miller 2004]

The government prohibits freedom of speech, the press, assembly, and association, and all forms of cultural and media activities are under tight control of the party. Radios sold in North Korea receive North Korean radio broadcasts only. CNN television is available in one Pyongyang hotel frequented by foreigners. Under these circumstances, little outside information reaches the public except the approved and disseminated by the government. [Miller 2004]

Criminal law makes the death penalty mandatory for activities "in collusion with imperialists" aimed at "suppressing the national liberation struggle." Some prisoners are sentenced to death for such ill-defined "crimes" as "ideological divergence," "opposing socialism," and other "counterrevolutionary crimes." [Miller 2004]

The state leadership perceives most international norms of human rights, and especially individual rights, as alien social concepts subversive to the goals of the State and Party. The government relies upon an extensive, multilevel system of informers to identify critics and potential troublemakers. Families must display pictures of the two Kims in their homes and must keep them clean. If inspectors find a family has neglected its photos, the punishment is to write self-criticism throughout an entire year. [Miller 2004]

The regime justifies its dictatorship with arguments derived from concepts of collective consciousness and the superiority of the collective over the individual, appeals to nationalism, and citations of "the Juche idea." The ability to act independently without regard to outside interference. [Miller 2004]

Although the Constitution provides for freedom of assembly, the government does not respect this provision in practice. The government prohibits any public meetings without authorization. Articles of the Constitution that require citizens to follow "socialist norms of life" and to obey a "collective spirit" take precedence over individual political or civil liberties. The regime only permits activities that support its objectives. The government attempts to control all information. Claiming that the country is under continuing threat of armed aggression, the government carefully manages the visits of foreign journalists. [Miller 2004]

At times, the government allows citizens to leave their villages to search for food, and there are reports of large-scale movement of persons across the country in search of food. The regime tightly controls access to civilian aircraft, trains, buses, food, and fuel. Only members of a very small elite have vehicles for personal use. [Miller 2004]

The Constitution states that "women hold equal social status and rights with men." However, although women are represented proportionally in the labor force, few women have reached high levels of the party or the government. Like others in society, children are the objects of intense political indoctrination; even mathematics textbooks propound party dogma. [Miller 2004]

Workers have no right to organize or to bargain collectively. Government ministries set wages. The state assigns all jobs. Ideological purity is as important as professional competences in deciding who receives a particular job. [Miller 2004]

North Korea seeks to ensure regime stability. It pursues unconventional policies, including information control to protect its citizens from "undesirable" capitalist influences; acquisition of food and economic aid to alleviate famine and economic hardships; adoption of nationalist ideology; and the pursuit of militarism combined with pragmatic diplomatic overtures to advance its security goals. [Miller 2004]

Nazi's Germany

Goebbels was appointed the head of the Propaganda Ministry on March 1933. His mission was 'to transform the very spirit itself to the extent that people and things are brought into a new relationship with one another.' The Ministry departments covered propaganda, the press, film, theater, and 'popular enlightenment.' Similar care was taken over the written word. All Socialist and communist papers were rapidly closed down and the remaining papers were controlled by the Reich Press Chamber. [Williamson 2002]

Consequently, Goebbels ensured that the public was fed a suitable cultural diet which conformed to Nazi ideology. In music and art, for instance, experiments in modern art forms were condemned, while in literature, books on war, the 'heroic' early days of the Nazi movement, Germany's historic mission in the east and similar topics were approved themes. [Williamson 2002]

The control of the educational system was vital for the inculcation of Nazi ideology. Educational syllabuses were radically revised in the light of Nazi racial, political and social prejudices. Special emphasis was placed in the school curriculum on history, biology and German as the three subjects which were particularly effective vehicles for Nazi propaganda. A key to the new priorities was given by Hitler's observation that 'the racial state must build upon its entire educational work ... not on the pumping in of empty knowledge but on the development of healthy bodies. Only in the second place comes the training of mental facilities.' [Williamson 2002]

Central to Hitler's policy for the 'Thousands Year Reich' was the need to increase dramatically the German population. The primary importance of women to the Nazis was their role as child-bearers and home-makers. Women were discouraged from full-time work or academic courses. They were prepared for domestic duties learning domestic science and preservation of their health. To train women for motherhood and marriage, the regime set up women's organizations. If it came to the choice, the Nazi priority was not so much the family as the procreation of healthy 'Aryan' children. It was considered reprehensible conduct to refrain from giving healthy children to the nation. This led to banning abortion in May 1933. [Williamson 2002]

The Hitler government attempted to ease women out of industry and commerce by making motherhood an attractive financial proposition through a series of grants, loans, tax-reliefs schemes and the introduction of family allowances. Working women were encouraged to attend courses on domestic science and child care in their spare time. The government also issued a series of laws restricting the number of hours women could work in factories and prohibiting them from undertaking heavy work in certain industries. The Nazi government 'found itself in a head-on collision with a long-term process of social en economic change,' because at a time of growing labor scarcity women were recruited to work in many of the new plants set up under the Four Year Plan. [Williamson 2002]

Holocaust

At the beginning of 1941, the prevailing thinking among Nazi planners was that the Jews would be deported to some distant and desolate land. Madagascar was considered but rejected. Operation Barbarossa offered a more viable location: in the territories of a soon-to-be-defeated Soviet Union. But before the end of the year, the invasion had stalled, and the Jewish question had taken a radical turn. Complete extermination would be in the works. [Wittman 2016]

For practical reasons, the Nazis decided to annihilate the Jews. Waiting for the Jews to emigrate by themselves will take time and would never finish; sending them to other countries was too visible, annihilation in their country was opaque to world critics.

It is a cliché that revolutions devour their children. Both Robespierre and Lenin were compelled to liquidate over-zealous revolutionaries whose opposition threatened their policies. Hitler was not spared of this process. The 'legal revolution' of 1933 could not implement the destruction of large-scale capitalism and the replacement of traditional bureaucracy with new, party-dominated structures. Ernst Rohm was an effective critic, his elimination was inevitable. [Williamson 2002]

Venezuela

Under Maduro's presidency (2013 to 2017), Venezuela has been almost totally destroyed. Consider this evidence, according to Gustavo R. Coronel:

According to former Secretary General of the United Nations Ban Ki-Moon, Venezuela is in a state of humanitarian crisis, with food and medicine severely restricted and thousands of Venezuelans leaving the country by land, air, and sea.

Medicine sent to Venezuela by charitable organizations is not allowed to enter the country, or it is confiscated by regime customs agents for their own purposes.

Inflation was at 500 percent for a few years, and now is over a million percent, the highest in the world.

The national murder rate is at some fifty-eight deaths per one hundred thousand inhabitants, the second highest rate in the world, while the murder rate in Caracas is 119 deaths per one hundred thousand inhabitants.

Large gangs of armed criminals called "colectivos" control large areas in the capital city of Caracas. In other cities, they are engaged in war with the armed forces.

In 2015, Venezuela was listed as the ninth most corrupt country in the world by Transparency International.

Venezuela was rated by the knowledge web-portal globalEDGE as having "the highest-risk political and economic situation and the most difficult business environment. Corporate default is likely."

PDVSA, the state oil company, has suffered a production drop of about eight hundred thousand barrels per day since 1998. The country needs the price of oil to be at least $80 per barrel to make ends meet, but the price of oil remains much lower than that, and no relief is in sight.

About a dozen high-level members of the government, including ministers, generals of the armed forces, and state governors, have been named by the U.S. government for violating human rights or for engaging in drug trafficking.

Members of the Venezuelan armed forces at all levels, including those in the National Guard and the Army, are significantly involved in drug trafficking, while the High Military Command is openly backing the unconstitutional government of Maduro. Diosdado Cabello considered the number two man in the government hierarchy, has been denounced as being the tzar of the Venezuelan military drug cartel by a former bodyguard who is currently in the United States as a protected witness.

Two nephews of Maduro, raised by his wife, Cilia Flores, have been convicted in a New York court of drug trafficking. They were holding Venezuelan diplomatic passports and enjoyed a lifestyle only possible as a privileged member of the Venezuelan regime.

The Supreme Court of Justice is completely made up of Maduro's followers. The president of the Tribunal, Maikel Moreno, was arrested in 1987 for murder.

The Supreme Court of Justice has systematically invalidated all activities of the Venezuelan National Assembly, duly elected in December 2015, to the point that opposition lawmakers denounced the actions as "a rupture of the constitutional order" in the country, and the secretary–general of the OAS, Luis Almagro, "threatened to invoke the Inter-American Democratic Charter, which could lead to sanctions being imposed on Venezuela."

Highlights for Chapter 14
- In China, the worst violations of human rights happen in the areas of democracy, freedom of thought and freedom of expression.
- The democracy movement, said Deng, had now "gone too far" and was no longer in the interest of "stability, unity, and the Four Modernizations."
- The party was implacably opposed to the right to basic human freedoms.
- Fang preferred "science, democracy, creativity, and independence."
- Liu Xiaobo viewed democracy and human rights as a matter of principle.

- Liu wrote, "We must attempt to change the government's long-standing inability to listen to the voice of the people."
- Liu's basic political philosophy was his vision of democracy and human rights.
- On June 2, Deng gave new orders to clear the square, by force if necessary.
- Deng instinctually returned to his Leninist roots, blaming the "Western imperialists" and denouncing the West's imposition of sanctions for human rights violations.
- Communist Party-run and Soviet Union-dominated states were unraveling one after another all across Eastern Europe.
- In Cuba, the emphasis was on moral incentives. Workers would be paid the same regardless of variations in effort or quality.
- The so-called volunteers – who often lacked the right to refuse – were deployed throughout the country rather ineffectively.
- Political criteria were among the factors in making decisions on student admissions in Cuba.
- The dual existence of the dollar and the peso economies was beginning to bring about a visible gap between the rich or the privileged and the poor.
- The Right to Your Own Things has been violated in Zimbabwe. Property rights – full legal ownership of the land – are non-negotiable.
- Where boundaries are moved and there is no respect for private property, hunger will result.
- The problem with not having ownership lies in the way that human nature works.
- The rule of law refers to a state of constitutionalism where the law (nor parliament) is supreme.
- Rule by law means the opposite. It refers to a police state in which the government invokes the law (indeed creates law) to "justify" excessive use of government force.
- During a period of tyranny, leaders need to be visionaries, with prophetic voices, who are able to rise above the present crisis and take a principled stand.
- The Right to Democracy in Zimbabwe is also affected. But democracy is not only about popular will.

- In Lagos, it is a daily occurrence – several times a day – and it's a growing phenomenon all over Africa, power cuts that shut down the lights and air conditioning and the start-up roar of the generator.
- The North Korean state directs all significant economic activity, and only government-controlled labor unions are permitted in this country of 22 million persons.
- The Government's human rights record remained poor, and it continued to commit numerous serious abuses. Citizens do not have the right peacefully to change their government.
- The government prohibits freedom of speech, the press, assembly, and association, and all forms of cultural and media activities are under tight control of the party.
- Although women are represented proportionally in the labor force, few women have reached high levels of the party or the government.
- Like others in society, children are the objects of intense political indoctrination; even mathematics textbooks propound party dogma.
- The control of the educational system was vital for the inculcation of Nazi ideology.
- The primary importance of women to the Nazis was their role as child-bearers and home-makers.
- In Venezuela, under Maduro's presidency (2013 to 2017), the country has been almost totally destroyed.
- Venezuela is in a state of humanitarian crisis, with food and medicine severely restricted and thousands of Venezuelans leaving the country by land, air, and sea.
- The national murder rate is at some fifty-eight deaths per one hundred thousand inhabitants, the second highest rate in the world.
- Members of the Venezuelan armed forces at all levels, including those in the National Guard and the Army, are significantly involved in drug trafficking.
- The Supreme Court of Justice is completely made up of Maduro's followers.

Chapter 15: Discrimination

The largest sources of discrimination for humanity came from religious misguidance and political wrongdoing. Many battles have been fought on the name of God or the homeland. Tolerance was not the supreme criterion to avoid bloodshed. Human beings have been persistent in discrimination and bigotry. Discrimination is the unjust or prejudicial treatment of different categories of people or things, especially on the grounds of race, age, or sex. Bigotry is the intolerance toward those who hold different opinions from oneself.

Because the status of women was much lower than that of men in tzarist Russia, women benefited more from egalitarian reforms of the revolution. Many women achieved great success in the middle ranks of Soviet life, although very few women obtained high-ranking positions in the Soviet government or in the Communist Party. [Streissguth 2002]

In Tsarist Russia, the function of women was to care for husband and children, and in the ranks of peasants and workers, which formed eighty percent of the population, to share man's physical toil. Among the peasants especially, women worked harder than men, because in addition to their responsibilities for "kids and cooking," as the Germans say, they had to work, and did work, in the fields. In consequence, they had intrinsically more to gain from a revolution than men and were more realist and less frustrated than men, when the Revolution confronted them with new problems and opportunities. [Streissguth 2002]

Although the Bolsheviks demolished all sex barriers, there were, and are still today, few women in the upper hierarchy of the Communist Party or Soviet Government. [Streissguth 2002]

In Cuba, the experience of women changed considerably under the revolutionary rule. The proportion of women in the labor force doubled from the late 1950s to the late 1970s, when they accounted for 30 percent of the labor force. Women's participation in politics lagged considerably. Women accounted for only 13 percent of the Central Committees of the Communist Party of Cuba chosen in 1980 and 1986. [Bethell 1993]

In 1975, Castro initiated a policy for affirmative action designed to increase the number of women in the PCC, the Popular Power system, the Communist Youth and the Confederacion de Trabajadores de Cuba. [Staten 2005]

Zimbabwe

In Zimbabwe, a different type of discrimination came about, white's discrimination. The land was stolen from whites for being white. The whites' wealth came from the land and from industries based on agricultural marketing and processing. The land bomb had been ticking away since independence. Although in terms of statistics, land ownership in Zimbabwe is probably as unequal as it is in Britain, the land had been at the heart of Zimbabwe's liberation war. Far more than human rights, democracy or self-rule, people had fought for their stolen land. But under the independence settlement, if the government wanted the land it had to pay full compensation in a currency of the seller's choice. Only unused land could be taken without compensation. [Dowden 2009]

For twenty years Mugabe did little about the huge discrepancy in land ownership and allowed the principles of the 1931 Land Apportionment Act to stand. That had decreed 48 million acres reserved for 48,000 whites and 25 million acres for one million black farmers. At independence, 6000 white commercial farmers held 39 percent of the land. In 1990, only 8 percent of this commercial land was owned by black farmers, most of them the politically well connected. [Dowden 2009]

Mugabe announced a 'third Chimurenga,' the third time the Shona people had gone to war to defend their land. The war vets marched onto farmland, killed animals, destroyed crops and burned buildings. Farmers and their families were beaten up, some were killed. [Dowden 2009] Mugabe declared in October 1976: "In Zimbabwe, none of the white exploiters will be allowed to keep a single acre of their land!" By 1978 there was, on average, one farm murder of a white civilian every three days. Every farm was a target. [Freeth 2011]

The whole thing was Hitleresque. Later, Mugabe said, "I am still the Hitler of our time. This Hitler has only one objective – justice for his own people, sovereignty for his own people, recognition of the independence of his people and their right to their own resources. If that is Hitler, then let me be a Hitler tenfold. Ten times Hitler, that is what we stand for." This time, though, Hitler was a black African cleansing his country of white Africans. [Freeth 2011]

The case of white farmers in Zimbabwe was a special case of white discrimination instead of the most common cause of black discrimination. Organizations are generally very happy to finance projects fighting discrimination when black people are being severely discriminated against, but when white people are the victims, nobody wants to get involved. It is too controversial. The fact that white people had been discriminated against in post-independence Africa for nearly fifty years didn't appear to make a difference. [Freeth 2011]

The issue of race in Africa is too strong, it can be either black, white or Asian. In the black nationalist and pan-Africanist ideologies, a white man cannot be an African. It is a matter for reflection, the history of a nation should not affect the personal lives of people caught a few generations later. Why white farmers, those living in Africa after many generations, had to be persecuted by the new rulers after independence. This has always seemed strange, because, taken to its logical conclusion, it means that white people cannot be Australian either, and nor can black people be American or Australian or British. This is terribly dangerous. No one really condemned the anti-Jewish programme in Nazi Germany. It is only afterward that people become brave. While terrible events are happening, they hunker down. [Freeth 2011]

There was talk about a new constitution for Zimbabwe. Mugabe's party, ZANU-PF, tried to sell the idea on the land issue, saying that the white man's land could be taken and the Zimbabwe government would not have to pay for it. This was supposed to be the sweetener to allow the further entrenchment of the president's power within the constitution. [Freeth 2011]

The constitution was changed to please the desires of the new leaders and white farmers were denied access to due process. Amendment 17 to the constitution denied whites access to the courts. This law was the "most crass measure" ever came across in thirty-two years. Another judgment in the Zimbabwe Supreme Court had held that parliament could do as it wished. [Freeth 2011]

There is enough land in Zimbabwe for everybody, there is no need to punish whites to please blacks. Human rights should be legally binding, however, for the government, Zimbabwe was a sovereign power in which property rights could be infringed in the public interest in order to redress colonial imbalances. [Freeth 2011]

People close to the Mugabe government started to take justice in their own hands. There were many instances of the police refusing to attend life-threatening situations because they were "political." There were lawless evictions by thugs of farmers, despite Tribunal protection. And also official army involvement in the evictions and the incriminating silence of the Zimbabwe government. [Freeth 2011]

The racial discrimination argument was won. However, it didn't last long. At his birthday on February 2009, President Mugabe was back on the warpath. "Land distribution will continue," he said. "It will not stop. The few remaining white farmers should vacate their farms, as they have no place here. Our land issues are not subject to the SADC Tribunal." He described the ruling as "nonsense" and "of no consequence." [Freeth 2011]

Farmers were trying to convince the invaders using any argument, including the word of God. "What is the one thing we have in common?" We all are going to die. "You've got a choice. Either you do things God's way or you don't. It's your choice, but if you don't do things God's way, what will happen to you when you face death?" I kept asking them questions and getting them to think about judgment day and the love of God who sent his only Son to die for us all so that we might have forgiveness and life. The invaders made threats: "We will burn your house! We will eat your children!" And then they were gone again. [Freeth 2011]

After losing their farms, farmers have managed to return a number of times without getting arrested. Now not a single borehole is operational and the pump at the river also hasn't worked since the invaders took over. Without being able to get to the orchards, it seems that none of the 40,000 trees have been irrigated or sprayed or fertilized, despite Minister Shamuyarira having taken over all the equipment and materials needed to carry on farming operations. As a result, many of the citrus orchards are dead or dying. [Freeth 2011]

But the repeating of history does not change the principle that if a man buys a piece of land and develops and uses it productively, he should be able to continue to utilize that piece of land; unless it is compensated for in accordance with international norms. [Freeth 2011]

But deep down in my heart, I knew that justice was coming and that those evil men knew it would too. I knew that there was a far bigger wave building, a little way off, which would sweep over our land and cleanse it. I knew that we all had a part to play, but it would only begin to happen when we all started to act with honesty and courage – and with God in our hearts. [Freeth 2011]

Soviet Union

During the late 1920s, a series of trials took place involving specialists workers who were either foreign or came from bourgeois backgrounds. They were accused of treason, acts of espionage and working to restore the capitalist system. In 1928, 53 engineers were arrested in the town of Shakhty in the Donets Basin. It was claimed that they were German agents and were accused of acts of industrial sabotage. [Evans 2005]

The last of the great show trials began in Moscow in March 1938. Now the time had run out for Nicolai Bukharin, Andrei Rykov and the former head of the secret police, Genrikh Yagoda. Across the Soviet Union, tens of thousands of people were purged and eliminated. By the end of 1938, the Russian Communist Party had lost a third of its members. Treachery was used as a means of acquiring promotion to a Party's position, or a property and a way of settling old scores. [Evans 2005]

In the 1950s, there was another purge where many high-ranking Party members, including former close associates of Zhdanov, were arrested and either imprisoned or executed. Thousands of officials, many of them long-serving and loyal Party members, were arrested to face unfounded charges of conspiracy and treason. There have been various estimates about the number of people who died in the death camps of the 'Gulag archipelago.' Some suggest about 9 million but it could reach between 12 and 24 million. [Evans 2005]

The political police was an instrument of control at the disposal of the top party leadership, though sometimes that meant just the top leader and at other times it meant the party leadership collectively. Although the political police was under the jurisdiction of the Communist Party leader, it was ultimately accountable to only one person, and that was Stalin, who remained the party chief. These forces could be used against party members, including very senior ones. [Brown 2009] What were the reasons for Stalin's purge of the Party? Had he become an unbalanced psychopath or was it, as some historians have stated, further evidence of Stalin's paranoia – his suspicion of those around him particularly the rising young leaders within the Party? [Evans 2005]

The Communist Party did not allow the slightest challenge to its own hegemony. The system was highly ideologized and the various campaigns were orchestrated by the Department of Propaganda and Agitation. The repression of Stalin's last years affected tens of thousands of people who were far removed from the party leadership. Often it was enough to be the son of 'an enemy of the people' – a child of one of those incarcerated for no good reason in the 1930s – for that person to be arrested and sent to a labor camp. [Brown 2009]

Soviets participated willingly on wrongful activities, they were accomplices of the regime. When I was entering the Party, in my application, I wrote, "I know and accept the Party Program and Regulations. I am prepared to devote all of my energy, and, if necessary, to give my life to my Motherland." And what do you think of me? That I'm an idiot? That I'm infantile …? Some of the people I know … They have outright laughed at me: emotional socialism, the ideas on paper … That's what I look like to them. Stupid! Down Syndrome! You're 'an engineer of human souls.' [Alexievich 2016]

This statement is really clear, of course, you are stupid, no other way around. Socialism is emotional and guided by religious precepts. It was your fault to get attached to a bad political system, it was your fault, you are the one to blame, socialism did not deserve to be in power for so many years; it is always the fault of those that support socialism, let us not forget that! It is the fault of the people!

The truth is that Russians contributed to sustaining socialism, even though it was wrong and harmful, "Two men sitting at a table got into an argument, shouting at each other until they were hoarse. The first one said, 'no matter what, I'm still a communist. We were supposed to build socialism. How could we have broken Hitler's spine without Magnitka and Vorkuta?' The second one: 'I've been talking to the local elderly … All of them worked or served – I don't know the right word for what they did – in the camps. They were the cooks, the guards, special agents. There was no other work out here, and those works paid well: salaries, rations, outfitting. That's what they call it, 'work.' For them, the camps were work! A job! And here you are talking about crimes against humanity. Sin and the soul. It wasn't just anyone doing time, it was the people. And the ones sentencing them and guarding them were the people, too – not foreign workers, not people brought in from outside – they were the very same people. Our own men. Kin. Today, you see everybody putting on the striped uniform. Now, everyone is the victim and Stalin alone is to blame. But think about it … It's simple arithmetic … Millions of inmates had to be surveilled, arrested, interrogated, transported and shot for minor transgressions. Someone had to do all this ... and they found millions of people who were willing to ..." [Alexievich 2016]

Many people accept mean responsibilities. Nobody knows the reason: fear, need, sadistic mood, greedy approach, survival instincts. Some may be even obeying orders, believing that they have no decisions to make. It is a wrong human condition, punishing others without knowing whether they deserve it or not.

Criticism to Soviets abound, however, some say it was the people's fault, "He was taken away for something very stupid ... Total nonsense ... He was at a store with his wife and said, "The Soviet regime has been around for twenty years, and they still can't make a decent pair of pants." Today, they say that everyone was against it, but I tell you – the people supported the mass arrests." [Alexievich 2016]

What a good testimony, at least one is saying some truths. Of course, it is people who accept the injustices of the government, who else? How are you going to accept a neighbor thrown to jail for saying the truth? Of course, the regime is incapable of doing any good to the population, it is not in their objectives.

It has been established that Russians are not kind. Russian's human nature demonstrates the lack of civilized approaches, "The Russian people are not at all kind. That's just a widespread misconception. They're maudlin, sentimental, but they are not kind. Someone killed a stray dog and made a video of it. The whole Internet blew up. People were ready to lynch the guy who did it. But when seventeen migrant workers were burnt alive at the market – their boss would lock them up in a metal wagon at night along with his goods – the only people who stood up for them were human rights advocates. People whose occupation it is to stand up for everyone. The general feeling was, "These people died, others will come to replace them." Faceless, voiceless ... strangers ..." [Alexievich 2016]

When a society is composed of unkind people, there is no justice. It happens all over the globe, people do not care for what happened to their neighbors, lest for some people suffering an injustice far away. There are no proportions, sometimes an animal is more valuable than a human being.

There was discontent within Russia against communists, denouncing communists during war occupation was common. During German occupation some denounced the Soviets, "His grandfather despised communists! Lenin and Stalin! As soon as he returned, he started taking his revenge. He'd point them out to the Germans: this one's a communist ... and that one ... those men would be taken off somewhere ... It took me a long time to understand what the war was ..." [Alexievich 2016]

It is normal when you suffer too much, you want to discharge your resentment, it is human nature. However, there must be some limits, at least a fair trial to determine what kind of injustices those men perpetrated; if there were killings, they must pay for them. Not because of their ideas they should be punished, but by their actions.

Distrust is a common sentiment in Russia. Confidence is not getting roots in Russia, distrust is ever present, "Russian people don't expect to ever be happy. Everyone sane is taking their children out of this country. A lot of my friends have already left ... They call me from Israel and Canada. I'd never thought about leaving before. Leaving, leaving ... I started considering it only after my daughter was born. I want to protect the people I love. My father will never forgive me. That I am sure of." [Alexievich 2016]

Cuba

Emigration in Cuba has been a constant during so many years now. Nearly 250,000 Cubans had fled the island between 1959 and October 1962. Almost all were members of the upper and middle classes and this contributed to the 'brain drain' and the lack of qualified personnel to help with the development of the country. Living standards that had improved tremendously the previous two decades were reversed. In 1992 and 1993, more than 7,000 balseros in boats or rafts made it to the United States from Cuba. According to interviews, the vast majority of the balseros were escaping economic hardships of the Special Period. [Staten 2005]

One reason why levels of coercion have been lower in Cuba than in a majority of communist states is that successive waves of emigration from the island have been permitted. Thus, several hundred thousand of the most disaffected citizens have been able to move either to the United States or to other parts of Latin America. [Brown 2009] Castro allowed almost 125,000 Cubans to leave the country via the port city of Mariel in 1980. Among these emigres were political prisoners, common criminals (less than 4 percent of the total), Cubans released from mental health facilities and Cuba's poor. This group differed significantly from the largely elite professionals and middle- and working-class immigrants who arrived in Miami during the first (1959-1962) and second (1965-1973) waves. [Staten 2005]

Africa

The emigration in Africa has also been huge. The exodus of people is even more alarming. There are an estimated 15 million Africans born in the continent now living outside it. Some 70,000 skilled people are reported to be fleeing the continent each year. Tens of thousands trek across the Sahara Desert in buses and lorries in the hope of finding a passage across the Mediterranean or leave in tiny boats from West African beaches and ports hoping to reach Spain or Portugal. [Dowden 2009]

The question for the majority black, 'colored' and Indian population of South Africa was how to wrest power from the white minority. The ANC had been a middle-class black organization since its foundation in 1912, formally admitting whites as members only in 1964. The Pan Africanist Congress advocated a more race-based approach: Africa for the Africans. The debate reflected the two strands, Africanist or Marxist, race or class, that ran through the struggle for Africa's liberation from imperial and white rule. [Dowden 2009]

In 1950 the South African Communist Party was banned and ten years later so was the ANC. Better organized, the SACP dictated ANC strategy. But white led, and with close links to Moscow, it could not advocate the expulsion of whites from the country. The SACP and ANC screamed for an uprising of the masses to smash imperialism, capitalism, and colonialism. In contrast, the Africanist tradition was more psychological and racial. It demanded Africa for the Africans and wanted to see black states and black leaders who could treat with the rest of the world on an equal footing. [Dowden 2009]

Since the race was the basis of the South African state and society and discrimination was the daily experience of ordinary black people in their everyday lives, this was a far more appealing ideology for many blacks than the broad, revolutionary, anti-capitalist aims of the ANC. The global struggle against capitalism did not motivate as fiercely as the struggle to regain lives and land now. [Dowden 2009]

In the 1970s the Africanist cause was reincarnated as Black Consciousness, a philosophy rather than a movement, forged by Steve Biko and other black intellectuals. Steve Biko, the most charismatic and articulate South African of his generation, was killed in jail by the police in 1977. The capture and imprisonment of Nelson Mandela and the leadership of the ANC in the early 1960s decapitated the black leadership for a generation. Biko complained that neither the ANC nor the Pan

Africanist Congress was doing anything that meant much to ordinary people; their language of class struggle did not touch the lives of ordinary Africans whose main problem was white racism. Being black, said Biko, was not a matter of skin color, it was a mental attitude. He wrote: 'Black people are those who can manage to hold their heads high in defiance rather than willingly surrender their souls to the white man.' [Dowden 2009]

The realization that blacks were complicit in their own oppression and only blacks could liberate themselves from it, struck a chord with the new generation. The message that Biko delivered with such articulacy was that each black South African must stand up and free himself or herself as an individual from mental apartheid as a starting point and an integral part of liberating their country. [Dowden 2009]

China

In China, there was also political discrimination, in the universities, the first burst of criticism came from academics who complained 'there is a tendency for political qualifications to override cultural and technical qualifications.' [Roberts 2003]

Venezuela

Political discrimination has long plagued Venezuela. For decades, government patronage and spoils were divided along party lines at the expense of large sectors of Venezuelan society. Chavez assumed the presidency in part on the promise to free Venezuela from its entrenched patterns of political exclusion. While his government managed to uproot the established system of political discrimination, it has replaced it with new forms of discrimination against real and perceived political opponents.

Material about discrimination can be obtained through the following link: https://www.hrw.org/reports/2008/venezuela0908/2.htm

The Chavez government proclaims a commitment to political inclusion but has openly discriminated against those who do not share its views. Government officials have removed scores of detractors from the career civil service, purged dissident employees from the national oil company, denied citizens access to social programs based on their political opinions and denounced critics as subversives deserving of discriminatory treatment. The Chavez administration's exclusion and harassment of those who voice their dissent belie its banner of democratic pluralism.

Political discrimination under Chavez was most pronounced in the aftermath of the 2004 recall referendum on Chavez's presidency. Citizens who exercised their right to call for the referendum—invoking one of the new participatory mechanisms championed by Chavez during the drafting of the 1999 Constitution—were threatened with retaliation and blacklisted from some government jobs and services.

In 2004, the Hugo Chavez regime in Venezuela distributed the list of several million voters who had attempted to remove him from office throughout the government bureaucracy, allegedly to identify and punish these voters. Since the Maisanta software contains the list of signers of the Petition for Recall, these individuals were more readily identified as political opponents by the Chavez regime after 2004.

In another case that suggests politically motivated discrimination, an employee at the National Council of Frontiers (Consejo Nacional de Fronteras, CNF) was told by her boss that she and three other employees had been fired solely because they signed for the recall referendum.

Since 1996, Rocío San Miguel had worked as a contract employee and legal counsel to the CNF, a government agency attached to the office of the vice-president. Four of the council's 22 employees—Magally Chang, Jorge Guerra, Thais Peña Rocío, and San Miguel—were fired on March 22, 2004. The dismissal letters gave no reasons for their termination.

Throughout 2005–2006 there were growing reports of the arrest or exile of opposition leaders and claims of widespread job discrimination against Chavez opponents, even among everyday citizens who held no leadership roles in the political opposition.

Chávez himself has sent mixed messages regarding political discrimination. At times he has recognized that discrimination is a problem and spoken out against it. For example, he directed employers to "bury" the Tascón list due to reports he received of employment discrimination (although he waited a full year after the list's implementation to do so). He also promoted a constitutional reform proposal to explicitly bar discrimination based on political orientation.

Political discrimination has been openly endorsed and practiced in the oil industry, which is one of the country's largest sources of employment and the backbone of the national economy. After a two-month-long strike in December 2002, the government fired close to half of the workforce from the state oil company, Petróleos de Venezuela, S.A. (PDVSA), and blacklisted them from future employment in the oil sector.

In following years, the government used participation in the strike much like it used participation in the recall referendum effort: to identify targets for discriminatory treatment. PDVSA blacklisted the dismissed employees from future employment in the oil sector as well as in its subsidiaries and contractors. The energy minister and Chavez suggested that all of the company's workers must support the government or leave. There is credible evidence that the discriminatory mindset reflected in these public statements also was embodied in actual employment policies in some departments of PDVSA.

Political discrimination has underpinned and tarnished the government's actions in a wide variety of areas. Political discrimination has affected government decisions with respect to the media, organized labor, and civil society. Legitimate criticism has been used by some government officials as the basis for excluding dissident voices from the airwaves, collective contract negotiations, and civil society meetings.

The Chavez government has punished media outlets for their criticism of the government. The government has also threatened legal action or administrative sanctions against opposition stations, and blocked applications by a station critical of the government for frequencies to extend its coverage.

In the most notorious case, the government refused to renew the license of the opposition television station RCTV in May 2007 because of its obstinate refusal to soften its editorial line. While the decision was nominally justified by the need to use the RCTV frequency to set up a new public channel, the government had other frequencies at its disposal and at the time had renewed the licenses of channels that supported the government or had moderated their criticism.

Labor unions which fall into disfavor with the government have faced obstacles to collective bargaining. Contrary to international law on the right to association in particular as it relates to trade unions, the government has denied established unions the right to bargain collectively until they hold state-supervised leadership elections.

Highlights for Chapter 15

- In Tsarist Russia, the function of women was to care for husband and children.

- Although the Bolsheviks demolished all sex barriers, there are still today few women in the upper hierarchy of the Communist Party or Soviet Government.
- In Cuba, the experience of women changed considerably under the revolutionary rule. However, women's participation in politics lagged considerably.
- In 1975, Castro initiated a policy for affirmative action designed to increase the number of women in the Communist Party.
- In Zimbabwe, a different type of discrimination came about, white's discrimination. The land was stolen from whites for being white.
- The war vets marched onto farmland, killed animals, destroyed crops and burned buildings.
- Mugabe declared in October 1976: "In Zimbabwe, none of the white exploiters will be allowed to keep a single acre of their land!"
- By 1978 there was, on average, one farm murder of a white civilian every three days.
- The issue of race in Africa is too strong, it can be either black, white or Asian. In the black nationalist and pan-Africanist ideologies, a white man cannot be an African.
- The constitution was changed to please the desires of the new leaders and white farmers were denied access to due process.
- The color of the skin was the only consideration when distributing land. The discrimination issue pointed out that the taking of land only affected white farmers.
- The problem was that, once the government had 'bought the farm,' the title deeds were vested in the state president and there was no actual on-the-ground owner any longer.
- The racial discrimination argument was won. They could no longer be discriminated against just because of the color of their skin. However, it didn't last long.
- "Land distribution will continue," Mugabe said. "It will not stop. The few remaining white farmers should vacate their farms. He described the ruling as "nonsense" and "of no consequence."
- The invaders made threats: "We will burn your house! We will eat your children!"

- If we wanted an end to Mugabe's tyranny, we had to face it and expose the things that were wrong.
- After losing their farms, farmers have managed to return a number of times without getting arrested. Now not a single borehole is operational and the pump at the river also hasn't worked since the invaders took over.
- If a man buys a piece of land and develops and uses it productively, he should be able to continue to utilize that piece of land.
- But deep down in my heart, I knew that justice was coming and that those evil men knew it would too.
- During the late 1920s, a series of trials took place involving specialists workers who were either foreign or came from bourgeois backgrounds.
- The last of the great show trials began in Moscow in March 1938. Across the Soviet Union, tens of thousands of people were purged and eliminated. Some suggest about 9 million but it could reach between 12 and 24 million.
- What were the reasons for Stalin's purge of the Party? Had he become an unbalanced psychopath or was it Stalin's paranoia?
- The repression of Stalin's last years affected tens of thousands of people who were far removed from the party leadership.
- It has been established that Russians are not kind. Russian human nature demonstrates the lack of civilized approaches.
- Emigration in Cuba has been a constant during so many years now. Nearly 250,000 Cubans had fled the island between 1959 and October 1962.
- In 1992 and 1993, more than 7,000 balseros in boats or rafts made it to the United States from Cuba.
- Castro allowed almost 125,000 Cubans to leave the country via the port city of Mariel in 1980.
- The exodus of people in Africa is even more alarming. There are an estimated 15 million Africans born in the continent now living outside it.
- Since the race was the basis of the South African state and society, discrimination was the daily experience of ordinary black people in their everyday lives.

- In the 1970s the Africanist cause was reincarnated as Black Consciousness, a philosophy rather than a movement.
- The realization that blacks were complicit in their own oppression and only blacks could liberate themselves from it was their motto.
- Political discrimination has long plagued Venezuela.
- Chavez invented new forms of discrimination against real and perceived political opponents.
- The Chavez administration's exclusion and harassment of those who voice their dissent belie its banner of democratic pluralism.
- Political discrimination under Chavez was most pronounced in the aftermath of the 2004 recall referendum on Chavez's presidency.
- Throughout 2005–2006 there were claims of widespread job discrimination against Chavez opponents.
- Chavez himself has sent mixed messages regarding political discrimination. At times he has recognized that discrimination is a problem and spoken out against it.
- Political discrimination has been openly endorsed and practiced in the oil industry.
- The energy minister and Chavez suggested that all of the company's workers must support the government or leave.
- The Chavez government has punished media outlets for their criticism of the government.
- In the most notorious case, the government refused to renew the license of the opposition television station RCTV in May 2007.
- Labor unions which fall into disfavor with the government have faced obstacles to collective bargaining.

Chapter 16: Corruption

Many people believe that corruption exists everywhere, that it should not be a topic for discussion. If you say that in a country corruption created poverty and famine and that it is the fault of politicians, people respond saying that it happens everywhere, that no country is immune to corruption. There is however a difference. when you are caught in Canada in corruption charges, your penalty is severe because the country enforces respect and the rule of law. What happens in under-developed countries is that the rule of law does not prevail, governments allow putrefaction of officials accepting bribes and abusing deviation of public funds.

Corruption can be defined as the misuse of public wealth for private gain, however, the broader definition of "misuse of entrusted power" is gaining popularity. Corruption has many forms: – the acceptance, soliciting or extortion of bribes; patronage, clientelism, use of informal arrangements, personal connections, service exchanges or contacts within the bureaucratic structure; theft of public funds or goods and political corruption. These alternative misuses of public funds may vary from country to country and differing realities but its roots lie in several factors that lead to the misuse of public office, they are relatively similar and take three main forms:

1. the overall level of public wealth available,
2. the risks inherent in corrupt deals, and
3. the relative bargaining power of the briber and the person being bribed.

The misuse of public office for private gain is the accepted definition of corruption, therefore, in that case, the public sector uses to be considered corrupt. This of course assumes that the population makes a distinction between public and private roles. The dominance of the party in organizing socialists and communists societies has led to the existence of a public sector officially the sole means of resource distribution.

Corrupt transactions are initiated consciously, challenging accountability and the rule of law. Profit and opportunity are weighed against the risks of being detected and the likelihood of the severity of punishment. Corruption takes place where there is a combination of opportunity and inclination. It can be initiated from either side of the transaction: a bribe being offered to an official, or the official requesting (or even extorting) an illicit payment. Those offering bribes may do so either because they want something they are not entitled to, and bribe the official to bend the rules, or because they believe that the official will not give them their entitlements without some inducements being offered.

However the problem does not lay in just developing a comprehensive program to fight corruption but in examining its causes and effects as well. The lack of hard data concerning the causes and effects of corruption in most countries harms the design and implementation of activities to curb corruption.

Corruption plays an important role in demonstrating how citizens relate to their governments. The duality of the corruption formula with two sides entering into an agreement for the provision of services leaves both sides as victims and perpetrators of corrupt acts. Corruption has been identified by many as being one of the most important factors in the undermining of democracy. Corruption can be seen as a symptom of poor governance and a crucial factor if reviewing the state/society relationship.

While political corruption can prompt public protest, the majority of the population endures wide-scale corruption and considers it an inevitable part of life in many countries. An "everyone does it" attitude prevails within certain sectors and assumes improper motives to those who try to expose corrupt practices.

Informal social networks form an integral factor in the corruption equation. The dominance of closed social networks, which allowed life under the planned economy in socialists and communists countries, has facilitated the emergence of a corrupted bureaucracy. Having been based on a valid method of achieving goals or "getting things done" within the economy, the continued use of social networks instead of "modern" methods of goal achievement have been proven extremely difficult to eliminate.

The idea of trust, a component of social capital, is an important glue holding society together. Certainly the international development community is increasingly recognizing the important role of social capital in development. The erosion of social capital or trust between the people and their governments has led to the undermining the democratic transitions of many countries. Mass tax evasion, capital flight, low electoral turnout and a gradual disinterest in the formation of policy and governance in general are but a few signs of this lack of faith in the governing powers. The causes of this lack of trust and its impact are many and directly lead to the spread of corruption.

The relative weakness and/or ineffectiveness of the State and its institutions are major sources of corruption and breed a lack of trust in the government to provide services. The inability of the State to hold public servants accountable and exerting control over their actions constitutes the most obvious feature.

With the existence of weak states unable to provide services, the connections and contacts between society and state are rapidly eroding. The government and those that govern are far removed from the daily lives of the population. Governments are perceived as corrupt and based on closed systems for the promotion of self-interests and the extortion of income flow.

The other side of corruption is how governments benefit from it for purposes of staying in power against the will of the people; in many cases using public resources to rig the elections. Africa is one of the continents where corruption has hit the population the most. Most of the time dictators benefit of their lack of accountability and wrongdoing to steal the public treasure. Corruption exists everywhere, not just Africa. It happens in Europe and America, in India and China, and do not forget Russia.

Zimbabwe

Way back in November 1984, during a time of prayer at our church in Chegutu, Anne Cranswick spoke the following prophetic words: "My people, listen to what I say. The state of this country will become worse and still worse. Corruption will be as you have never seen it before. Law and order, education, medical facilities, agriculture, transport and finance will break down, be chaotic. People will be in a state of despondency. My tribe will be scattered..." Less than a decade and a half later, the prophecy was coming true. [Freeth 2011]

John Robertson, a Zimbabwean economist, says, 'We imagine corruption to be like a tick on a dog. There are some places in Africa where the tick is bigger than the dog.' [Dowden 2009]

Staying in power is a way of life in Zimbabwe. Becoming a politician allows people to get rich. Gradually, the ZANU party leaders became like the pigs in Animal Farm, an elite above the law, in total political control and living the lifestyle of the world's richest. They awarded themselves huge salaries and grotesque allowances, using their political positions to gain contracts and take over the business. They became as far removed from the lives of their fellow black Zimbabweans as any white Rhodesian had ever been. [Dowden 2009]

Because Mugabe had a relatively decent performance in his initial years as president, people do not believe what happened afterwards. One of the usual reactions of outsiders to Mugabe is, 'He's gone mad, hasn't he? The common impression is that Mugabe used to be a good guy and Zimbabwe did well in the early years. Then he went crazy and ruined it. Some have suggested that he was always evil, murdering rivals, manipulating supporters. [Dowden 2009]

Mugabe had not gone mad. Nor was he always bad. His transformation happened over many years. During his mandate he tried to retain power and use propaganda in his favor. He had to convince his followers taking justice on their own hands against the White Africans. He is a complicated schizophrenic man, driven both by respect for the Western mentality for logic and order and a passionate sense of injustice and rejection by whites. He has both a vision of wrongs to be righted, even revenged, and by the lust for power. [Dowden 2009]

Angola

The elite ruling class that had been at the heart of the slave trade for centuries found no difficulty setting up a communist command economy. For them it was simply a continuation of the monopolies they had enjoyed in the good old days. They managed the economy in a way that made them exceedingly rich. Government officials and ministers were able to obtain dollars for travel or contracts overseas. They received the dollars at the official rate and then go the street and sell them at the black market rate 40 times higher. Fortunes were made on this currency round-tipping. [Dowden 2009]

Angola's few principled Marxists were sidelined or retired. Those who remain in government call themselves 'pragmatic.' Many of them are extremely wealthy. The IMF says that between 1996 and 2001 nearly 40 percent of state expenditure was not accounted for and that in 2001 nearly $ 1 billion went missing from government accounts. According to the IMF, Angola is expected to grow by 15-20 percent a year for the next decade and maybe beyond. But the money stays with the top 5 percent of the population. Spread out among all Angolans each one would receive about $2000 a year, putting it 63rd in the list of countries ranked by income per head and above Romania. But in the Human Development Index, Angola lies at 161st place out of 177 countries, and falling. Ninety-five percent of Angola's 16 million people live on less than a dollar a day. [Dowden 2009]

An IMF report states that oil-rich African countries have no better record of lifting their populations out of poverty or reaching the Millennium Development Goals than countries without oil. Oil creates an enclave economy: the money comes directly into the treasury straight from oil companies and no mechanism exists to spread it around. Angolans gain nothing from their country's oil riches, and if they want to change their lives they will have to fight. [Dowden 2009]

Congo (Zaire)

When Mobutu's rule ended in 1997, Zaire as a nation state was dead. Theft and corruption ruled. Once the system is corruption and corruption is the system, it is impossible to operate without it. At present no company, local or foreign, can do business in Congo and avoid corruption. [Dowden 2009]

The only national organization that survived Mobutu and the looting was the Catholic Church. Its voice is still powerful and it creates an uncorrupted space for discussion and debate. The Church is also the largest 'aid agency' and provider of health and education in the country. [Dowden 2009]

Despite the politics of theft, violence and patronage, Congo still inspires great patriotism among its long-suffering citizens. They may have little loyalty to institutions or a ruler, but Congolese believe desperately in the Congolese nation and a few are prepared to fight its looting bosses. [Dowden 2009]

Kenya

'There is a need for healing of the nation. The process of national healing and reconciliation is unlikely to proceed as long as society is still polarized,' a report said. It pointed out the impunity of politicians from past crimes and dwelt on corruption, the nature of presidential power, and the need for devolution and a new constitution. The report called for a 'much-needed political compromise.' [Dowden 2009]

Murderous local wars fueled by politicians have often broken out, particularly at election times after multi-party democracy was reintroduced. Kenya's politics are the most ethnicized and monetarized of any on the continent. The primary job for an MP is seen as delivering goodies to his or her own ethnic group. The people vote for the corrupt politicians because they are obviously the Strong Man who have goodies to bring from the government. [Dowden 2009]

In Kenya, no single commodity provided the bulk of the wealth. To get rich in Kenya you have to work. So how could politicians get rich? Foreign aid was one source, and because Kenya was such a close political ally, no-one investigated how much Western aid went missing. A few politicians set up genuine businesses but the majority had to graft and beg, exchanging government contracts for bribes. [Dowden 2009]

The looting of Kenya by its rulers dragged its economic growth rate down from 4.5 percent in the late 1980s to 1 percent in 1991 and less than 1 percent in subsequent years. The whole country paid the price of their rulers' greed. From 1992 poverty and infant mortality rated increased rapidly and life expectancy and school enrollment fell. [Dowden 2009]

In 2002 there was a change of government. In the lead-up to the election a new constitution was proposed and the whole country joined in to draw it up. After months of debate and wrangling a draft was agreed at a conference center near Nairobi called Bomas. It introduced checks and balances, provided for devolution and a powerful Prime Minister and other reforms that diluted the powers of the presidency. The new government was going to investigate the previous regime for corruption. [Dowden 2009]

The government set up a huge public inquire into the Goldenberg fraud. Moi, his sons and business partners Gideon and Phillip, Kamlesh Pattni, the mastermind behind the schemes and the man who set up the Goldenberg Bank, and his bagman, Ketan Somaia, whose Delphis Bank handled much of the money. Lawyers cross-examined civil servants, bankers and Pattni himself. Day by day they sat bug-eyed as the thieves fell out and implicated each other, revealing the astounding tale of the theft of Kenya by its rulers and their business associates. [Dowden 2009]

Nigeria

Corruption exists everywhere, not just Africa. It happens in Europe and America, in India and China. But Nigeria's hilariously brazen corruption puts it in a different league. Elsewhere it is conducted behind closed doors or by nods and euphemisms. In Nigeria it is open and it is everywhere. Internationally the word 'Nigeria' has come to mean corruption and dodgy dealing. The country regularly appears top of the list of the world's most corrupt countries, according to Transparency

International. Nigeria is also home to the famous 419 scams named after the law that is supposed to ban them. [Dowden 2009]

Many Nigerians will tell you that it takes two to tango and corruption needs a giver as well as a receiver. They like to blame corruption on foreigners. On the rare occasions when grand corruption has been exposed in Africa there has been an outsider connection: either European or American companies have paid bribes or their banks have received stolen money without question. [Dowden 2009]

If, on the other hand, corruption comes from within Africa, what traditions within Africa could have evolved into today's ubiquitous systems? In parts of precolonial Africa if you wanted to please a king, you brought him a gift. In return he looked after you, fed you and protected your family. In such an exchange a social bond was created and symbolically cemented by constant gift-giving and receiving between ruler and ruled. There is nothing traditional about a Swiss bank account, said President Obasanjo. [Dowden 2009]

And the colonial legacy? Both Nigeria and Congo began as territories seized by Europeans for pillage. They were estate states. Congo was created and owned by King Leopold of Belgium. Much of Nigeria was owned and ruled by George Goldie's National Africa Company, chartered by the British government to exploit thousands of square miles and rule hundreds of thousands of Africans. The estate states were created to extract commodities for Europe as cheaply as possible and they made their ruler-owners rich beyond imagining. It is hardly surprising that those who inherited these states imitated their founders. [Dowden 2009]

After seventeen years of military rule Nigeria was close to being like Mobutu's Zaire. All its institutions – the civil service, the law, hospitals, schools, the army, police, business, academics – had become so corrupt that, although Nigeria looks like a functioning state, it is just a shell. It still holds the shape of a nation state from the outside, but within, corruption has become the institution. [Dowden 2009]

On corruption and human rights Obasanjo commissioned reports when he came into office. But he never published them. Unwillingly to make the thieves accountable to the Nigerian people, he preferred to use the information to blackmail political rivals. In time, senior members of the government were summoned for questioning. However, it became clear that although many people were investigated, only those opposed to Obasanjo were brought to account. [Dowden 2009]

Colin Powell, the American Secretary of State, once let slip the opinion that all Nigerians are crooks. All? Maybe not, but a lot of Nigerians dedicate their lives to fulfilling the stereotype. And being Nigerian they are also often world class. An official of the US Drug Enforcement Agency spoke in awe of the Nigerian drug smuggling gangs. 'We thought we knew most of the tricks of the drug trade until we came up against the Nigerians,' 'Then we realized we were just beginners.' [Dowden 2009]

In 1996 a commission of inquiry discovered that the $12 billion surplus revenue from oil resulting from the high price during the Gulf War was missing. Much of it was in offshore accounts controlled by President Ibrahim Babangida. None of it was ever recovered. When Babangida's successor, Sani Abacha, died in 1998, his family were forced to pay back $2 billion stolen during his five-year reign. But they were allowed to keep the $100 million that he stole before he seized power. Many Nigerians think that $2 billion is small change compared to what he actually stole. [Dowden 2009]

The root of the problem is that the Nigerian state depends not on a constitution but on a commodity: oil. Nigeria's oil comes from the Niger Delta. In the nineteenth century the Delta produced another desperately needed oil, palm oil. In 1884, the British National Africa Company created a monopoly to purchase and export palm oil from the Niger River. The monopoly wiped out the African middlemen and Africa ended up with little to show for its prized commodity. It was forced at gunpoint to become a primary producer for a British company. History is repeating itself. Nigeria's first oil was discovered at Olubiri, a village in the Niger Delta. Ogoni activists tried to force the oil companies and the government to give more oil revenue to the local people. Their strategy was a direct confrontation, the leader convicted by military tribunal and executed in 1995. [Dowden 2009]

Nigeria's oil is the story of Midas. Nigeria was suddenly rich. The African country with the most people was blessed with an endless cheap source of energy and wealth. But it turned Nigeria into a nation of junkies. The sweet back juice oozed everywhere, into everything. It suffocated the economy, generated greed, fed regional jealousy, funded terrible regimes, started a war. Oil dreams wrecked Nigeria. [Dowden 2009]

King Oil destroyed almost every other economic activity in Nigeria. In 1966 less than 10 percent of the government's revenue came from oil.

By 1990 oil provided 97 percent. There is no alternative source of wealth to fund political opposition. In some years the oil revenue doubled. Today it provides more than a third of Nigeria's GDP and three-quarters of government revenue. In the 1970s Nigeria was once so awash with petrodollars that the then President, Yakubu Gowon, said that Nigeria's only problem was how to spend the money. Mostly was stolen or wasted. [Dowden 2009]

Meanwhile Nigeria's poor get poorer. In 2006 the country contained the largest number of absolutely poor people in the world after China and India – 70 percent of all Nigerians, some 84 million people. [Dowden 2009]

Compare Nigeria with Indonesia, another oil producer which came from a similar economic base. Both suffered dictatorships from the 1960s which both ended in 1998. Both were corrupt dictatorships but the difference was that Indonesia's rulers invested in the country and its people. They developed Indonesia and cared about its future, education and health. The Nigerian elite did not believe in Africa. They stole whatever they could and shipped the money out of the country, letting schools, universities and hospitals collapsed. In a country awash with oil they did not even keep an oil refinery going and had to import fuel. [Dowden 2009]

Nigeria is now like eighteenth-century Britain, deeply corrupt and with an abyss between classes. The elites, the 'Chosen' as Wole Soyinka, Nigeria's playwright, calls them, are treated as gods by their fawning subjects. The elite owns and runs Nigeria. An elite has wealth and power, though not necessarily education. Individual elites can come unstuck, but only once did a President try to attack them as a class. In the 1990s the military dictator, Sani Abacha, took them on head-on. [Dowden 2009]

His predecessor, General Ibrahim Babangida, who ruled from 1985 until 1993, used the opposite policy to stay in control. He kept the elite happy. Every politically important Strong Man was given a chance to get the trough and eat. He said he was trying to find a new system of democracy for Nigeria and a new type of Nigerian to run it. In the end he set up two political parties, one slightly to the right, one slightly to the left, wrote constitutions and manifestos for each, selected their leaders and called it democracy. [Dowden 2009]

In Nigeria money is power and power is money. That is no different from the rest of the world but it is more naked, more total in Nigeria. Like a lot of dictators Abacha made state funds his own, not to have fun but to buy people. He had to have more money than anyone else to ensure he could outbid anyone for the souls of Nigerians. [Dowden 2009]

Feeding all the elites was expensive. Abacha resorted to awarding bogus contracts to keep them happy. There were two different rates of exchange for importing goods, one was eighty naira to the dollar, the other was twenty-two for essential goods. That required the permission of the President. Once you had been given an import contract at the lower rate, you hurried off to the Central Bank, obtained your dollars and sold them on the open market, you fetched four times the rate at which you had bought them. [Dowden 2009]

Abacha was murdered in 1998. Under considerable international pressure after Abacha's death, the military decided to return the country to civilian rule. The coming of democracy in 1999 did not change the Nigerian system: the king is dead, long live whoever-has-got-the-oil-money. Policies and principles were non-existent. Politics were about personal alliances. [Dowden 2009]

Cuba

Corruption among high-level government officials and military personnel was publicly exposed during the period of rectification. They used their preferential access to key resources for their own personal benefit and many lived beyond the means of the typical Cuban citizen. Public trials combined with long-term prison sentences and some executions of top government officials were designed to deter future corruption. The most sensational and noteworthy trial was that of General Arnaldo Ochoa Sanchez, who was condemned to death for treason. He was a military hero in Angola, Ethiopia and Nicaragua. [Staten 2005]

In the summer of 1989 Fidel Castro recognized that corruption had spread throughout the upper echelons of the regime. Military personnel was arrested and shot for having committed acts of corruption. [Bethell 1993]

Corruption had increased and was clearly associated with the growth of the peasants' markets. Corruption took the form of stealing or diverting resources from state-run enterprises for private gain, the selling of the poorest crops to the state with the best crops being sold at the farmers' market, the selling of illegal products on the black market and the illegal use of state goods in the construction of houses by private individuals. [Staten 2005]

China

The cause of the disastrous Cultural Revolution was the "taint" of "thousands of years of feudalism," which in the end corrupted the party itself, "as manifested in such things as the personality cult, the patriarchal ways or styles of work, and the life tenure of cadres in leading posts." [Schell 2013]

To make matters worse, party cadres started taking advantage of the difference between state-set prices and market-based prices to line their own pockets. "Red envelopes" - the elegant Chinese term for bribes – became an increasingly standard operating procedure for getting things done in the new economy. From setting up an enterprise or making an investment to getting a favorable article in the press or securing a loan, corruption became endemic. [Schell 2013]

"This is what lies behind the economic miracle: the miracle of systematic corruption; the 'miracle' of an unjust society; the 'miracle' of moral decline; and the 'miracle' of a squandered future," Liu Xiaobo wrote caustically. "The damage – to the economy, the human rights, to the entire society – is incalculable. Will we ever be able to recover? If so, that would be the miracle!" [Schell 2013]

Accidents at work killed 101,480 people in China in 2007. In the same year there were 229 people killed at work in Great Britain. It is related more to the absence of democratic and legal accountability in China. Unsafe practices as well as corruption (a major problem in the Asian communist states, not least in China) flourish in the absence of democratically elected politicians and an independent judiciary who can hold both economic and political executives to account. [Brown 2009]

Venezuela

Venezuela had been subjected to an unprecedented level of corruption, placing the country among the twelve most corrupt countries in the world in the Perception of Corruption Index prepared every year by Transparency International. The concentration of decision making in a very small government oligarchy inevitably led to a total breakdown of transparency and accountability in the country.

Gustavo R. Coronel has publlished some material about corruption in Venezuela in the following link:

https://www.cato.org/commentary/corruption-democracy-venezuela

Hugo Chavez was elected president of Venezuela in December 1998 on the strength of three main promises: convening a Constituent Assembly to write a new constitution and improve the state, fighting poverty and social exclusion, and eliminating corruption. A few years later, it was evident that the Constituent Assembly was a vehicle to destroy all existing political institutions and replace them with a bureaucracy beholden to his wishes. In 2013, Nicolas Maduro was appointed the president of Venezuela. He followed the same steps of his predecessor. Poverty and social exclusion remain as prominent as before, while the levels of government corruption are higher than ever.

Corruption has been a problem in Venezuela for centuries. In the early 20th century, the long dictatorship of Juan Vicente Gomez was plagued by high corruption, but it was limited to the dictator's immediate collaborators. A similar situation prevailed during the military dictatorship of Marcos Perez Jimenez, from 1948-58. This situation of administrative disarray was replaced during the 1960s by a period of high transparency in the management of public wealth at the hands of democratic presidents Rómulo Betancourt, Raúl Leoni and Rafael Caldera.

In the mid 1970s, the management of national assets deteriorated significantly, as the country experienced a sudden oil windfall that tripled fiscal income. The ordinary men in charge of the government were exposed to extraordinary temptations. By 1980, the country had fallen into debt to the international banks, a victim of the so-called "Dutch disease" that affects Third World petroleum states that depend almost solely on oil exports for national income.

From 1980 onwards, Venezuelan corruption has remained high. Particularly grave was the administration of Pres. Jaime Lusinchi from 1984-94, which saw some $36,000,000,000 pilfered or stolen mainly through a corrupt exchange control program. In 1997, a non-governmental organization estimated that some $100,000,000,000 in oil income had been wasted or stolen during the last 25 years.

In the first nine years since Chavez came to power, an estimated $300,000,000,000 of oil income had entered the national treasury. In parallel, during Chavez's tenure, national debt increased from $22,000,000,000 to about $70,000,000,000. Together with income tax revenues, the total income of Venezuela during Chavez's presidency has been approximately $700,000,000,000. This formidable amount of money is nowhere to be seen in terms of public works or effective health and education programs.

In 2007, three parallel budgets existed, totaling more than $80,000,000,000: the formal one, for some $55,000,000,000 (including additional amounts), approved by the submissive National Assembly; a second one, amounting to $10,000,000,000, derived from the international monetary reserves taken from the Venezuelan Central Bank, in violation of the laws of the country; and a third, in the amount of $15,000,000,000, built from the funds siphoned out of Petroleos de Venezuela, monies which were required for investment and maintenance of the petroleum industry. None of these budgets were discussed publicly or subject to accountability.

Between 2007 and 2012, total political power was firmly in the hands of Chávez. During this period of increasingly authoritarian rule, the management of Venezuelan national wealth went from unsatisfactory to chaotic. Oil income had been steadily increasing. In 1998, the average price of oil had been $10 per barrel; in 2007, it was $65 per barrel; and, in 2008, it jumped to $87 per barrel, staying at around that level until 2012. During this six-year period, Chávez had access to about $500 billion in oil income, and he utilized this extraordinary windfall to consolidate his political power at home and abroad.

At the presidential level, the nature of corruption was mostly political, although significant amounts of cash were kept without control at the presidential palace, to be utilized as necessity dictated. The presidential palace was the place where violations of the constitution were decided and the president exercised his abuse of power. In the palace, Cubans controlled sensitive intelligence matters, illegal financing of foreign electoral campaigns occurred, bribes of friendly leaders in the hemisphere were allocated, and political strategies were agreed upon with brotherly dictatorships in Cuba, Belarus, Syria, Iran, Libya, and Zimbabwe, and with authoritarian regimes in Argentina, Bolivia, and Nicaragua.

By 2009, close to $40 billion had already been distributed by Chávez to foreign governments in order to buy political loyalties. By 2012, the number of handouts abroad had increased to no less than $150 billion, particularly to Castro's Cuba, since one hundred thousand barrels per day of Venezuelan oil were being sent to Cuba, to be paid back in sports training, medical services, and other services. This arrangement allowed the Castro government to send some fifty thousand Cubans to Venezuela, many of whom went to control strategic areas of Venezuelan public administration, including identification and economic matters. Chávez instituted a system of domestic handouts that put money in the pockets of the poor but did not solve the structural problems of poverty.

Irregularities abounded in the management of public funds: more than $22,500,000,000 in dollar transfers have been made to foreign accounts, maintains the Venezuelan Central Bank, and at least half of that money remains unaccounted for. Jose Guerra, a former Central Bank executive, indicates that some of this money has been used by Chavez "to buy political loyalties in the region ... and some has been donated to Cuba and Bolivia, among other countries."

By 2008, the oil petroleum company of Venezuela (PDVSA) was no longer a conventional oil company but a "social" company engaged in diverse businesses that ranged from importing and distributing food to building low-quality housing. Contracts without bidding were often assigned to friends of the regime. Kickbacks became customary. The management of the company and the national comptroller systematically ignored PDVSA's scandals, such as 2010 contracting of the offshore drilling rig Aban Pearl to a ghost company, rampant overpricing in procurement contracts to benefit contractors and company insiders, and the illegal use of the employee's pension fund for speculative purposes. The president of the company, Rafael Ramirez, was also the minister of energy and petroleum, and he systematically diverted PDVSA's funds from the company into the pockets of the executive branch, to be used without accountability. By 2012, PDVSA was deep into debt in spite of high oil prices, since its income was diverted to partisan political activities. Due to lack of proper infrastructure investment, oil production and the condition of plants and equipment had deteriorated significantly, causing refinery accidents and numerous oil spills due to leaking pipelines.

A 2009 report by the U.S. Government Accountability Office to the U.S. Congress reported increasing corruption among the Venezuelan military, especially the national guard. Corruption, said the report, had reached the ministerial level of the government. In particular, the links of the Venezuelan military and the Colombian terrorist and drug trafficking group known as the FARC (Revolutionary Armed Forces of Colombia) had been clearly established, as proven by the contents of the laptops belonging to deceased FARC leader Raul Reyes. The U.S. government named three high members of the government as drug kingpins for providing material support to the FARC. Gen. Henry Rangel Silva, Gen.

Hugo Carvajal, and former Minister of the Interior Ramon Rodriguez Chacin are still active members of the Venezuelan regime.

The twenty years of Chavez and Maduro's presidency led to the highest levels of government corruption ever experienced in Venezuela. The main reasons were: the record oil income obtained by the nation, money going directly into government's pockets; a mediocre management team working without transparency or accountability; the ideological predilections of Chavez and Maduro, which led them to try to play a messianic role in Latin America, and even world affairs; and the policies of handouts put in place by Chavez and Maduro to keep the Venezuelan masses politically loyal.

Chavez and Maduro's record show a significant gap between their promises to end corruption and the current reality. Immense amounts of money belonging to the Venezuelan people have been misused in furthering an anti-U.S. alliance in the Western Hemisphere and beyond.

Three major areas of corruption had emerged during the Chavez and Maduro presidencies: grand corruption, derived from major policy decisions made by the presidents; bureaucratic corruption, at the level of the government bureaucracy; and systematic corruption, taking place at the interface between the government and the private sector.

Examples of grand corruption are:
- Expenditures and promises made to political leaders and countries of the Western Hemisphere, in order to buy their political loyalties.
- Social programs run by the military during all these years.
- Government contracting is done without bidding.
- Corruption at the National Electoral Council.
- High levels of mismanagement at the state-owned petroleum company, Petroleos de Venezuela.
- The emergence of a new, rich, "revolutionary bourgeoisie" that drives Hummers, sports Cartier and Rolex watches, and wears Ermenegildo Zegna suits.
- Private corporations that deal with the government are owned by government officers.
- Drug trafficking.

It is clear that no meaningful victory against corruption can be won in Venezuela while the Chavez-Maduro government is in power. Only a democratic government, fully accountable to the people, and fully transparent, will be able to minimize this malady.

Highlights for Chapter 16
- Corruption can be defined as the misuse of public wealth for private gain.
- Considerations on the misuse of public funds: level of public wealth available, risks inherent in corrupt deals, and bargaining power of the briber and the person being bribed.
- The dominance of the party in socialists and communists societies is the sole means of resource distribution.
- Corruption takes place where there is a combination of opportunity and inclination.
- The idea of trust, a component of social capital, is an important glue holding society together.
- The relative weakness and/or ineffectiveness of the State and its institutions are major sources of corruption.
- Governments are perceived as corrupt and based on closed systems for the promotion of self-interests and the extortion of income flow.
- The other side of corruption is how governments benefit from it for purposes of staying in power against the will of the people; in many cases using public resources to rig the elections.
- A Zimbabwean economist, said, 'We imagine corruption to be like a tick on a dog. There are some places in Africa where the tick is bigger than the dog.'
- Staying in power is a way of life in Zimbabwe. Becoming a politician allows people to get rich.
- The elite ruling class in Angola that had been at the heart of the slave trade for centuries found no difficulty setting up a Communist corrupted command economy.
- The IMF says that in Angola, between 1996 and 2001, nearly 40 percent of state expenditure was not accounted for and that in 2001 nearly one billion dollars went missing from government accounts.
- In Angola, oil creates an enclave economy: the money comes directly into the treasury straight from oil companies and no mechanism exists to spread it around.
- Angolans gain nothing from their country's oil riches, and if they want to change their lives they will have to fight.
- At present no company, local or foreign, can do business in Congo and avoid corruption.

- The only national organization that survived Mobutu and the looting was the Catholic Church.
- In Kenya, a report pointed out the impunity of politicians from past crimes and dwelt on corruption, the nature of presidential power, and the need for devolution and a new constitution.
- The primary job for a Kenyan MP is seen as delivering goodies to his or her own ethnic group.
- In Kenya, no single commodity provided the bulk of the wealth. To get rich you have to work. So how could politicians get rich? Foreign aid was one source.
- The looting of Kenya by its rulers dragged its economic growth rate down from 4.5 percent in the late 1980s to 1 percent in 1991 and less than 1 percent in subsequent years.
- Nigeria regularly appears top of the list of the world's most corrupt countries, according to Transparency International.
- Many Nigerians will tell you that it takes two to tango and corruption needs a giver as well as a receiver. They like to blame corruption on foreigners.
- In parts of precolonial Africa if you wanted to please a king, you brought him a gift. There is nothing traditional about a Swiss bank account, said President Obasanjo.
- In Nigeria, all its institutions – the civil service, the law, hospitals, schools, the army, police, business, academics – had become corrupt.
- Nigeria still holds the shape of a nation state from the outside, but within, corruption has become the institution.
- The root of the problem is that the Nigerian state depends not on a constitution but on a commodity: oil.
- King Oil destroyed almost every other economic activity in Nigeria. In 1966 less than 10 percent of the government's revenue came from oil. By 1990 oil provided 97 percent.
- Meanwhile Nigeria's poor got poorer.
- The Nigerian elite did not believe in Africa. They stole whatever they could and shipped the money out of the country, letting schools, universities and hospitals collapsed.
- The elite owns and runs Nigeria. An elite that has wealth and power, though not necessarily education.

- In Nigeria money is power and power is money. That is no different from the rest of the world but it is more naked, more total in Nigeria.
- In the summer of 1989 Fidel Castro recognized that corruption had spread throughout the upper echelons of the regime.
- In Cuba, public trials combined with long-term prison sentences and some executions of top government officials were designed to deter future corruption.
- Corruption had increased and was clearly associated with the growth of the peasants' markets.
- In China, the Cultural Revolution corrupted the party itself, "the personality cult, the patriarchal ways or styles of work, and the life tenure of cadres in leading posts."
- Party cadres started taking advantage of the difference between state-set prices and market-based prices to line their own pockets.
- In Venezuela, during the Chavez and Maduro regime, poverty and social exclusion remain as prominent as usual, while the levels of government corruption are higher than ever.
- From 1980 onwards, Venezuelan corruption has remained high. Particularly grave was the administration of Pres. Jaime Lusinchi from 1984-94.
- In the first nine years since Chavez came to power, an estimated $300,000,000,000 of oil income had entered the national treasury.
- The twenty years of Chavez and Maduro's presidency led to the highest levels of government corruption ever experienced in Venezuela.

Chapter 17: Socialism and Communism in Extinction

The worker's utopia dreamed of and promised by Lenin turned out to be a failure. Although his revolution was probably the single most important event of the twentieth century, by the end of that century it had been completely swept away. There is no country in the world to be named communist. All the existing countries considered communist have altered the basic ideas for a better society. [Streissguth 2002]

Russia and the former Soviet republics continue to struggle with faltering economies, corruption, declining health standards, and sharply stratified societies, legacies of the revolution that was supposed to bring their people to a bright, happy, and egalitarian future. [Streissguth 2002]

All intellectuals in the world, even if some do not recognize it, know that socialism or communism does not work, it does not provide the benefits of a just society. One experience after the other demonstrates the failure of these existing systems called socialist or communist. Even communists must have been somewhat shaken by such testimonies as that of Max Eastman, Lenin's old friend, who found himself compelled to admit that "instead of being better, Stalinism is worse than fascism, more ruthless, barbarous, unjust, immoral, anti-democratic, unredeemed by any hope or scruple." And when we find the same author recognizing that Stalinism is socialism, his conclusion clearly achieves wider significance. [Hayek 1994]

All socialist or communist countries that have tried to impose their ideals, have gone through development stages where politicians try to improvise a working, prosperous society, without succeeding. And most of the time the Strong Man concept takes precedence over ideals. It is the next leader who decides the luck of the population. The Soviet Union was a far less fearful place to inhabit in the Brezhnev era than it was in the late 1930s. Poland and Hungary throughout the communist period were manifestly undemocratic, but life there was qualitatively less oppressive and thuggish than it was in China during the years in which the Cultural Revolution was wreaking havoc. [Brown 2009]

Socialism and Communism in the World

It is well known that the Soviet Union was the first nation to impose some kind of socialism or communism in the world. After consolidating their power, the leaders decided to be involved in similar enterprises over the world. The newly independent nations of Asia and Africa were turning to communist ideology for guidance and to the Soviet Union for arms and economic aid. With its enormous stretches of land and natural resources, the Soviet Union to many seemed the country of the future. [Streissguth 2002]

Among the followers of Karl Marx there were doctrinal differences. From the outset, there was tension between socialists who believed in the importance of parliamentary means and those for whom revolutionary class struggle was a higher priority. The First International, founded in London in 1864, split in several different directions and was formally disbanded in 1876. The Second International (also known as Socialist International) was founded in Paris in1889. The international was composed of national political parties and trade unions, many of whose members had been influenced by Marxist teaching. [Brown 2009]

There is, after all, no longer an international communist movement. Of the six defining characteristics of a communist system, it is the last two ideological features which have almost completely disappeared. One of these was the sense of belonging to such an international communist movement. That transnational movement has gone, and so has the aspiration to build a communist society. [Brown 2009]

Politicians always promise better times, it is the only way to stay in power. However, why is so difficult to achieve their promises. While the standard of living within the Soviet Union stagnated, Brezhnev and the party promised that better times and true communism were just around the corner – just as the Western countries were enjoying sharp rises in their economic production, living standards, and health and education levels. [Streissguth 2002]

After several years, the Soviet Union became Russia, and in the process made a transformation towards free-market policies. This had an impact on the rest of East Europe; those countries with some ties to the Soviet Union rapidly started to withdraw from socialism or communism. Very little is left of communism in Europe where the movement began. As recently as the mid-1980s, half of Europe was controlled by Marxist-Leninist parties. Today, no state in that continent is ruled by Communists, nor are they close to coming to power. [Brown 2009]

Over time, the successes as well as the failures of communism increased the system's vulnerability. In the Soviet Union of 1939, only 11 percent of the population had received more than an elementary education. By 1984 the percentage who had attended at least secondary school had risen 87 percent. The more educated the population became, the more they were inclined to seek information denied to them by the party-state authorities. [Brown 2009]

There are few countries that still consider themselves socialists or communists. In the established communist states left standing – China, Cuba, Laos, North Korea and Vietnam – the leading role of the party and democratic centralism remains intact. Indeed, that is the chief justification for calling them communist. However, they differ greatly in the extent to which they still possess the defining features of a communist system economically – state ownership of the means of production and a command, rather than market, economy. [Brown 2009]

This raises the question of why four communist states in Asia and one in the Caribbean have survived for so long. It goes without saying that they have the same supports which worked effectively for seven decades in the Soviet Union – powerful institutions, starting with a disciplined ruling party, an omnipresent secret police, and a rigorous censorship. China and Vietnam have not taken the risk of embarking on a fundamental political reform. What all five states have succeeded in doing, however, is linking communism and nationalism. The development of a strong state is part of their appeal to national pride. [Brown 2009]

China, so far as ownership is concerned, is already a mixed economy, and it has become in the main a market economy. Vietnam has followed in China's post-Mao footsteps. From 1986 onward it, too, embraced marketizing reform. Inequality has greatly increased in China, especially the urban-rural divide. There is, in fact, increasing concern about the size of the gap between rich and poor. [Brown 2009]

In Laos and Cuba have been modest movements away from the classical command economy, which, in Stalinist form, is now to be found only in North Korea. Yet neither Laos nor Cuba has gone anything like as far down the road to the market as have China and Vietnam. [Brown 2009]

End of Socialism in the Soviet Union

Mikhail Gorbachev became the most revolutionary leader since Lenin. He believed that the solution to the malaise that gripped the country was to return the USSR to its Leninist roots. Perestroika ('reconstruction and reform'), glasnost ('publicity and openness'), and demokratizatsiia ('democratization') were to rejuvenate the socialist system and make it more efficient. [Freeze 1997]

Gorbachev attacked the Soviet Union's many problems with zeal and optimism. He quickly attached two bywords to his remaking of the Soviet system: glasnost (openness), which would permit criticism of the system and its shortcomings, and perestroika (restructuring), which would allow larger family farmings plots and private business cooperatives but keep large enterprises and natural resources in the hands of the state. [Streissguth 2002]

The Soviet Union, being the first experience of a socialist or communist society, was the first one to determine that it was not taking the right path. However, they could not recognize bluntly their mistake, they hid their intentions of reform within the system such that the population did not react against them. It was the same party in power the one that decided that change was necessary. Reform was the mechanism of change.

As an alternative way of organizing human society, communism turned out to be a ghastly failure. The population did not improve over the years. The final goal was never attained, only promises and promises, the facts demonstrated failure. Partly because, however, its ideology included some genuinely humanistic aspirations, trampled on though they were by the party-state authorities, reformers were able to begin to make changes by arguing from within the ideology, choosing their quotations carefully. [Brown 2009]

It soon appeared that of all the problems confronting the new rulers, the economy was the most difficult and complicated. A retreat from a planned economy toward a market economy was unprecedented at the time. It happened also in China and Vietnam, but only in later years. [Laqueur 2015]

The greatest stimulus to change is failure' according to a Czech economist. If only a minority of radical reformers within the Communist Party (CPSU) joined the party with express intention of changing the system, that raises the question of what changed the minds of the party reformers. Some of the influence of the party reformers came directly from the West. People within the political elite and leading specialists in various fields, who were also party members, had much more chance of traveling to Western countries and what they saw and heard had an impact. [Brown 2009]

Intra-party reform was more decisive than pressures from outside the party ranks in changing the system in highly significant ways. What made possible largely peaceful change away from communism in the Soviet Union was a similar evolution in the views of a small minority of party officials and a larger minority of party intellectuals while they were already in positions of responsibility. [Brown 2009]

Like Gorbachev, various officials had in their youth taken most of the official doctrine in Stalin's USSR for granted. By the second half of the 1980s, their political evolution had brought them close to social democracy. [Brown 2009]

Gorbachev built up a new team that shared the consensus that an understanding with the West had to be based on a halt to rearmament. The Afghan war continued during the 1980s like a wound that did not heal. By 1987 it became clear that the Soviets would leave the country. Soviet withdrawal began on May 15, 1988. [Laqueur 2015]

Gorbachev passed a sweeping reform of the highest echelons of Soviet government. It established the offices of president and vice president and adopted a cabinet of ministers who would report to the president. A new constitutional article passed in 1990 ended the monopoly of the Communist Party in favor of a multi-party state. [Streissguth 2002]

Gorbachev's 'new thinking' explicitly downgraded the class struggle and asserted 'the priority of all human values, a world without violence and wars, diversity of social progress, dialogue and cooperation for the sake of development and preservation of civilization, and movement towards a new world order.' [Streissguth 2002]

Change in the ideas of the leaders who already occupied positions of institutional power was of exceptional importance. Thus, Gorbachev came to believe that the kind of order which existed in the democracies of Western Europe was order of a qualitatively higher kind than that imposed by the KGB in the Soviet Union, and that what had been called 'socialism' in the Soviet Union was a perversion of socialist ideals. [Brown 2009]

But hardly anyone was thinking of privatization; Gorbachev seems to have believed in models of worker cooperatives. True, Gorbachev and most of his advisers were not thinking in such radical terms. But gradually they understood that half measures would not save the country. They had inherited a situation that was untenable in the long run. In addition, they faced a sudden deterioration affecting Soviet industry and, to an even greater extent, agriculture. [Laqueur 2015]

These changes meant that the party was quietly dropping its insistence on the primacy of the class struggle and the building of socialism in favor of 'all-human values,' the rule of law and international peace. [Streissguth 2002] By 1990-91, Gorbachev no longer aspired to build something which had not been seen on earth, but a society which had produced a tangible enhancement of the quality of political life and which would, he hoped, produce comparable improvements in the standard of living. In other words, the model had become that of the European social democracies or the kind of social market economy which existed in West Germany. [Brown 2009]

What perestroika demonstrated, however, was that communism could not survive with radical reform of its political system. What had been the most powerful institutions in the country – the Politburo and Secretariat of the Central committee – began to send mixed signals to the society, as their members visibly pulled in different directions. Once democratization had affected the ruling party, it could not be confined to it. [Brown 2009]

The political monopoly of the Communist Party had not yet been broken, but there was no action. A powerful anti-Gorbachev faction emerged, demanding the preservation of the status quo, which eventually led to an anti-Gorbachev coup in August 1991 (he resigned in late December 1991) and the rise of Yeltsin – but it also led to the collapse of the old Communist Party. [Laqueur 2015]

Perestroika and Glasnost meant not only greater freedom to publish novels but also action – in the economy, in domestic political life, in foreign policy – an end to the Cold War. [Laqueur 2015]

Had perestroika really been necessary, and if so, could it not have been carried out in a less painful way? Why was the transition in China less painful and, as far as the economy was concerned, more efficient? The brief answer is that Russia was not China, it was not a multinational state, and by and large the Chinese perestroika had been limited to the economy, with no intentions to introduce a multiparty system. [Laqueur 2015]

Is Communism still around?

One of the weaker reasons sometimes given for the persistence of communist and other authoritarian regimes in Asia is that 'culture is destiny.' That is not to say that political culture does not matter, but rather to emphasize that political cultures change, although this rarely happens overnight. The argument that countries of Confucian traditions are ill-suited to the development of democracy was effectively rebutted by Kim

Dae Jung, the president of South Korea. The example of South Korea, Taiwan and Japan illustrates the point. [Brown 2009]

More generally, it can be said that a state's political culture inheritance makes democratization a much more uphill task in some countries than others. It was, indeed, readily predictable that the Baltic states would make a rapid transition from communism to democracy. And it is no surprise that the former Central Asian republics of the Soviet Union have exchanged one form of authoritarian rule for another. [Brown 2009]

Modern China

China fully retains the monopoly of power of the party and the strictly hierarchical organization and discipline associated with democratic centralism. In many ways, however, China today is a hybrid system. So far removed from communist orthodoxy has its economy become that it has even been described as an example of 'party-state capitalism.' [Brown 2009]

For the rest of the six defining features of a communist system, China, then, does not meet neither the economic nor the idealistic features. Since Mao's death it has moved substantially away from the economic criteria. Its concessions to the market have been on such scale that it cannot be considered a command economy. So far as ownership is concerned, there is still a large state sector, but by 2006 private enterprise in China accounted for almost half of the country's GDP and more than two-thirds of its industrial output. [Brown 2009]

China and Vietnam have the advantage over the other remaining communist states of relative economic success. They both have become important participants in the global marketplace. [Brown 2009]

As a result of Vietnam's economic reform, which has earned it membership of the World Trade Organization, the country's relations even with the United States have improved. [Brown 2009]

China's extraordinarily fast rate of economic growth in recent decades is also a double-edged sword for the communist system. If the growth continues unabated, there will be a very large class of relatively prosperous people, increasingly well informed about the outside world. These may be the seeds of their own destruction. [Brown 2009]

Modern Russia

In the words of a Russian, My father was an honest communist. I don't blame the communists, I blame communism. I still can't decide how to feel about Gorbachev … or that Yeltsin … You forget about the long lines and empty stores faster than you do about the red flag flying over the Reichstag. [Alexievich 2016]

In Russia they believed in a revolution, they thought their life was going to improve. It is the people who are mistaken, because they believe socialism is a good political system; they did not grasp how wrong they were. The government was directed by a bunch of fanatics without a clear agenda; only staying in power is their motto. In Venezuela there are a bunch of thugs in charge of the government, people do not believe in a revolution, everything is only propaganda. However, the government stays in power.

Soviets were idealists, no doubt, promoting the bad system of course, "Idiots! They call us. 'Why did they have a revolution?' But the things I remember … I remember people with fire in their eyes. Our hearts were on fire! No one believes me! But I still have my wits about me … I remember … Yes … Those people didn't want anything for themselves, it wasn't like today, when everyone puts himself first. A pot of cabbage soup … A little house, a little garden … It was about the collective 'We'! We! We!!!" [Alexievich 2016]

Of course Soviets were idiots. Because of people like them the regime maintained power, do not you see that! It has already been said, the collective is a fantasy invented by the Politburo. The individual must move towards independence whereas governments must move towards organizing the society to facilitate transactions to manufacture and distribute food, goods and supplies.

Idealists and the poor made the explosive mix that generated the Soviets, "How can you not fall in love with a dream like that! Poor people, those who had nothing, believed in Bolsheviks. They won the support of the youth. We walked through the streets crying, 'Meltdown the church bells! Turn them into tractors!' The only thing we knew about God was that there was no God. We mocked the priests, and at home we destroyed icons. Instead of sacred processions, we held demonstrations with red banners ..." [Alexievich 2016]

That is common in socialist and communist beliefs, benefiting from whatever has been produced, instead of producing it by themselves. Expropriation of land, factories, banks, and so on, a common practice in those regimes, punishing the owners instead of organizing workers to start new businesses. The laziness of socialism and communism will mean their end, without production a society does not progress.

Today, some still believe the idea was not wrong, "Communism is denigrated! Socialism trashed! People say to me, "but who take Marxism seriously today? Marx's place is in the history textbooks." And who among you can say you've ever read the later works of Lenin? That you know all of Marx? There's early Marx … and Marx at the end of his life … What people today disparage as socialism has no relation to the socialist idea. The idea is not to blame." [Alexievich 2016]

Sorry, it has been demonstrated that the socialist idea is wrong, it is the socialists that have not demonstrated that the idea is right. To do it, you do not need to read Marx or Engels, what you need is to demonstrate that a socialist society is going to function according to human nature realities. Social, psychological, economic, and spiritual considerations should be structured into a comprehensive analysis of the society. Up to now, nobody has done that, there is no intellectual capable of producing such a monumental framework. The society needs producers, intellectuals and guardians to accomplish its needs.

Most ideas do not match up with human nature, " … It was a beautiful idea! But what are you going to do with human nature? Man hasn't changed since the days of ancient Rome ..." [Alexievich 2016]

Well, at least a sensible statement. I would not say ancient Rome but at least since the days of Christ. It is the first time I hear something about human nature, this is an important turning point. Political systems must consider human nature and organize society around its characteristics, do not force people into untested perfectionism. Human being are not perfect, on the contrary, they are absolutely imperfect, ruled by the hazardous genetic roulette.

Soviets thought they were building socialism, "I remember the thirties … People like me came of age in those years. Tens of millions of us. And we consciously built socialism. We were prepared to make any and all necessary sacrifices. I don't agree with general Volkogonov, who wrote that the only thing that existed in those pre-war years was Stalinism. He is an anti-communist." [Alexievich 2016]

Here we start to find different opinions. There will be defendants of communism all the time, but that does not demonstrate its viability. Viability must be demonstrated theoretically and practically. Neither of them have been demonstrated, socialism and communism do not work, they are not made for human beings. Human nature is totally different to the ideas of socialism and communism.

Soviets sacrificed themselves during those years of socialism, "My mother is from the generation of the pre-war intelligentsia. She's one of the people whose eyes sparkled with tears whenever the Internationale played. She lived through the war and never forgot how a Soviet soldier had hung a red flag on the Reichstag. 'Our country was victorious in such a horrible war!' Ten, twenty, forty years passed ... and she would still repeat those words to us like an incantation. Like a prayer ... It was her prayer. 'We had nothing, but we were happy!' My mother's conviction in this was absolute." [Alexievich 2016]

Where are all these wrongful sentiments coming from? How people believe in the impossible system? Socialism is not going to solve people's problems, it is going to make them worse. I have thought many times about it, and the only answer is that society is plenty of unfairness. During a life cycle, people face many situations, depending on their decisions, they succeed personally or not. Those that do not succeed start to become angry against the political system, blaming it for their unsuccessful past. People have no way to complain and they start to make up their fantasies, one of them is believing that socialism is a good alternative.

Soviet life was harsh but they were to stand up for it, "Everything was simpler in our old life: one pair of boots for all seasons, one coat, one pair of pants. We were raised like young warriors in ancient Sparta: if the Motherland called, we'd sat on a hedgehog for her." [Alexievich 2016]

In their old life, Soviets were idealistic, believing in non-viable ideas. They thought they were doing a revolution, what a mistake. And many of them still dream of coming back to the same bad socialist system. What is going on with those people?

Soviets lived dreaming, believing in a better society, "Everyone dream of a new life ... Dreams ... People dream that tons of salami would appear at the stores at Soviet prices and members of the Politburo would stand in line for it along with the rest of us. Salami is a benchmark of our existence. Our love for salami is existential ... Twilight of the Idols! The factories to the workers! The soil to the peasants! The rivers to the beavers! The dens to the bears! Mexican soap operas were the perfect replacement for Soviet parades and live broadcasts of the First Congress of People's Deputies. I stayed in college for two years and then dropped out. I feel sorry for my parents because they were told flat out that they were pathetic sovoks whose lives had been wasted for less than a sniff of tobacco, that everything was their fault, beginning with Noah's Arc, and that now, no one needed them anymore. Imagine working that hard, your whole life, only to end up with nothing." [Alexievich 2016]

I would say that they deserved their fate. Some are dreamers, others are profiteers, humans beings are not so naive. Diversity is our nature, people are not equal, there are many viewpoints. That there are some that are stupid, of course, it always happen, some benefit from them. At the end, they wake up from the dream and find out the reality.

Old generations are still wondering about the past, "As for Papa himself? He's an old man now, but old age has taken him unawares. He should be savoring every moment, gazing up at the sky, admiring the trees. Playing chess or collecting stamps … Matchboxes … Instead, he's glued to the television: Parliamentary sessions, leftists, rightists, rallies, demonstrations with little red flags. That's where you'll find my father! He staunchly supports the communists." [Alexievich 2016]

The greatness of the Empire was also a factor, Russians need something to believe in … something lofty and luminous. Empire and communism are ingrained in us. We seek out heroic ideals. With socialism, the people were participating in history … they were living through something great ... [Alexievich 2016]

It is clear that the Russians were cheated by the system, they believed in a better life but nothing demonstrated socialism was the right system. How people suffer so much during so many years and are not capable of rebellion? People use to get trapped in the lies of socialism and communism; they always expect things to change over time but nothing happens. If you are poor, you think it is justice to steal from the rich. In fact, justice is opportunity, socialists break down the system by brute force and do not provide the basic needs to the people. Socialists do not give opportunities to their people they just incarcerate those that dissent.

Many believed socialism was a great cause, "I get indignant whenever people start talking about Marxism with disdain and a knowing smirk. … Socialism isn't just labor camps, informants, and the Iron Curtain, it's also a bright, just world: everything is shared, the weak are pitied, and compassion rules. Instead of grabbing everything you can, you feel for others." [Alexievich 2016]

A just world must be built with people's effort, laziness does not enter the equation. Whoever agrees with sharing its wealth can do it in any political system, including capitalism, it is not necessarily socialism or communism the solution. In a capitalist system it can be done, people get welfare and benefits from governments. Socialism should go ahead and demonstrate it works but do not force everybody to the same policy, unless its viability is demonstrated. Trial and error at the level of a country must not be tolerated, untested approaches should affect the least of people, the whole population does not deserve a bad government..

Soviets believed they were doing something great, "Our Soviet life ... you could say that it was an attempt at creating an alternative civilization. If you want to put it in dramatic terms ... The power of the people! I can't calm down about it!" [Alexievich 2016]

It is an excellent slogan, The power to the people!, but the results were meager, people did not improve. It is incredible to hear old soviets speak well of socialism, after more than sixty years socialism did not solve their problems.

Today things have changed for the worst according to many, "A bottle of vodka costs as much as a coat used to. And something to snack on? Half a kilo of salami is half a month's pension. Drink up that freedom! Eat it up! What a country they surrendered. An empire!! Without a single shot fired ... The thing I don't understand is, why didn't anyone ask us? I spent my life building a great nation. That's what they told us. They promised." [Alexievich 2016]

It is clear that many Soviets thought they were building a good society, but everything was just good desires, it is impossible to build a good society with socialists principles.

There are some people that still believe in the Soviets, The Great October Revolution! Today, they're calling it a military coup, the Bolshevik conspiracy ... The Russian catastrophe ... Saying Lenin was a German agent and the Revolution was brought about by deserters and drunken sailors. I cover my ears, I don't want to hear it! It's more than I can take ... My whole life, I've believed that we were the luckiest people on earth, born in the most beautiful and extraordinary country in the world. There's no other one like it! [Alexievich 2016]

What a pity, not knowing where are you standing up. Great? There is nothing great in the Soviet Union. Do you want to be powerful and please the government? Or do you want to live well and happy with your family and please yourself? Of course it was a Russian catastrophe, people did not improve at all.

Soviets were a bunch of idealists, and ideals must be supported by pragmatism, "More than a century ago, Dostoevsky finished writing The Brothers Karamazov. He wrote of the eternal "Russian Boys" who will always debate the big questions, nothing less: Is there a God, is there immortal life? As for those who don't believe in God, they take up the subject of socialism and anarchism, remaking humanity according to a new model. Don't they see that all they'll end up with is the devil? It's always the same questions, no matter how they are posed." [Alexievich 2016]

Under capitalism, the big questions can be answered, Freedom allows minds to wonder and come up with better solutions. Socialism has the wrong approach, it forces people under the same policies for all; when a population has divided opinions, the best solution is that which offers more freedom. The individual versus the collectivity is always going to be eternal discussion, individual freedom versus forced community. Let us choose the solution that satisfies both groups, capitalism offers that solution by allowing freedom and community initiatives whereas socialism eliminates freedom favoring only the community approach.

New generations have turned down ideas, they have became pragmatics, "I was in no hurry to get married, have kids, I've always put my career first. I value myself, my time, and my life. And where did you ever get the idea that men are looking for love? Ooh, love … Men consider women game, war trophies, prey, and themselves hunters. Those are the rules that have been developed over the course of centuries. And women aren't looking for their knight in shining armor to come galloping in on a white horse – they want him on a sack of gold. A knight of indeterminate age … even a "daddy" will do … So what? Money rules the world! But I'm no prey, I'm a huntress myself ..." [Alexievich 2016]

This is a wrong interpretation of capitalism, it is the money-oriented view. It is a pity that women fell under the same trap that older generations felt many years ago. I guess men are evolving into a new generation that would respect women for their values and not for their body. However, it takes time for these new ideas to finally settle down; new generations have not that viewpoint about women built up into their genes, it requires constant remainder through generations. The human brain does not automatically switches from one generation to the next, it may require dozens of generations before those ideas become routine.

Cuba's Future

Some scholars argue that Cuba will follow the same path as the East European countries or the former Soviet Union. A post-Castro leadership will eventually arise that is less committed to real democracy and more committed to restructuring the economy and take advantage of a possible massive privatization. [Staten 2005]

Highlights for Chapter 17

- The worker's utopia dreamed of and promised by Lenin turned out to be a failure.
- "Socialism is worse than fascism, more ruthless, barbarous, unjust, immoral, anti-democratic, unredeemed by any hope or scruple."
- The sense of belonging to an international communist movement has disappeared, and so has the aspiration to build a communist society.
- After several years, the Soviet Union became Russia, and in the process made a transformation towards free-market policies.
- Over time, the successes as well as the failures of communism increased its system's vulnerability.
- In the established communist states left standing – China, Cuba, Laos, North Korea and Vietnam – the leading role of the party and democratic centralism remains intact.
- What all these states have succeeded in doing, however, is linking communism and nationalism. The development of a strong state is part of their appeal to national pride.
- China and Vietnam, so far as ownership is concerned, are already a mixed economy, and they have become in the main a market economy.
- Inequality has greatly increased in China, especially the urban-rural divide.
- In Russia, Perestroika ('reconstruction and reform'), glasnost ('publicity and openness'), and demokratizatsiia ('democratization') were to rejuvenate the socialist system and make it more efficient.
- In Russia, it was the same party in power the one that decided that change was necessary. Reform was the mechanism of change.
- A retreat from a planned economy toward a market economy was unprecedented at the time. It happened also in China and Vietnam, but only in later years.
- Gorbachev's 'new thinking' explicitly downgraded the class struggle and asserted 'the priority of all human values.

- By 1990-91, Gorbachev no longer aspired to build something which had not been seen on earth, but a society with quality of political life and improvements in the standard of living.
- An anti-Gorbachev coup in August 1991 and the rise of Yeltsin also led to the collapse of the old Communist Party.
- China fully retains the monopoly of power of the party and the strictly hierarchical organization and discipline associated with democratic centralism.
- China and Vietnam have the advantage over the other remaining communist states of relative economic success.
- In Russia they believed in a revolution, they thought their life was going to improve.
- Expropriation of land, factories, banks, and so on, a common practice in socialist regimes, punishing the owners instead of organizing workers to start new businesses.
- Socialism and communism do not work, they are not made for human beings.
- Soviets lived dreaming, believing in a better society, "Everyone dream of a new life ... Dreams ... People dream that tons of salami were available."
- Some scholars argue that Cuba will follow the same path as the East European countries or the former Soviet Union.

Final Notes

I hope it has been demonstrated that Absurd Socialism follows a common pattern of development with the intention of luring the population and implementing its erroneous approach. Socialist and communist systems promote a strictly regulated society using democracy as a parapet to promote insane policies to gain the consent of the majority of the population without solving their problems. Over the centuries, hundreds of thousands of people have been sacrificed in the name of the stability of socialism or communism.

Socialist and communist countries are characterized by strong states governed by the party and the Strong Man syndrome. Societies are ruled in a tyrannical way spreading fear among the population. People are weak and afraid, this helps perpetuate the regime for many generations. All socialist and communist experiences have followed the Strong Man approach.

Christianity has had a large impact in socialist ideals, primarily collectivization. The notions of sacrifice, solidarity and collaborations have been surrounding religion for many centuries. Usually, poor people are the most vulnerable to accept these ideals. The welfare of people, like the happiness of a man, depends on a great many things that can be provided in an infinite variety of combinations.

The immense power given to the state or to the party in power by socialist and communist regimes has always been a source of conflict. The cult of personality is utilized by these systems to impose the mythical viewpoint of the strong man. Propaganda is used to promote socialist and communist ideology. Identifying its enemies allows total control of the population. Gathering information about every single citizen according to their loyalty gets its maximum expression in these regimes.

"Hitler did not have to destroy democracy; he merely took advantage of the decay of democracy." Absurd Socialism uses the democratic infrastructure to impose its ideas on the population. The rule of law is preserved in democracies while the rule by law is implemented in tyranny. Socialism and communism use the rule by law to twist the rules using their immense power seized over the kidnapping of all the institutions.

In Venezuela, the Strong Man in power started by seizing democratically the presidency and little by little taking control of all the institutions until it was possible to manage all decisions from his presidential palace. It has been a hard fight for the opposition to gain spaces in the political arena, the government had all the power and bought the support of the people by giving them crumbs without resolving their problems. To topple the president using democracy means has been almost impossible because the Electoral Power and the Supreme Court are in the hands of partisans of the party in power. Leaders need to be visionaries, with prophetic voices, and able to rise above the present crisis and take a principled stand. It is important to identify any opportunity to regain power because normally the people do not dare to face the Strong Man position.

Socialism and communism are non-democratic, even though they talk about democratic centralism – the party in power – and definitively are non-market based. Social democracy is a market-based approach, and it is different from socialism and communism. For socialists, the capitalist class is a minority that derives profit from employing the working class through private ownership of the means of production. China and Vietnam, so far as ownership is concerned, are already a mixed economy, and they have become, in the main, a market economy.

The interaction of individuals, possessing different knowledge and different views, is what constitutes the life of thought. What our generation has forgotten is that the system of private property is the most important guaranty of freedom. Absurd Socialism destroys public enterprises to centralize all productive activities in the hands of the state and become the monopoly of food, medicine, and services for the population.

Collectivization and individuality are complementary instead of opposites. All socialist and communist regimes started by collectivizing the land, industries and any other social activity. By the mid-1980s, collectivized agrarian socialism was withering away, while rural standards of living and household incomes were improving dramatically. It was demonstrated in practice that collectivization did not work. Deng Xiaoping had made good on his slogan "Poverty is not socialism."

Nazism had in common with Russian communism 'a total ideology, a single mass party, terrorist secret police, a monopoly of mass communications, a monopoly of weapons, and a centrally directed planned economy.' Freedom and socialism do not mix, therefore, socialism must be authoritarian to stay in power. All socialist and communist regimes, including Venezuela, share the same pattern of power as Nazis and Soviets.

The constitutions of some communist countries illustrate the 'leading role of the party.' The constitution used to be changed to please the desires of the new leaders. Central Planning leads to dictatorship because it is the most effective instrument of coercion and enforcement of ideals. "In dealing with ideology problems we must never use coercion," said Deng Xiaoping. One strange case happens in Venezuela, the government calls itself 'Socialist' without any legal authority of the constitution.

In order to identify enemies of the Revolution, gossip became an arm of state power. Alert and suspicious, the working-class constituted a vast spy system. In Venezuela, the government offers benefits to the population if they register in a national database that promotes cheaper food supplies. Fidel Castro said, 'Within the revolution, everything; against the revolution, nothing.' In Venezuela, Hugo Chavez said the same and persecuted the opposition, people on the list of defectors of the regime lost their jobs or had to earn lower salaries thanks to his discrimination.

In China, the worst violations of human rights happen in the areas of democracy, freedom of thought and freedom of expression. The Right to Your Own Things has been violated in Zimbabwe. Property rights – full legal ownership of the land – are non-negotiable. Where boundaries are moved and there is no respect for private property, hunger will result. In Venezuela, private enterprises were expropriated and democracy was eliminated to follow more of a centralized democrat pattern where the Strong Man was the ruler.

The exodus of people in Africa is alarming. There are an estimated 15 million Africans born in the continent now living outside it. was their motto. In Zimbabwe, a different type of discrimination came about, white's discrimination. Political discrimination has long plagued Venezuela. Chavez invented new forms of discrimination against real and perceived political opponents. More than 3 million Venezuelans have left the country in the last 4 years.

The relative weakness and/or ineffectiveness of the State and its institutions are major sources of corruption. In many failed states, oil creates an enclave economy: the money comes directly into the treasury straight from oil companies and no mechanism exists to spread it around. At present no company, local or foreign, can do business in failed states and avoid corruption. Venezuela has been under the oil monopoly, Hugo

Chavez thought oil revenues were enough to feed the population without producing any additional goods or services.

Reports of failed states pointed out the impunity of politicians from past crimes and dwelt on corruption, the nature of presidential power, and the need for devolution and a new constitution. The looting of failed states by its rulers dragged its economic growth rate down. Failed states regularly appear top of the list of the world's most corrupt countries, according to Transparency International. In Venezuela, the looting of the country's treasure is closer to one thousand billion dollars during the Chavez-Maduro regime.

An economist in Africa, said, 'We imagine corruption to be like a tick on a dog. There are many places in the world where the tick is bigger than the dog.' In China, the Cultural Revolution corrupted the party itself, "the personality cult, the patriarchal ways or styles of work, and the life tenure of cadres in leading posts." In Venezuela, during the Chavez and Maduro regime, poverty and social exclusion remain as prominent as usual, while the levels of government corruption are higher than ever.

The greatest stimulus to change is a failure' according to a Czech economist. Socialists promises have failed, and after so many years in power, they have not been able to deliver. The expropriations of food and the seizures of private business and factories had their effects: Expropriation of land, factories, banks, and so on, a common practice in socialist regimes, punishes the owners instead of organizing workers to start new businesses. After the disaster of the Chavez-Maduro regime, it is time for a change, a bad government cannot last so long, the Venezuelan Spring is coming.

The worker's utopia dreamed of and promised by Lenin turned out to be a failure. China fully retains the monopoly of power of the party and the strictly hierarchical organization and discipline associated with democratic centralism. A way of perpetuating power is linking communism and nationalism. The development of a strong state is part of their appeal to national pride. In Venezuela, Chavez and Maduro have been promoting differences with the United States to maintain a conflicted attitude that shifts away from the population the real problems.

States don't fail overnight. The seeds of their destruction are sown deep within their political institutions. What is tragic in most cases is that the failure is by design. These states collapse because they are ruled by what it is called "extractive" economic institutions. Countries' failure is characterized by the betrayal of its leadership; ideals not been accomplished; the political system does not promote the rule of law; the economic systems do not perform well. In Venezuela, it took Chavez several years to destroy democracy and private enterprises; Maduro inherited the disaster and is now paying the penalty.

A partial list of failed states incapable of delivering their promises follows:

RUSSIA: Originally the Soviet Union between 1922 to 1991, it was a socialist one-party state, governed by the Communist Party. Once becoming Russia, there have not been major improvements for the people. The oil boom is the only source of their stability.

CHINA: Its society is dominated by the Communist Party and the democratic centralism approach. Even though its economic improvements have been excellent, people still suffer and it is unclear if the decades of suffering have been worthwhile.

VIETNAM: The Vietnamese Communist Party is the sole source of leadership for the state and society. However, much more authority is delegated to the president and to the cabinet; enthusiasm for free-markets runs higher in communist China and Vietnam.

LAOS: The party is the "leading nucleus" of the political system, providing for a National Assembly; the economy of Laos is essentially a free-market system with active central planning by the government, similar to the Chinese and Vietnamese models.

NORTH KOREA: It is a highly centralized one-party state and it got a terrible score for the legitimacy of the state. Human rights violations are rampant, and aid organizations estimate more then 2 million have died since the mid-1990s over food shortages alone.

UGANDA: Uganda's worst tally is from mounting demographic pressures. 6.5% of the adult population has HIV or AIDS.

KENYA: About 50% of the Kenyan population lives below the poverty line and roughly 40% of the nation is unemployed.

NIGERIA: Nigeria is plagued by corruption, poor employment, and terrible infrastructural development.

ZIMBABWE: It was headed by one of the world's worst dictators, Robert Mugabe. Zimbabwe has more than 1 million citizens living with HIV/AIDS. Inflation is so bad, the government considered minting a $100 trillion bill.

SOUTH SUDAN: Recently liberated from Sudan, the new country is peppered with unexploded landmines and has trouble with basic vaccinations. With its very existence relies on U.N. support, South Sudan got the worst possible score for foreign intervention — as well as for group grievances and refugees.

SUDAN: Home to the brutal genocide in Darfur, Sudan got the worst possible scores for refugees, group grievances, factionalized elites, and external intervention.

CONGO: With rampant AIDS, malnutrition, pollution, and disease, Congo alone got the worst possible score for demographic pressures.

CUBA: It is a totalitarian communist state. The Communist Party is the main leading force with the Strong Man syndrome perpetuated. Market reforms of recent years would be incorporated into the new 2019 constitution with private property regulated in a limited way.

VENEZUELA: It is currently undergoing a large economic crisis which is largely deemed to be a result of socialism. Venezuela's current regime is a self-deprecating expression of extreme socialist ideas, that when applied for the first time in Russia 100 years ago, called itself communism.

Bibliography

[Alexievich 2016] Svetlana Alexievich, "Secondhand Time, The Last of the Soviets," Random House / New York, 2016.

[Bethell 1993] Leslie Bethell, Editor, "Cuba, A Short History," Cambridge University Press, 1993.

[Boloix 2017] Germinal Boloix, "Socialist Bingo: A Knowledge Distorted Journey," Germinal Boloix, editor, 2017.

[Boloix 2018] Germinal Boloix, "Socialism is Dead, Nietzsche is Eternal," Germinal Boloix, editor, 2018.

[Brown 2009] Archie Brown, "The Rise and Fall of Communism," Doubleday Canada, 2009.

[Dowden 2009] Richard Dowden, "Africa, altered states, ordinary miracles," Public Affaires, 2009.

[Evans 2005] David Evans, "Stalin's Russia," Contemporary Books, McGraw-Hill, 2005.

[Fleming 2008] Thomas Fleming, "Socialism," Marshall Cavendish Corporation, 2008.

[Freeth 2011] Ben Freeth, "Mugabe and the White African," Lion Hudson plc, 2011.

[Freeze 1997] Gregory L. Freeze, Editor, "Russia a History," Oxford University Press, 1997.

[Hayek 1994] F. A. Hayek, "The Road to Serfdom," The University of Chicago Press, Chicago 1994.

[Laqueur 2015] Walter Laqueur, "Putinism, Russia and its Future with the West," Thomas Dunne Books, St. Martin's Press, New York, 2015.

[Miller 2004] Debra A. Miller, Book Editor, "North Korea, the History of Nations," Greehaven Press, 2004.

[Roberts 2003] J.A.G. Roberts, "The Complete History of China," Sutton Publishing Limited, 2003.

[Schell 2013] John Delury and Orville Schell, "Wealth and Power," Random House, Inc., New York, 2013.

[Scruton 2017] Roger Scruton, "On Human Nature," Princeton University Press, 2017.

[Staten 2005] Clifford L. Staten, "The History of Cuba," Palgrave MacMillan, New York, 2005.

[Streissguth 2002] Thomas Streissguth, Book Editor, "The Rise of the Soviet Union," Greehaven Press, Inc., San Diego, California, 2002.

[Williamson 2002] D. G. Williamson, "The Third Reich," Pearson Education Limited, 2002.

Epilogue

At the beginning of 2019, events in Venezuela are unfolding rapidly. January the 23rd, 2019 has become an important date for the future of the country. Juan Guaido is becoming the next president of Venezuela because Nicolas Maduro is not the president anymore, the 10th of January 2019 was the end of his mandate, therefore the National Assembly had the responsibility of appointing a new president.

Using the fraudulent 'constitutional national assembly,' Maduro elected himself as new president without following the rules of the Constitution of the country. The opposition was waiting for the opportunity to take matters into their own hands on January 10th. For Chavistas, this has been a big blow on their stomach they had been defining their own laws using the Supreme Judicial Court to punish the National Assembly. It is time to make justice.

There should be a transitional government to last for a short period and presidential elections would be held next. The transition is going to be difficult, the new government must appoint new heads of institutions, primarily the Electoral Power, change the members of the Judicial Supreme Court and start rebuilding the society through increases in employment. International aid would be necessary to finance the transformation of the state as well as the humanitarian aid for the population.

The problem right now is that there are two governments struggling to stay in power, Maduro is a communist dictator and Guaido is a Democrat, it is clear who should maintain the power in the country. Events are in progress and the community is hoping Maduro resigns for the good of the people. Democracy must be reestablished in Venezuela as soon as possible. Two governments functioning in parallel cannot last long. Guaido is being recognized by most international governments and the only support Maduro endures is the military. I hope a final event would twist the balance of forces and Guaido finally steps up as the sole interim president of Venezuela.

Germinal Boloix
February 2019.

www.ingramcontent.com/pod-product-compliance
Lightning Source LLC
Chambersburg PA
CBHW021045090426
42738CB00006B/187